Treatment in Crisis Situations

Treatment Approaches in the Human Services

FRANCIS J. TURNER, Editor

Donald F. Krill, *Existential Social Work*
Arthur Schwartz, *The Behavior Therapies*
Herbert S. Strean, *Psychoanalytic Theory and Social Work Practice*
Francis J. Turner, *Psychosocial Therapy*
Richard A. Wells, *Planned Short-Term Treatment*
Harold D. Werner, *Cognitive Therapy*

Treatment in Crisis Situations

Naomi Golan

THE FREE PRESS
A Division of Macmillan Publishing Co., Inc.
NEW YORK

Collier Macmillan Publishers
LONDON

The Free Press
A Division of Macmillan Publishing Co., Inc.
866 Third Avenue, New York, N.Y. 10022

Collier Macmillan Canada, Ltd.

Library of Congress Catalog Card Number: 77–85350

Printed in the United States of America

printing number

12   13   14   15   16   17   18   19   20

Library of Congress Cataloging in Publication Data

Golan, Naomi.
    Treatment in crisis situations.

    (Treatment approaches in the human services)
    Bibliography: p.
    Includes index.
    1. Crisis intervention (Psychiatry) I. Title.
II. Series. [DNLM: 1. Crisis intervention.
2. Psychotherapy. WM401 G617t)
RC480.6.G64   362.2   77–85350
ISBN 0–02–912060–8

    Grateful acknowledgment is extended for permission to use the following:
Leona Grossman, "Train Crash: Social Work and Disaster Services." Condensed with
per mission of the author and the National Association of Social Workers from *SocialWork*,
Vol. 18, No. 5 (September 1973), pp. 38–44.
    Excerpts from "Rape—A Personal Account." Reprinted with permission of the
National Association of Social Workers from *Health and Social Work*, Vol. 1, No. 3
(August 1976), pp. 84–95.
    Portions of Reva Wiseman, "Crisis Theory and the Process of Divorce," from *Social
Casework*, Vol. 56, No. 4 (April 1975), pp. 205–212. Reprinted with permission of the
author and the Family Service Association of America.
    Frances H. Scherz, "Maturational Crises and Parent-Child Interaction." Condensed
with permission of the Family Service Association of America from *Social Casework*,
Vol. 52, No. 6 (June 1971), pp. 362–369.
    Excerpt from Barbara Bender, "Management of Acute Hospitalization Anxiety,"
from *Social Casework*, Vol. 57, No. 1 (January 1976). Reprinted with permission of
the author and the Family Service Association of America.

To Lydia Rapoport, 1923–1971

Teacher, colleague, and friend who first stirred my interest in crisis intervention. By generously sharing her extensive knowledge and experience, her intense involvement in issues of practice and teaching, and her warm personal charm, she provided the inspiration for this work, both before and after her untimely death.

Contents

Part 2 The Basic Practice Model

Part 3 Intervention in Typical Crisis Situations

Foreword

"Treatment Approaches in the Human Services" is the first series of professional texts to be prepared under the general auspices of social work. It is understandable that the editor and authors of this endeavor should be enthusiastic about its quality and prospects. But it is equally understandable that our enthusiasm is tempered with caution and prudence. There is a presumptuousness in attempting to be on the leading edge of thinking and aspiring to break new ground, and our professional experience urges us to be restrained.

The first suggestion for this series came from the editorial staff of the Free Press in the spring of 1975. At that time, the early responses to *Social Work Treatment** were available. It was clear from the responses that, useful as that book appeared to be, there was a wish and a need for more detail on each of the various thought systems covered, especially as regards their direct practice implications. These comments led to a proposal from the

*Francis J. Turner, ed., *Social Work Treatment* (New York: Free Press, 1974).

Free Press that a series be developed that would expand the content of the individual chapters of *Social Work Treatment* into full-length books with the objective of providing a richer and fuller exposition of each system. This idea is still germane to the series, but with the emergence of new thought systems and theories it has moved beyond the notion of expanding the chapters in the original collection. New thinking in the helping professions, the diversity of new demands, and the complexity of these demands have increased beyond the expectations of even the harbingers of the knowledge explosion of the early 1970s. No profession can or should stand still, and thus no professional literature can be static. It is our hope that this series will stay continuously current as it takes account of new ideas emerging from practice.

By design, this series has a strong orientation to social work. But it is not designed for social workers alone; it is also intended to be useful to our colleagues in other professions. The point has frequently been made that much of the conceptual base of social work practice has been borrowed and that social work has made few original contributions to other professions. That is no longer true. A principal assumption of this series is that social work must now accept the responsibility for making available to other professions its rich accumulation of theoretical concepts and therapeutic strategies.

The responsibility to share does not presume that professions with a healing and human-development commitment are moving to some commonality of identity and structure. In the next decade, we are probably going to see clearer rather than more obscure professional identities and more rather than less precise professional boundaries, derived not from different knowledge bases but from differential use of shared knowledge. If this prediction is valid, it follows that each profession must develop increased and enriched ways of making available to other professions its own expanding knowledge of the human condition.

Although the books in this series are written from the viewpoint of the clinician, they will be useful for the student-professional, the senior scholar, and the teacher of professionals as well. On the principal that no dynamic profession can tolerate division among its practitioners, theory builders, and teachers, each book is intended to be a bridging resource between practice and theory development. In directing this series to colleagues whose principal targets of practice are individuals, families, and groups, we take the other essential fields of practice as given. Thus the community-development, social-action, policy, research, and service-delivery roles of the helping professions are not specifically addressed in these books.

One of the risks of living and practicing in an environment characterized by pluralism in professions, practice styles, and theoretical orientations is that one may easily become doctrinaire in defending a particular perspective. Useful and important as is ongoing debate that leads to clarification of similarities and differences, overlaps and gaps in thought systems and theories, the authors of these books have been asked to minimize this function. That is, they are to analyze the conceptual base of their particular topic, identify its theoretical origins, and explain and describe its operationalization in practice, but avoid polemics in behalf of "their" system. Inevitably, some material of this type is needed for comparisons, but the aim is to make the books explicative rather than argumentative.

Although the series has a clear focus and explicit objectives, there is also a strong commitment that it be marked with a quality of development and evolution. It is hoped that we shall be responsive to changes in psychotherapeutic practice and to the needs of colleagues in practice and thus be ready to alter the format of subsequent books as may be necessary.

In a similar way, the ultimate number of books in the series has been left open. Viewing current practice in the late 1970s, it is possible to identify a large number of influential thought systems that need to be addressed. We can only presume that additional perspectives will emerge in the future. These will be addressed as the series continues, as will new developments or reformulations of existing practice perspectives.

The practice of psychotherapy and the wide spectrum of activities that it emcompasses is a risky and uncertain endeavor. Clearly, we are just beginning a new era of human knowledge and improved clinical approaches and methods. At one time we were concerned because we knew so little; now we are concerned to use fully the rich progress that has been made in research, practice, and conceptualization. This series is dedicated to that task in the humble hope that it will contribute to man's concern for his fellows.

It is particularly appropriate that Dr. Naomi Golan's book on crisis treatment is the first to be published in the series. First, it immediately brings to the foreground an international flavor, one of the goals to which the series aspires. Dr. Golan has skillfully intermeshed her teaching, practice, and research experience in the United States with her more recent experience in Israel and thus demonstrates that theories of human behavior, when soundly based, are transferable across national and cultural lines. This helps put to rest the frequently voiced challenge that our therapeutic activities are class, race, and nationally bound.

Second, Dr. Golan's book serves as an excellent example of an area in which social work has made a distinct theoretical contribution. Certainly, social work cannot claim to be the originator or indeed even the main contributor to crisis theory. As in many other areas, we have learned much from our colleagues in other disciplines about this important aspect of human problem situations. But we have done much more than borrow and learn; we have enlarged, enriched, and made more precise some of the conceptual bases of crisis understanding as well as the scope of strategic and effective intervention in a growth-enhancing way.

That social work has been particularly interested and competent in distinct crisis situations is not surprising. Crisis has always been a part of the purview of social work practice, although it has not always been recognized as such. Indeed, once practitioners became clearer about the nature and diversity of crisis situations and thus about the relevance of these concepts for their own practice, there was a danger that crisis theory would become the sole theoretical base for some practitioners. Such overenthusiasm has now passed. Nevertheless, crisis concepts continue to be most helpful for all practitioners as a way of understanding what is happening to many people and learning how to intervene effectively in situations that a few years ago would not have been handled so sensitively. Dr. Golan has made a major contribution to practitioners both in explicating a basic practice model and in applying it to different aspects of crisis phenomena.

A third aspect of the timeliness of this book relates to our current life realities. As we become increasingly aware and accepting of the reality that as members of the family of man our lives and fates are closely interrelated with those of others, we are beginning to learn that the crises of other people and groups are in some ways our own. Crisis is a part of our daily living. When it is recognized and dealt with properly, our functioning can be facilitated and enhanced; when it is not recognized and appropriately handled, we can become debilitated and incapacitated.

In an exemplary way, Dr. Golan's book captures the depth and breadth of the concept of crisis. She presents an excellent analysis of its historical development in other disciplines and a companion analysis of its development in social work. She examines the many-faceted manifestations of crisis as they occur developmentally, situationally, or as large-system disasters. Of particular interest for social workers is her exposition of how crisis theory can enable us to help the victims of large-scale disasters involving many people. Apart from a few social workers whose practice is directly related to providing services in such situations, few of us have had a theoretical understanding of what happens in these circumstances and hence how to be most helpful. Dr. Golan's excellent discussion of this component of social work practice represents a major contribution to the literature.

In addition to the content, the extremely rich bibliography represents an excellent resource that will be much appreciated by practitioners and scholars.

Thus, this book makes an important contribution to the professional literature. It is an incisive presentation of the current state of psychotherapeutic treatment in crisis situations that provides an authoritative resource to practitioners in virtually all types of settings.

FRANCIS J. TURNER

Acknowledgments

The decision to write a book about crisis treatment can, in itself, become a hazardous event. Throughout the various phases of preparation, this situation often appeared on the verge of erupting into states of active disequilibrium. That I was able to cope with the various threats and challenges and finally bring the book to completion was due in large measure to the active networks of colleagues, friends, fellow workers in the field, and, above all, my patient, forbearing family, who all combined to provide support and encouragement throughout the process.

To all of these helpers, my heartfelt thanks.

NAOMI GOLAN

Haifa, 1977

Part 1

Theoretical Framework

Introduction

CRISIS INTERVENTION HAS BECOME a major treatment approach to helping individuals, families, and groups during stressful situations. Over the past thirty years or more, practitioners in the helping professions have been searching for both a viable theoretical framework and the appropriate techniques and strategies to deal with this volatile, high-risk population.

Today, social workers, psychologists, psychiatrists, doctors, nurses, vocational counselors, marriage therapists, and others have absorbed elements of this approach and are using them at varying levels of sophistication. Much of the ongoing treatment in family and child-welfare social agencies, in medical complexes and hospital settings, in psychiatric clinics and correctional services, is geared to this level of intervention.

In addition, carefully trained multidisciplinary teams operate special crisis stations within, or in conjunction with, ongoing mental health services, admission wards in general hospitals, and broad-based community outreach programs. Twenty-four-hour "hotlines" carry on a continuous campaign of billboard and radio advertising, inviting troubled persons to telephone for help with critical problems. Round-the-clock walk-in services and emergency shelters offer immediate aid on a no-screening, few-questions-asked basis. Self-help and mutual-help programs are mushrooming and proliferating.[1]

By now, the theoretical foundations for the crisis approach appear to be fairly well laid down. Out of the various conceptualizations which have emerged, combined, and sometimes diverged again, a basic framework has been developed about which there seems to be general agreement, irrespective of setting, discipline, or situation.[2]

In contrast, the application of the theory is far less clearly articulated. Until now, the criteria have been hazy and undiscriminating, depending more often upon the practitioner's personal bent or the limitations imposed by policy or problem than on specific guidelines for the employment of crisis intervention as the treatment of choice.

Goals for intervention in crisis situations have been defined as follows:

> (1) to alleviate the immediate impact of disruptive stressful events; and (2) to help mobilize the manifest and psychological capabilities and social resources of those directly affected . . . for coping with the effects of stress adaptively.[3]

Yet the tactics and techniques by which these goals are to be implemented tend to be haphazard and not carefully thought out, on the one hand, or overspecified, on the other. In either instance, the person, problem, place, and process, to use Perlman's classic configuration[4], are often lost sight of.

This volume is an attempt to bridge the gap between theory and practice. In this first section, two parallel streams of development will be traced briefly: the multiple academic, theoretical, and professional contributions which combined to form what is known today as "crisis theory," and the practice trends which have led to current crisis-oriented brief treatment programs.

In the second section, a basic model of crisis practice will be offered which, to our mind, is attuned to the underlying dynamics in crisis situations and can be applied creatively.

The final section will deal with three broad categories of stress-induced situations in terms of their specific phase developments. An attempt will be made to adapt variations of the basic model to resolution of typical crises in each category. This, we feel, can provide a format for applying the theory to practice with a variety of clients in crisis.

Obviously, it would be both presumptuous and futile to try to offer an all-enveloping design for treatment. It should be specified at the outset that our approach is set in the framework of social work practice. As such, crisis intervention is seen as *one form* of social treatment, to be employed selectively and with discrimination. Although other helping persons may find parts of the book useful, it is intended primarily for social work students and practitioners who are already familiar with the profession's knowledge, values, and skills base and are aware of the issues that arise in their application.

This is not to underestimate the other professionals, para-professionals, non-professionals, and volunteers who often carry the major load of direct intervention. Rather, it is a recognition of the basic fact that, when faced with the need to make significant practice judgments and decisions, one generally tends to operate out of one's own frame of reference and experience. I hope this book will help to articulate that base of operation.

The focus will be on direct work with clients. Two other impinging areas will be touched upon only tangentially and in passing: the use of the crisis approach in dealing with broad social-policy issues such as poverty, urban decay, and racism, and its employment within the epidemiological framework of primary, secondary, and tertiary prevention. Both issues are important, yet a full consideration would take us too far afield from our central concern.

In her discussion of the common base of social work practice, Bartlett states that relevant clusters of social science knowledge must be integrated with the broad range of interventive methods gleaned from workers' extensive practice wisdom to develop predictive measures of how people behave in certain situations and how they can be helped most effectively.[5] In another context, she points out that two recent directions of thinking have stimulated the emergence of social work concepts in stress situations. One is the conceptualization of human growth and development as the successive mastery of particular problems presented to the individual by each stage through which he passes in the life cycle. The second is the crisis concept, wherein these problems are conceived as tasks that must be met and coped with in some adaptive way. "Task," in Bartlett's usage, denotes any of the critical demands or sets of demands made upon people by various life situations. This definition leads directly to the concept of "coping," the way in which people deal with the tasks that confront them.[6]

This is the approach used in this volume. The concepts of task and coping are central to our viewpoint and will be discussed more extensively in Chapter 4, in relation to our basic treatment model.

Notes

1. A recent compilation of articles and papers, Howard J. Parad, H. L. P. Resnik, and Libbie G. Parad, eds., *Emergency and Disaster Management: A Mental Health Sourcebook* (Bowie, Md.: Charles Press, 1976), gives a comprehensive picture of the various settings and types of services in which the crisis approach is employed to varying degrees and in different ways.

2. See Howard J. Parad, "Crisis Intervention," in Robert Morris, ed., *Encyclopedia of Social Work,* 16th issue, Vol. 1 (New York: National Association of Social Workers, 1971), pp. 196–202; Lydia Rapoport, "Crisis Intervention as a Mode of Brief Treatment," in R. W. Roberts and R. H. Nee, eds., *Theories of Social Casework* (Chicago: University of Chicago Press, 1970), pp. 267–311; Gerald F. Jacobson, "Programs and Techniques of Crisis Intervention," in Silvano Arieti, ed., *American Handbook of Psychiatry,* 2nd ed., Vol. 2 (New York: Basic Books, 1974), pp.810–825; Naomi Golan, "Crisis Theory," in Francis J. Turner, ed., *Social Work Treatment: Interlocking Theoretical Approaches* (New York: Free Press, 1974), pp. 420–456.

3. Parad, 1971, p. 196.

4. Helen H. Perlman, *Social Casework: A Problem-Solving Process* (Chicago: University of Chicago Press, 1957), p. 4.

5. Harriett M. Bartlett, *The Common Base of Social Work Practice* (New York: NASW, 1970), pp. 70–84.

6. Ibid., pp. 93–97.

Chapter 1

The Crisis Approach to Practice

The Current Scene

Basic Tenets Of Crisis Theory

The heart of the crisis approach, as it is currently used, lies in a series of basic propositions and statements which seem to have stood the test of time and application. Many of these were first expressed by Erich Lindemann and Gerald Caplan in their work at the Harvard School of Medicine's Department of Psychiatry and at its School of Public Health. These were further developed, modified, and amended by other theoreticians such as Lydia Rapoport, Howard Parad, David Kaplan, Gerald Jacobson, Marvin Strickler, and Peter Sifneos.

The theory is embodied in the following ten points:

1. Crisis situations may occur episodically throughout the normal life span of individuals, families, groups, communities, and nations. They are usually initiated by some *hazardous event*,

7

which may be a finite, external stressful blow or some less bounded internal pressure. It may be a single catastrophic occurrence or a series of successive mishaps which build up a cumulative effect.

2. The impact of the hazardous event disturbs the individual's homeostatic balance and puts him in a *vulnerable state*. To regain his equilibrium, he goes through a series of predictable phases: first he attempts to use his customary repertoire of problem-solving mechanisms, with an accompanying rise in tension. If this is not successful, his upset increases and he mobilizes new, emergency methods to cope with the situation.

3. If the problem continues and cannot be resolved, avoided, or redefined, tension rises to a peak, and a *precipitating factor* can bring about a turning point, during which self-righting devices no longer operate and the individual enters a state of disequilibrium and disorganization. This is the state of *active crisis*.

4. During the course of the developing crisis situation, the individual may perceive the initial and subsequent stressful events primarily as a *threat*, either to his instinctual needs or to his sense of autonomy and well-being; as a *loss* of a person, an ability, or a capacity; or as a *challenge* to survival, growth, or mastery.

5. Each of these perceptions calls forth a characteristic emotional reaction which reflects its subjective meaning to the individual: *threat* elicits a heightened level of anxiety; *loss* is expressed through feelings of depression, deprivation, or mourning; *challenge* stimulates a moderate increase in anxiety plus a kindling of hope and expectation. Different persons may react to the same stressful situation in different ways or to varying degrees, depending on their subjective interpretation of the event.

6. A crisis situation is neither an illness nor a pathological experience; it reflects instead a realistic struggle in the individual's current life situation. However, it may reactivate earlier unresolved or partially resolved conflicts so that he responds in an inappropriate or exaggerated fashion. Crisis intervention in such cases may provide a multiple opportunity: to resolve the present

difficulty, to rework the previous struggle, and to break the linkage between the two.

7. Each particular type of crisis follows a series of predictable stages which can be mapped out and plotted. Emotional reactions and behavioral responses at each stage can be generally anticipated. Fixation at a particular phase or the omission of a stage may provide the clue as to where the person is "stuck," what lies behind his inability to do his crisis work and master the situation.

8. Although the total length of time between the initial blow and the final resolution of the crisis may vary, depending upon the specific nature of the situation, the cognitive, affective, and behavioral tasks that have to be accomplished and the situational supports and resources available, the actual state of active disequilibrium is time-limited, usually lasting up to four to six weeks.

9. During the resolution of the crisis, the individual tends to be particularly amenable to help. Customary defense mechanisms have become weakened, usual coping patterns have proved inadequate, and the ego has become more open to outside influence and change. A minimal effort at this time can produce a maximal effect; a small amount of help, appropriately focused, can prove more effective than more extensive help at a period of less emotional accessibility.

10. During this *reintegration* phase, new ego sets may emerge and new adaptive styles learned which will enable the person to cope more effectively with other situations in the future. However, if help is not available during this critical period, inadequate or maladaptive patterns may be adopted which can result in weakened ability to function adequately in the period ahead.

PRINCIPAL ADVOCATES AND PROPONENTS

Crisis intervention, as carried out by professional social workers, is considered to represent one form of the problem-solving approach developed by Perlman. It is used in direct work with clients who apply for help with common situational and developmental difficulties. Siporin reports:

> ...When faced with excessive stress and crisis and when needed resources are inadequate to the requirements of the tasks involved, people have difficulty in social functioning and problems in social living; their coping abilities break down or are impaired. Problems may take the form of interpersonal conflicts, inadequate or unsatisfying role performance, lack of needed resources, inability to make life-cycle stage transitions or to cope with accidental crises and disaster situations.
>
> ... People are believed to be able to regain equilibrium, to recover from their demoralization, and to resume optimal functioning when their competence is restored or strengthened and when requisite social resources and welfare services are provided. The processes of problem solving and of crisis or conflict resolution ideally require rational planning and decision procedures with individuals and groups, involving a phased sequence of tasks.[1]

With this as our starting point, a review of the relevant literature shows that the crisis approach is being applied increasingly in work with clients in traditional family and child-welfare agencies and is frequently offered in conjunction with short-term treatment for a wide range of individual and interpersonal problems.[2]

Sometimes this may simply reflect the idiosyncratic approach of one particular worker in an agency[3]; at other times it is a basic shift in agency emphasis.[4] It may involve the setting up of a type of service delivery, as in the case of the "Quick Response Units" of the Jewish Family Service of New York, which provide quick availability, crisis intervention, and planned short-term treatment within a six-week period.[5]

Public welfare departments are utilizing the crisis aspects of particular stress situations in special programs to facilitate change.[6] Child-placement agencies have developed innovative means to deal with crises in family situations[7] and to provide services to children in their own homes, even though the term *crisis* may not be specifically mentioned.[8]

Social workers in secondary settings, operating as part of a professional team, use crisis intervention as an integral strategy in their armamentarium of services. Child-guidance clinics, once the banner-carriers of long-term treatment geared to basic personality change, have tended in recent years to shift their focus somewhat to a limited, crisis-oriented approach, either as part of their overall stance or through the use of special crisis facilities within their broader framework. The Crisis Clinic of the Framingham Youth Guidance Center is geared to this type of service:

> During working hours throughout the week, one or more of the psychology or social work staff of the clinic is on duty to receive new applicant families. Since applications are nearly always made by telephone, an appointment with a specific worker at a specific time is offered for the same or the next day. If there is a walk-in application, one of the workers on duty is responsible for seeing the applicant, at least briefly.
>
> The applicant calling—usually the mother—is told that the worker will see the family "for up to four hours of interview time in order to help you understand the problem and figure out what to do about it."
>
> ...For the first interview, mother, father, child, and occasionally other family members or friends are expected to be present. Length of interviews, members to be present during portions of each interview, and intervals between interviews are planned purposefully by the worker in consultation with the chief of service. Each family is seen by a single worker, rather than by a team. . . . With the family's permission, early and frequent consultation by the worker with such ancillary professional persons as school personnel and local physicians as well as with welfare and public health resources is strongly encouraged.[9]

Mental health clinics for adults have been among the foremost advocates of the crisis approach. Gerald Jacobson, director of the Los Angeles Psychiatric Service (LAPS), notes that the two primary characteristics of such crisis programs are *ready access* and *brief treatment*.[10] The Benjamin Rush Centers for Problems of

Living, part of the LAPS, offer services to all applicants, regardless of diagnostic, financial, age, or other considerations.

Treatment begins in the first hour, is not sharply differentiated from diagnosis, and lasts from four to six visits. Although referrals for hospitalization and day care are sometimes made, approximately 95 percent of applicants are treated in the facility. Whenever possible, treatment begins on the day of application, with the focus on the immediate crisis problem. The goal of treatment is to restore the individual to at least his precrisis level of functioning.[11]

Social workers, operating within inpatient and outpatient medical facilities, often intervene at points of crisis, almost as a matter of role definition. Two medical workers report that they *think* in terms of crisis theory:

> ... At the University of Illinois Neonatal High Risk Nursery, which receives infants from numerous other hospitals in the area, social workers frequently have the assignment of helping parents face such crises. An infant is often transferred so shortly after birth that personnel from the sending hospital have had little chance to talk to the parents . . . . The mother is still in the transferring hospital and the father comes alone for the painful visit. It becomes the social worker's role to help the parents adjust to the child's potential for retardation, physical handicaps, or even death. It is the social worker who must be wise enough to be realistic and yet know how much to say without frightening the parents.[12]

Both in direct counseling with the parents and in interpretive joint interviews with parents and the physician, the social worker helps the family obtain answers to medical aspects of the situation and, at the same time, explores the emotional issues involved. Since the social problems of the patients reflect those of an inner-city population, issues of drug addiction, mental illness, and poverty are also raised. When child abuse and neglect are brought up, agencies outside the hospital are involved in coordination and joint planning of social services.[13]

Work with terminally ill patients and their families assumes crisis dimensions during certain phases of the illness, such as when parents first learn that their child has contracted leukemia. David Kaplan points out that the professional's most important function at this time is to share the anguish, the grief, and the fears of these families without "turning them off".[14] At the Children's Hospital of Los Angeles, the social worker in the Division of Hematology finds that meeting with parents, together and as part of a group, helps them begin the process of anticipatory mourning.[15]

Admission services in general hospitals, usually manned by medical and nursing personnel, have in recent years begun to include social workers as part of their staff. Workers in the emergency room of the Strong Memorial Hospital in Rochester, N.Y., are available personally from 8:00 A.M. to 10:00 P.M. and around the clock by telephone. The social worker's role as crisis intervener assumes particular importance in this context, where the immediacy of the problem, the pressure in the emergency room to act quickly to alleviate stress and to empty beds for more acutely ill patients, and the need to move them on to more appropriate settings require rapid and innovative responses.[16]

Sometimes social services are structured to meet the special needs of a group subjected to particularly stressful situations. As part of the birth-control counseling carried out at the Student Health Center of the California State University at Sacramento, social workers have developed a model for work with immature, sexually active college students struggling with the shock of unwanted pregnancy:

> The intitial interview with the woman is usually held at the time her pregnancy is confirmed. [This] . . . often precipitates a crisis situation, as her former coping strategies prove inadequate. . . . The task of the worker . . . is to engage the woman in a helping relationship that enables her to begin to move toward taking control of her situation. The model uses the basic existential stance of individual responsibility and control, with the worker in the role of helper. . . .Knowing of the dependency which characterizes these clients, the worker consciously assigns decision making to the client with concomitant support and recognition of the difficulties posed.[17]

At times a group of agencies will join together to offer a coordinated service to deal with an acute problem too ramified for any one of them to deal with singly. As a result of lack of community resources, four helping organizations banded together in the Pasadena area in 1974 to establish an interlocking network of services for rape victims. The Pasadena-Foothill Valley YWCA trained and supervised volunteers to operate a 24-hour hotline as well as to give support and information, to accompany victims to the hospital, the police station, or to court, and to provide informal counseling and referrals. The Huntington Memorial Hospital provided medical care as well as information on follow-up care and testing, medical evidence for corroboration in court. The Foothill Family Service offered immediate appointments for crisis, short-term, long-term, and joint treatment. Pasadena Planned Parenthood furnished some follow-up testing and counseling, particularly regarding venereal disease and pregnancy. In addition, the network provided public education programs concerning rape and services for rape victims.[18]

Community-based suicide-prevention centers are perhaps the most widely known example of special crisis-intervention services staffed by combined professional and non-professional teams and structured to meet a specialized problem situation, although in recent years some centers have broadened their scope to encompass other stressful problems. In most centers, volunteers man hotlines, give immediate support and counsel, and refer callers to appropriate community services. Professionals act as consultants, trainers, and back-up personnel. In some cases they provide short-term in-person treatment and community interpretation.[19]

Flexibility in scope and structure, with a minimum of red tape and paper work, is the keynote of the Crisis Intervention Service of the Dane County Mental Health Center in Madison, Wisconsin. The core staff of graduate-level mental health professionals offers a wide range of immediate assistance, directly to individuals and groups and indirectly through consultation to other community caregivers. They work extensively on the telephone, see persons at the center, or travel to points in the area in respond to requests for help. They operate closely with police, hospital personnel, and volunteers in the community, according to an established ranking of priorities: suicide attempts, high-risk suicide threats, potential involuntary mental-hospital commitment, family trouble situations, consultation to other services, work with families of suicide victims, and other types of crises.[20]

At times a social agency will collaborate actively with another community service to set up a new program. The Family Service Society and the Police Department of Pawtucket, Rhode Island, cooperate in a joint community outreach program, aimed at aggressive intervention in family and juvenile crisis situations. Social workers and police officers form "police crisis teams" which go out, usually to clients' homes.

The bulk of referrals comes from the police, who receive the calls at the station and relay them immediately by radio to the team, which in many cases responds at once. Situations usually involve family problems, juvenile shoplifting, running away, school difficulties, alcohol-and drug-related problems, and neighborhood disturbances. Once entry into the home is gained, the social worker usually conducts the major part of the interview, involving the police member of the team where there is question of criminal behavior or a need to sanction a particular plan. With families, the main goal is frequently to defuse the situation, to help the participants see the crisis as part of an ongoing pattern of difficulties within the family. If these patterns can be identified, an attempt is made to effect some kind of immediate resolution and, when possible, to refer the family to appropriate community services.[21]

Present Status of Crisis Intervention

Despite the drying up of financial support for a number of demonstration projects and a shift in their legal status, which has somewhat deflected programs from their original thrust,* crisis

*See section on "Mental Health Policies and Programs," Chapter 2, for a discussion of this aspect.

intervention appears to be "alive and well." Evidence from the field indicates that this approach has increased in appeal for professionals in established primary and secondary settings and in new types of services tailored to this form of intervention.

On the one hand, this crisis-intervention approach addresses itself to acute problem situations with a broad appeal and often universal applications. Clients ask for help at moments of high anxiety, when they are open to and motivated for change. Resolution comes quickly and often dramatically, in marked contrast to the slow, uneven pace in long-term treatment. On the other hand, this approach offers both practitioners and agencies relief from the pressures of long waiting lists and limited caseloads through its rapid access and quick turnover features.

Whether crisis intervention can achieve its potential as a primary treatment modality for social workers, however, depends to a large extent on the degree to which it can become integrated into practice in the many fields and problem areas for which it would appear appropriate.[22] This may hinge, in the final analysis, as much on whether it is taught in schools of social work and staff-development seminars as a major intervention form as on whether agencies and sponsors adjust their policies and programs to accommodate this form of service. And this, in turn, may depend on the extent to which its application can be made consonant with other practice trends and principles being taught and with the overall thrust of current social work practice.

Notes

1. Max Siporin, *Introduction to Social Work Practice* (New York: Macmillan, 1975), p. 147.
2. James Krider, "A New Program and Its Impact on a Small Agency," *Social Casework* 50 (November 1969): 508–512.
3. Personal discussion with Gloria Randall, caseworker at Jewish Family and Children's Service, Milwaukee, Wis., July 1976.

4. Personal discussion with David L. Hoffman, Executive Director, Family Service of Milwaukee, July 1976.

5. Judith Lang, "Planned Short-Term Treatment in a Family Agency," *Social Casework* 55 (June 1974): 369–374.

6. Betty Morris, "Crisis Intervention in a Public Welfare Agency," *Social Casework* 49 (December 1968): 612–617.

7. John F. Simonds, "A Foster Home for Crisis Placements," *Child Welfare* 52 (February 1973): 82–90.

8. Josephine S. Hirsch, Jacquelynne Gailey, and Eleanor Schmerl, "A Child Welfare Agency's Program of Service to Children in Their Own Home," *Child Welfare* 55 (March 1976): 193–204.

9. Patricia L. Ewalt, "The Crisis Treatment Approach in a Child Guidance Clinic." *Social Casework* 54 (July 1973): 406–411.

10. Jacobson, 1974, p. 812.

11. Brochure on Benjamin Rush Centers Division of Didi Hirsh Community Mental Health Center, 1976, pp. 4–5.

12. Mary S. Sheridan and Doris R. Johnson, "Social Work Services in a High-Risk Nursery," *Health and Social Work* 1 (May 1976): 87, 91–92.

13. Ibid., pp. 92–95.

14. David M. Kaplan, Aaron Smith, Rose Grobstein, and Stanly E. Fischman, "Family Mediation of Stress," *Social Work* 18 (July 1973): 60–69.

15. Vrinda S. Knapp and Howard Hansen, "Helping the Parents of Children with Leukemia," *Social Work* 18 (July 1973): 70–75.

16. Anne S. Bergman, "Emergency Room: A Role for Social Workers," *Health and Social Work* 1 (February 1976): 32–75.

17. Betty Russell and Sylvia Schild, "Pregnancy Counseling with College Women," *Social Casework* 57 (May 1976): 324–329.

18. Grace Hardgrove, "An Interagency Service Network to Meet the Needs of Rape Victims," *Social Casework* 57 (April 1976): 245–253.

19. Richard D. McGee, *Crisis Intervention in the Community* (Baltimore: University Park Press, 1974), pp. 21–33; Sheila Fisher, *Suicide and Crisis Intervention: Survey and Guide to Services* (New York: Springer, 1973).

20. Personal visit and staff discussion, July 1976.

21. Bruce B. Burnett, John J. Carr, John Sinapi, and Roy Taylor, "Police and Social Workers in a Community Outreach Program," *Social Casework* 57 (January 1976): 41–49.

22. Howard J. Parad, Lola Selby, and James Quinlan, "Crisis Intervention with Families and Groups," in Robert W. Roberts and Helen Northen, eds., *Theories of Social Work with Groups* (New York: Columbia University Press, 1976), pp. 304–330, offers a whole new range of possibilities for the use of the crisis approach with natural and formed groups.

Chapter 2

Historical Perspectives:
Social Science and
Mental Health Contributions

To be fully understood, present-day crisis treatment must be viewed as the product of convergence and interplay between two mainstreams of developments since World War II. On the one hand, selected concepts, hypotheses, and hunches have been drawn from psychodynamic personality theory, observations on children's development, experimental findings on stress and disasters, sociological studies on family and community reactions to pressures and stress, developments in military and civilian psychiatry, and formulations in learning and behavioral psychology. As noted earlier, these elements have been joined, in an electic fashion under the heading of "crisis theory." On the other hand, evolutionary developments within the social work profession since the beginning of the century have brought about significant changes in the nature and orientation of traditional casework practice, resulting in an increased emphasis on short-term and

19

task-oriented treatment, particularly during periods of heightened stress and emergency.

While a comprehensive examination of these parallel trends lies outside of the scope of this volume, this chapter will briefly scan some of the highlights of the theoretical, research, and legislative contributions. Chapter 3 will examine developments within social work practice leading to the present crisis-oriented approach.

Psychodynamic Theory

Classical psychoanalytic theoreticians, regardless of their particular loyalties, tended to concentrate on the psychopathology of their patients, interpreted in terms of the inherent conflicts between id, ego, superego, and external reality. Since the late 1930s, however, second-generation metapsychologists[1] such as Heinz Hartmann, Ernst Kris, and Rudolf Loewenstein have turned their attention to the executive, conflict-free areas of the ego. Hartmann's concept of ego autonomy,[2] amplified and further developed by Rapaport,[3] gave a new thrust to formulation of the role of the ego in personality functioning.

Hendrick[4] discussed the "inborn ability to master a segment of the environment," while Kardiner[5] noted that successful and gratifying experiences, rather than frustration, can lead to increasingly integrated action and ego growth. Mittelmann[6] felt that motility (motor development) is one of the central functions of the ego. Rado[7] emphasized the importance of examining failures in current adaptation, their causes, and how they can be overcome.

Alexander, long a stormy petrel in the psychoanalytic field, suggested that treatment can best be understood in terms of the two components of the learning process: motivation and the acquirement of new patterns of behavior. Changes in the individual's life call for the unlearning of old response patterns and the learning of new and more adequate ones.[8] In another context he suggested that supportive methods of treatment are primarily indicated when the ego is temporarily impaired as a result of acute emotional distress. Therapeutic tasks at such times would include gratifying the patient's dependency needs, reducing stress by giving him the opportunity for abreaction (bringing into consciousness repressed material), providing intellectual guidance by helping him review the acute stress situation and assisting him in making judgments, supporting his defenses until the ego can handle the emotional discharges, and actively participating in manipulation of his life situation.[9]

Lewin's concept of the individual's lifespace[10]—the field of forces within which he developed—and Maslow's concern with self-actualization and the drive for growth[11] added to this increasing interest in the healthy aspects of the ego as therapeutic tools. Among the most significant contributions in this area were White's concepts of effectance and competence, both considered independent ego energies, with the accompanying feelings of efficacy and sense of competence.[12]

During this period, Erikson, working independently, developed his eight-stage epigenetic approach to the life cycle. One of his central propositions was that the individual's ability to solve the key psychosocial crises posed by each developmental stage could either enhance or weaken his ability to master crises in subsequent stages.[13]

At about this time, child psychologist Jean Piaget was examining in minute detail the intellectual and motor processes of children to determine experimentally at which stages they developed their capacities to organize and incorporate new experiences and to solve problems.[14] Escalona studied intensively the normal developmental patterns of infants to measure their adaptation to and interaction with their environment as shaping factors in their personalities.[15] Murphy, following up on Escalona's infants, observed them for twenty years to map the unfolding abilities of children and adolescents to evolve patterns of coping and mastery. She distinguishes between two types of coping: the "capacity to make use of the opportunities, challenges, and resources of the environment and to manage the pain, frustration, difficulties and failures with which he is confronted,'' and the ''capacity to maintain internal integration along with the resilience or potential to recover after a period of disintegrative response to stress.''[16]

Experimental Psychology

General psychologists and physiopsychologists were drawn into consideration of coping and mastery patterns, initially through their interest in responses to threat and sensory deprivation. Early researchers examined reactions under stress-inducing field situations such as isolation in the Antarctic and in prison camps and under simulated laboratory conditions of high stress and sensory deprivation. The list of researchers in this area is far too long to be included, but three must be mentioned.

Selye, a pioneer for many years in this field, used the concepts of homeostasis and equilibration to observe the individual's performance under various stress conditions. He proposed a series of three stages: first an *alarm reaction,* consisting of successive shock and countershock phases; then *resistance,* during which maximal adaptation is attempted; and finally *exhaustion,* when adaptive mechanisms collapse.[17]

Janis's work on stress started out with an interest in patients' responses to high-threat situations such as impending surgery. He noted that the effectiveness of warning depends on who sends the message (the communication source), what the message says (information on how to cope with the threat), and the distinctive characteristics of the individual to whom the message is given.[18] More recently, he has turned his attention to decisions made under stressful conditions. He sees such decision making as involving appraisal of the challenge, evaluation of recommended alternatives, a tentative decision in favor of the best available policy, commitment to the new policy, and adherence to it despite challenge.[19]

In his research on the cognitive factors in coping with stress, Lazarus differentiates between direct actions and intrapsychic thought processes. He emphasizes the need for appraisal of both the threatening condition and the potential avenues for solution and mastery.[20] He gives a useful definition of coping as "problem-solving efforts made by an individual when the demands he faces are highly relevant to his welfare (that is, a situation of considerable jeopardy or promise) and when these demands tax his adaptive resources."[21]

Learning Theory

Along with the developments in psychodynamic theory and experimental psychology, learning theorists were using a cognitive perspective, with its emphasis on information processing, to look at coping and decision making.[22]

Thus Taplin describes the person experiencing a crisis as having previously been able to perceive, think, remember, evaluate, respond, and make decisions; now these processes have been interrupted as the result of some physical or psychological "overload." The new situation demands that he acquire new information, build new cognitive maps, and develop the capacity to design and select from among possible coping strategies at times of breakdown. Even after the crisis peak is passed, these new strategies can stand him in good stead in the future.[23]

Behavioral modification theorists see treatment at periods of crisis as part of their overall approach: the unlearning of old, unsuccessful, or damaging patterns of interaction and the learning of new, constructive ones. Emphasis is placed on the cognitive aspects of experience, on teaching the individual how to change and to recognize how others perceive him. The cause-effect aspect of behavior is stressed: if the person changes what he does, others will change in response. Behavior is shaped toward helping him engage in more socially acceptable and less pain-producing activities and learn more productive ways to deal with problem situations.[24]

Sociological Studies

Sociologists during this period were preparing the background for the crisis approach in two areas: the examination of families under stress, and the observation of reactions to large-scale disasters.

Family sociologists, starting in the 1930s and 1940s, began to look at the effect of stressful events on families. Hill found three interacting elements which appeared to determine whether a given event would bring about a family crisis: the crisis-precipitating event ("stressor"), the internal organization of the family, and the family's definition of the event as stressful. He contrasted adequacy in usual family functioning with crisis-proneness in multiproblem families.[25]

Burgess recognized that sudden changes in family status and conflict among family members in their conceptions of their roles added to family crises.[26] Spiegel noted that discrepancies in cognition, in role assignment or complementarity, in distribution of instrumental means, or in cultural value orientation can all lead to role conflicts within the family and, eventually, to disequilibrium.[27] Bell and Vogel pointed out that the family's designation of an emotionally disturbed child as the scapegoat at times reduces internal tension and allows it to maintain its internal equilibrium.[28]

A long series of research projects examined the impact on families of various types of developmental and transitional crises such as marriage,[29] parenthood,[30] and old age.[31] Others recorded the eroding effects of such crisis-inducing elements as poverty, deprivation, and alienation on family functioning,[32] as well as of physical and psychiatric illness.[33]

In Eliot's work, later amplified by Hill, family crises were classified along the axes of dismemberment, accession, demoralization, and aggrievement.[34] Other sociologists developed parallel classification systems, Elaine and John Cumming, a sociologist-psychiatrist team, suggested three broad types of crises: those that are biologically tinged and therefore inevitable, such as adolescence and menopause; those that are environmentally tinged and to some extent avoidable, such as migration and bereavement; and those that are adventitious or purely chance events, such as accidents and disasters.[35] (The Cummings, it might be mentioned, viewed ego growth as essentially a series of disequilibrations and subsequent re-equilibrations between the person and his environment. Crisis resolution promotes ego growth by increasing the individual's repertoire and differentiation of ego sets.)

In a little-noticed research study on the effect of the birth of a retarded child on the mother, Farber described two types of operational crises: the *tragic crisis,* which tends to be percipitated at the time of diagnosis of retardation and resembles the bereavement process, and the *role-organization crisis,* which refers to the coping with the seemingly interminable care problems of the child.[36]

A number of sociologists carried out field studies on large-scale disasters such as floods, tornadoes, and war.[37] Tyhurst, examining civilian disasters, noted three predictable stages in the patterns of response: first psychological and physical turmoil; then painful preoccupation with the past; and finally remobilization of activity and adjustment.[38] Powell and Rayner observed that, while each type of disaster follows its own unique pattern, seven definable phases can be discerned: warning, threat, impact, inventory, rescue, remedy, and recovery.[39]

Psychiatric Developments

Linking the field studies on disasters with developments in military medicine, psychiatrists within the armed forces during and after World War II[40] and the Korean conflict[41] attempted to predict the performance of soldiers under combat conditions. It was found that persistent dysfunction could be reduced by treating the men as close to the front line as possible, focusing upon the immediate situational crisis, and returning them to combat duty within a short time in order to reduce regression and restore self-confidence.[42]

Lindemann's initial work on bereavement was the outcome of his observations of the grief reactions of survivors of the Cocoanut Grove nightclub fire in Boston in 1943, in which hundreds of people, including many servicemen, perished. He concluded that the duration and severity of bereavement depend upon the extent to which each survivor can successfully carry out his "grief work" by emancipating himself from his bondage to the deceased, readjusting to an environment from which the dead one is missing, and being able in time to form new relationships.[43]

Somewhat later, Lindemann's conclusion that certain inevitable events in the life cycle of individuals generate emotional strain and stress which can either lead to mastery of the new situation or turn into crisis led to the establishment, in 1948, of the Wellesley Human Relations Service, a community-based project aimed at preventive work in typical hazardous family situations.[44]

Parallel to and interwoven with Lindemann's work is that of Caplan, who developed his interest in crisis situations out of his early work with immigrant mothers and children in Israel after World War II.[45] During the 1950s and early 1960s, at the Harvard School of Public Health, his approach was set in the public health format of primary, secondary, and tertiary levels of intervention.[46] A series of investigations was carried out under his direction at the Family Guidance Center and elsewhere in the Boston area on various types of situational and maturational crises, such as the premature birth of a child.[47]

At one point, the traditional medical model of sickness and cure was questioned and an alternative approach, that of the *acute situational disorder,* was proposed. Here a crisis is seen as similar to an infectious disease state, which is frequently self-limiting and which may occur in a healthy person or be superimposed on a long-term chronic disease condition. Intervention in such cases is confined to the alleviation of the acute (crisis) situation without attempting to change the basic personality or to deal with the underlying pathology.[48]

During the 1950s and 1960s much of the core theory on crisis intervention was developed.[49] More recently, at the Harvard Department of Psychiatry's Laboratory of Community Psychiatry, Caplan and his colleagues have carried out studies on widowhood[50] and reactions to death.[51] For the past several years Caplan has focused his attention upon the natural and mutual support systems in the community which can be used to prevent and/or ameliorate the destructive aspects of crisis situations.[52] He used this approach in his work as consultant to the government of Israel during and after the 1973 Yom Kippur War.[53]

Suicide Prevention

Suicide-prevention services, one of the most active of the community mental health programs, developed their own frame of reference of "suicidology," the "scientific and humane study of self-destruction in man."[54] Much of the pioneering work was carried out first by Dublin and then by Shneidman, Farberow, and their associates at the Los Angeles Suicide Prevention Center (LASPC) in the late 1950s and 1960s. Here many of the theoretical concepts and rationale for this particular approach, which relies heavily on volunteers and lay groups for support, were formulated.[55]

Specific features include the extensive use of a twenty-four-hour telephone service, the immediate mobilization of community resources, the incorporation of volunteers into the core staff, and the establishment of an attitudinal stance which maximizes the use of authority, extensive activity, and the help of significant others. The LASPC's development of the "psychological autopsy" in the case of death is considered a major contribution. Not only does it provide important medical and legal data for the certification of death, but it serves as a means of easy access to crisis intervention with suicide survivors.[56]

As the suicide-prevention movement spread, the Center for Studies of Suicide Prevention was set up in 1966 to concentrate activities and exchange information. Community-based centers sprang up rapidly, frequently outside of established community mental health facilities, until by 1972 almost 200 such programs had been established throughout the United States. McGee, one of the most active proponents in this area, notes that many of these suicide-prevention centers have evolved over the past few years into more general crisis-intervention programs.

Mental Health Policies and Programs

In the thirty-odd years since the end of World War II, sweeping legislative changes occurred which have had a profound influence on the mental health field in the United States. The war alerted the country to its mental health needs and provided the momentum for the search for new approaches to the treatment of psychiatrically disabled soldiers.[57] The introduction of powerful new psychotropic drugs and the growing awareness of the detrimental effects of long-term hospitalization resulted in a major shift in focus in the treatment of the mentally ill and disabled from traditional hospital and institutional settings to community facilities.[58]

The first piece of mental health legislation, the Mental Health Act of 1946, authorized the provision of federal funds for the training of psychiatric personnel, for increased research on the nature and causes of mental illness, and for the development of community mental health services. The National Institute of Mental Health (NIMH), established in 1948, subsidized and monitored many of the theoretical and applied research projects which used the public health frame of reference and provided the arena for testing the hypotheses and propositions of crisis intervention.

One important study authorized by the Joint Commission on Mental Illness and Health, set up by the American Psychiatric Association and the American Medical Association, undertook to survey the entire mental health needs of the country.[59] The commission, through the work of its ten task forces and its final report, *Action for Mental Health*,[60] supplied the knowledge and impetus which led to many of the innovative programs of the Kennedy and Johnson years.

The Community Mental Health Centers Act of 1963, which grew out of President Kennedy's call for a bold new approach to mental illness and mental retardation, authorized the setting up of comprehensive community mental health centers. Ten elements of comprehensive services had to be available for such centers to qualify for federal assistance. Five of these services were considered essential at the outset: inpatient care, outpatient care, partial hospitalization (day, night, and weekend care), emergency, and consultation and education. Five more were to be instituted over time: diagnostic, rehabilitative, precare and aftercare, training, and research and evaluation services.[61]

A number of changes in venue and support have occurred in the community mental health field since the 1963 Act became implemented in 1965. After a preliminary period of reorganizing existing programs, building and expanding physical facilities, reorienting staff and recruiting of new personnel, community mental health centers (including crisis intervention services) began to proliferate under federal, state, and/or local auspices.

Mechanic, a medical sociologist specializing in the mental health field, has pointed out that, during this period, the social-stress perspective was being used increasingly to establish and direct public policy in both the military and the community mental health areas. This view assumes that every person has his breaking point and that mental illness and psychiatric disability are largely the outcome of the accumulated pressures in people's lives which eventually overcome their coping abilities. Thus, intervention to help alleviate these stresses so that the individual can continue to function without breakdown becomes an important societal tool. Treatment is aimed at enhancing the client's social and psychological resources through instruction, support, encouragement, and even, at times, intimidation.[62]

With the retrenchment and reorganization of federal fiscal policy which began in the Nixon administration, major shifts in the delivery of health services occurred. In 1972, NIMH established the Mental Health Emergencies Center, an outgrowth of the Center for Studies of Suicide Prevention which centralized the activities of the community suicide-prevention centers.

Meanwhile the Department of Health, Education, and Welfare was itself being reorganized and the Health Services Administration established in 1973. One of its branches, the Emergency Medical Services (EMS), was set up to provide both physical and psychological emergency care for all persons in such specific problem areas as suicide, alcohol and drug abuse, child abuse, rape, and psychosis. Many of the earlier crisis-intervention programs were shifted from NIMH sponsorship to the EMS. Services for victims of community disasters were considered separately and accorded high priority under the Disaster Relief Act of 1974.[63]

Under the reorganization and routinization of mental health programs, much of the innovation and excitement of the 1950s and 1960s appears to have subsided. What seems to remain, however, is a core of practice-tested services and a distinctive crisis-oriented approach, particularly in the area of emergency care.

Notes

1. Technically, *metapsychology* or *psychodynamic theory* refers to the theory of personality, while *psychoanalysis* is used for the theory of treatment.

2. Heinz Hartmann, *Ego Psychology and the Problem of Adaptation* (New York: International Universities Press, 1958).

3. Merton M. Gill, *The Collected Papers of David Rapaport* (New York: Basic Books, 1967), pp. 722–744.

4. Ives Hendrick, "The Instinct to Master," *Psychoanalytic Quarterly* 12 (1943): 561–565.

5. Abraham Kardiner, *The Individual and His Society* (New York: Columbia University Press, 1939).

6. Bela Mittelmann, "Motility in Infants, Children, and Adults," *Psychoanalytic Study of the Child,* vol. 9 (New York: International Universities Press, 1954).

7. See Franz Alexander, "Sandor Rado: The Adaptational Theory," in F. Alexander, S. Eisenstein, and M. Grotjahn, eds., *Psychoanalytic Pioneers* (New York: Basic Books, 1966), pp. 240–248.

8. Franz Alexander, "Psychoanalytic Contributions to Short-Term Psychotherapy," in L. R. Wolberg, ed., *Short-Term Psychotherapy* (New York: Grune and Stratton, 1965), pp. 84–101.

9. Franz Alexander, *Psychoanalysis and Psychotherapy* (New York: W. W. Norton, 1956), pp. 53–55.

10. Kurt Lewin, *Field Theory in Social Sciences* (New York: Harper, 1951).

11. See Frank G. Goble, *The Third Force: The Psychology of Abraham Maslow* (New York: Grossman, 1970).

12. Robert W. White, "Strategies of Adaptation: An Attempt at Systematic Description," in G. V. Coelho, D. A. Hamburg, and J. E. Adams, eds., *Coping and Adaptation* (New York: Basic Books, 1974), pp. 47–68.

13. Erik H. Erikson, *Identity and the Life Cycle,* Mono. 1 (New York: International Universities Press, 1959).

14. Jean Piaget, *The Origin of Intelligence in Children* (New York: W. W. Norton, 1963).

15. Sibylle K. Escalona, *The Roots of Individuality: Normal Patterns of Development in Infancy* (Chicago: Aldine, 1968).

16. Lois B. Murphy, "Preventive Implications in the Preschool Years," in G. Caplan, ed., *Prevention of Mental Disorders in Children* (New York: Basic Books, 1961), pp. 218–248. Also, Lois B. Murphy and Alice E. Moriarty, *Vulnerability, Coping, and Growth* (New Haven: Yale University Press, 1976).

17. Hans Selye, *The Stress of Life* (New York: McGraw-Hill, 1956).

18. Irving L. Janis, *Psychological Stress* (New York: John Wiley and Sons, 1958).

19. Irving L. Janis, "Vigilance and Decision Making in Personal Crises," in Coelho, Hamburg, and Adams, 1974, pp. 139–175.

20. Richard S. Lazarus, *Psychological Stress and the Coping Process* (New York: McGraw-Hill, 1966).

21. Richard S. Lazarus, James R. Averill, and Edward M. Opton, Jr., "The Psychology of Coping: Issues of Research and Assessment," in Coelho, Hamburg, and Adams, 1974, pp. 250–251.

22. We cannot go into this extensive area here. For the general approach, see E. Hilgard and G. Bower, *Theories of Learning*, 4th ed. (New York: Appleton-Century-Crofts, 1974); Jerome Bruner, *Studies in Cognitive Growth* (New York: John Wiley and Sons, 1966); and U. Neisser, *Cognitive Psychology* (New York: Appleton-Century-Crofts, 1967).

23. Julian R. Taplin, "Crisis Theory: Critique and Reformulation," *Community Mental Health Journal* 7 (March 1971): 13–23.

24. Joel Fischer and Harvey L. Gochros, *Planned Behavior Change* (New York: Free Press, 1975), pp. 4–9. Also, Robert D. Carter and Richard B. Stuart, "Behavior Modification Theory and Practice: A Reply," *Social Work* 15 (January 1970): 37–50.

25. Reuben Hill, "Generic Features of Families Under Stress," *Social Casework* 39 (February–March 1958): 139–150. Also reprinted in Howard J. Parad, ed., *Crisis Intervention: Selected Readings* (New York: FSAA, 1965), pp. 32–52.

26. Ernest W. Burgess, "Family Living in the Later Decades," in M. B. Sussman, ed., *Sourcebook in Marriage and the Family*, 2nd ed. (Boston: Houghton Mifflin, 1963), pp. 425–431.

27. John Spiegel, "The Resolution of Role Conflicts within the Family," in Norman W. Bell and Ezra F. Vogel, *The Family* (New York: Free Press, 1960), pp. 361–381.

28. Ezra Vogel and Norman W. Bell, "The Emotionally Disturbed Child as the Family Scapegoat," in Bell and Vogel, 1960, pp. 382–397.

29. Rhona Rapoport, "Normal Crises, Family Structure, and Mental Health," *Family Process* 2, no. 1 (1963). Reprinted in Parad, 1965, pp. 75–87.

30. E. E. LeMasters, "Parenthood as Crisis," *Marriage and Family Living* 25, no. 3 (1963), reprinted in Parad, 1965, pp. 324–338; Daniel F. Hobbs, Jr., "Parenthood as a Crisis: A Third Study," *Journal of Marriage and the Family* 27 (August 1965): 367–372.

31. Morton A. Lieberman, "Adaptive Processes in Late Life," in Nancy Datan and Leon H. Ginsberg, eds., *Normative Life Crises* (New York: Academic Press, 1975), pp. 139–159.

32. See Eleanor Pavenstedt and Viola W. Bernard, eds., *Crises of Family Disorganization* (New York: Behavioral Publications, 1971), particularly Sec. 2 on "Parents Under Unmanageable Stress," pp. 43–69. Also Catherine S. Chilman, *Growing Up Poor* (Washington, D. C.: U. S. Dept. of Health, Education, and Welfare, 1966), and Lola M. Irelan, ed., *Low-Income Life Styles* (Washington, D. C.: HEW, 1966).

33. See the long series of research studies in Barbara S. and Bruce P. Dohrenwend, eds., *Stressful Life Events: Their Nature and Effects* (New York: John Wiley and Sons, 1974). Also Fred Davis, *Passage through Crisis: Polio Victims and Their Families* (Indianapolis: Bobbs-Merrill, 1963).

34. Thomas D. Eliot, "Handling Family Strains and Shocks," in Howard Becker and Reuben Hill, eds., *Family, Marriage, and Parenthood* (Boston: Heath and Co., 1955); William W. Waller, *The Family: A Dynamic Interpretation*, revised by Reuben Hill (New York: Dryden Press, 1951). Both quoted in Hill, 1958, p. 37.

35. John and Elaine Cumming, *Ego and Milieu* (New York: Atherton Press, 1966), 46–50.
36. Bernard Farber, "Some Effects of a Retarded Child on the Mother," in Sussman, 1963, pp. 324–333.
37. George H. Grosser, Henry Wechsler, and Milton Greenblatt, eds., *The Threat of Impending Disaster* (Cambridge: M. I. T. Press, 1964); James B. Taylor, L. A. Zuicher, and W. H. Key, *Tornado: A Community Responds to Disaster* (Seattle: University of Washington Press, 1970).
38. James Tyhurst, "The Role of Transition States—Including Disasters—in Mental Illness," *Symposium on Preventive and Social Psychiatry,* (Washington, D.C.: Walter Reed Army Institute of Research, 1957), pp. 149–167.
39. J. W. Powell and J. Rayner, "Progress Notes: Disaster Investigation, Army Chemical Center, 1952," quoted in Richard I. Shader and Alice J. Schwartz, "Management of Reactions to Disaster," *Social Work* 11 (April 1966): 100–101.
40. Roy R. Grinker and John P. Spiegel, *Men Under Stress* (New York: Blackeston Press, 1945).
41. F. G. Harris and R. W. Little, "Military Organizations and Social Psychiatry," in *Symposium, on Preventive and Social Psychiatry,* 1957, pp. 173–184.
42. J. M. Caldwell, "Military Psychiatry," in A. M. Freedman, H. I. Kaplan and H. S. Kaplan, eds., *Comprehensive Textbook of Psychiatry* (Baltimore: William and Wilkins, 1967).
43. Erich Lindemann, "Symptomatology and Management of Acute Grief," *American Journal of Psychiatry* 10 (September 1944). Reprinted in Parad, 1965, 7–21.
44. Donald C. Klein and Erich Lindemann, "Preventive Intervention in Individual and Family Crisis Situations," in G. Caplan, ed., *Prevention of Mental Disorders in Children* (New York: Basic Books, 1961), pp. 283–306.
45. Gerald Caplan, "A Public Health Approach to Child Psychiatry," *Mental Health* 35 (1951): 235–249.
46. Gerald Caplan, *Principles of Preventive Psychiatry* (New York: Basic Books, 1964).
47. Gerald Caplan, Edward A. Mason, and David M. Kaplan, "Four

Studies of Crisis in Parents of Prematures," *Community Mental Health Journal* 2, no. 2 (Summer 1965): 150–159.

48. David M. Kaplan, "A Concept of Acute Situational Disorders," *Social Work* 7 (April 1962): 15–23.

49. Howard J. Parad and Gerald Caplan, "A Framework for Studying Families in Crisis," *Social Work* 5 (September 1960), reprinted in Parad, 1965, pp. 53–72; Lydia Rapoport, "The State of Crisis: Some Theoretical Considerations," *Social Service Review* 36 (June 1962), reprinted in Parad, 1965, pp. 22–31.

50. Phyllis Silverman, Dorothy MacKenzie, Mary Pettipas, and Elizabeth Wilson, eds., *Helping Each Other in Widowhood* (New York: Health Services, 1974).

51. Ira O. Glick, Robert S. Weiss, and C. Murray Parkes, *The First Year of Bereavement* (New York: John Wiley and Sons, 1974).

52. Gerald Caplan, *Support Systems and Community Mental Health* (New York: Behavioral Publications, 1974).

53. Naomi Golan and Batya Vashitz, "Social Services in a War Emergency," *Social Service Review* 48 (September 1974): 422–427.

54. Richard McGee, *Crisis Intervention in the Community* (Baltimore: University Park Press, 1974), pp. 18–19.

55. Louis I. Dublin, *Suicide: A Sociological and Statistical Study* (New York: Ronald Press, 1963); Edwin S. Shneidman, Norman L. Farberow, and Robert E. Litman, *The Psychology of Suicide* (New York: Science House, 1970); Norman L. Farberow and Edwin L. Shneidman, *The Cry for Help* (New York: McGraw-Hill, 1961).

56. McGee, 1974, 3–9.

57. David Mechanic, *Mental Health and Social Policy* (Englewood Cliffs, N. J.: Prentice-Hall, 1969), pp. 56–61.

58. Naomi Golan, "Federal Participation in Mental Health Programs: From Mann to Mental Health Centers," unpublished paper for School of Social Service Administration, University of Chicago, 1965.

59. Gerald Gurin, Joseph Veroff, and Sheila Feld, *Americans View Their Mental Health* (New York: Basic Books, 1960).

60. Joint Commission on Mental Illness and Health, *Action for Mental Health* (New York: John Wiley and Sons, 1961).

61. Public Health Service, *National Mental Health Programs and the States,* Pub. 629, rev. (Washington, D. C.: U. S. Government Printing Office, 1962).

62. David Mechanic, "Social Structure and Personal Adaptation: Some Neglected Dimensions," in Coelho, Hamburg, and Adams, 1974, pp. 32–44.

63. H. L. P. Resnik and Harvey L. Ruben, eds., *Emergency Psychiatric Care* (Bowie, Md.: Charles Press, 1975), preface.

Chapter 3

Historical Perspectives: Social Work Developments

Practice in Stress

EARLY ROOTS

Helping people in distress has been an integral aspect of social work practice since the early days of the "friendly visitor" from the Charity Organization Societies at the turn of the century.[1] Writing about her first job as intake secretary at the Boston Children's Aid Society in 1913, Bertha Reynolds recalled how the staff learned to become sensitive to the anxiety with which people in trouble approached the agency. She described the first summer course in psychiatric social work, started at Smith College a few years later, in the summer of 1918, "to contribute to the war effort by training workers for the rehabilitation of shell-shocked soldiers."[2]

In the 1921 unemployment crisis, representatives from more than thirty states met to "discuss the practicability of various emergency measures, the desirable relations between public and private agencies in such a crisis and the contribution family social workers might be expected to make."[3]

During the 1920s, as social work began to establish its practice base, psychiatrically trained, clinically oriented caseworkers drew a careful distinction between the "intensive" case, in which the agency assumed responsibility for "making a full inquiry into the social conditions of the patient and his family and endeavor-[ing] to secure the largest measure of social well-being possible for both [him] and his family," and the "slight service" case, in which "assistance is given without inquiring beyond the apparent facts or responsibility taken beyond the immediate service."

This division, though ostensibly drawn together in Mary Richmond's "two-pronged approach," was to continue to mark the profession for the next thirty years. For example, she declared firmly that the basic function of family casework was long-term intensive care. Reynolds, on the other hand, pointed out the positive treatment values in the single-contact interview focusing on "the problem of most concern at the moment."[4]

THE GREAT DEPRESSION

The widespread distress and disruption of the 1930s, as part of the Great Depression, brought home forcibly the need to cope, often within public relief settings, with the many-faceted effects of socioeconomic disaster:

> Even more difficult than the financing of relief has been the task of actually dealing with the day to day applications for assistance from thousands of families who were seeking outside aid for the first time; the task of giving an unhurried, individualized interview to those thousands of applicants, supplying leadership and direction in some plan by which they might keep their home intact and their family life as normal as possible . . .[5]

A report from family service agencies during this period showed that families in hard times tended to withdraw from cus-

tomary contacts with church, friends, and recreational opportunities, not only because they lacked money and consequently
lacked clothes, but because they had "no heart for such things."

> To some families this has come to mean a greater dependence
> on one another, a finding of new resources in the home. To others
> this withdrawing has increased family irritation, quarreling, nag-
> ging to the point where one or another—usually the father or an
> adolescent child—leaves home either temporarily or perma-
> nently.[6]

During this period the Travelers Aid Society, which primarily
operated out of railroad and bus stations to provide short-term
emergency care for stranded transients, developed its specialized
approach for dealing with frightened, upset, disheartened clients.
The society's manual, issued in 1937, stated:

> A crisis which has just arisen is much easier to resolve quickly
> than one less abrupt in development. The sudden crisis presents a
> challenge to the client; friends and family recognize the need to
> rally to his reinforcement. But the problem which has been slowly
> developing over a period of months or years and which is now
> deeply rooted requires a different approach. While the latest point
> of difficulty may be treated in the short contact, the more funda-
> mental problem may have to remain untouched.[7]

This and subsequent Travelers Aid reports emphasized the
beneficial effects of delineating limited goals which are tangible
and reachable and the neeed for immediate treatment, beginning
as soon as the client comes into the office.

THE WAR YEARS

World War II resulted in some easing of the economic difficulties caused by the Depression but brought widespread family disruption, separation, and upset, as Cohen has observed:

> The entire nation, in one way or another, was affected by the
> war . . . . The disruption of family life, the entrance of women into

industry on a large scale, the increase in divorces and in the number of unwed mothers, the rising rate of juvenile delinquency, and the myriad emotional problems arising from the fear of losing loved ones in the service provided a more than average load for casework services.[8]

These new pressures on family life provided both an opportunity and a challenge to local family agencies:

> A number of the societies gave consultation service to mothers who wanted to take jobs in industry . . . and to give them information about resources for the care of their children. Casework services to day nurseries helped both the mother and the . . . personnel when problems arose in the children's adjustment or in connection with the mother's work . . . .
> The private agencies undertook to give personal service to selectees and their families. They were particularly concerned with the men who were rejected for reasons of physical and emotional health and, later, the men discharged as unfit soon after induction . . . . The breakup of families due to separation, the tensions and anxieties arising from the war, the hasty, often impulsive marriages of young men about to be inducted into the armed forces, called for skilled casework services in helping husbands and wives work out their problems.[9]

It became obvious, noted Cohen, that more would have to be done to meet the growing psychosocial needs of the population; not only would new methods of treatment have to be instituted, but new programs of prevention would have to be developed.

Within the armed services, military psychiatric social work, which started in 1942, dealt with the problems of soldiers who were having difficulty in adjusting to their soldierly duties. This necessitated adaptations in the usual casework approach: interviews had to be focused on the immediate problem and conducted over short intervals of time with recording kept to a minimum. Group counseling and group therapy emerged as methods for dealing with large numbers of servicemen grappling with similar types of problems.[10]

POSTWAR DEVELOPMENTS

As the 1950s progressed, social agencies became concerned about the broadening discrepancy between the growing number of requests and the increasing length of time before service could be offered. Some set up separate "information, consultation, intake, and referral services" to offer help to those who "in normal situations are not neurotic and who can usually handle their problems without difficulty. Due to increased strains and tensions they may need temporary help."[11]

Some agencies resorted to preliminary screening of applicants by telephone, working out a priority system for those who could not afford to wait more than a day or two, those who could "hang on" if they had a specific appointment within two weeks, and those who could sustain a long wait.[12] Still others set up study groups to re-examine their intake practices and re-evaluate their criteria and tools for service.[13]

In one office of the Community Service Society of New York, it was found that many persons sought only limited help. If this was given, they could mobilize strength to cope with other aspects of their lives. To those clients who wanted such specific help, intake procedures were cut down to a single interview in which a quick, penetrating study of the immediate critical situation was carried out, including evaluation, clarification, and, if indicated, referral to appropriate community resources.[14]

By the early 1960s, agencies were feeling acute pressure between growing waiting lists and staff shortages, on the one hand, and frequent dropouts and unplanned terminations, on the other. Research studies brought forth the startling information that one out of three clients applying to family agencies did not return after the first interview,[15] and four out of five discontinued by the fifth.[16]

Efforts to deal with this situation ranged from minor modifications in service arrangements[17] to complete renovations of agency programs, objectives, and practices.[18] The Parads found evidence of considerable experimentation with the use of short-term, planned treatment—often within the newly emerging crisis framework—in their comprehensive survey of family service agencies and psychiatric clinics carried out during 1965–1966.[19] Social agencies began to study new approaches and to hold staff development seminars to learn to apply them, including crisis theory concepts.[20]

In casework with the aged, clients frequently were seen during periods of crisis, and treatment involved planning how to preserve their forms of independent living or how to adjust to new settings.[21] Wasser pointed out:

> The psychotic or critically ill aged person, particularly the one who is alone and isolated, is likely to come to the community's notice only when his symptoms have become blatantly obvious and to be referred to a social agency as the result of a crisis situation. When the worker deals with the case quickly and skillfully, further deterioration can often be prevented.[22]

As mentioned earlier, social workers in some types of settings had always dealt with persons in stressful situations; they now found a theoretical framework to justify and give structure to what they previously had been doing intuitively and on an ad hoc basis. Medical social services,[23] university counseling centers,[24] and those working with hard-to-reach clients[25] all found the crisis-intervention approach compatible with their practice in high-stress situations.

Much of the early innovation carried out by multidisciplinary teams within mental health settings, such as the Langley-Porter Neuropsychiatric Institute in San Francisco,[26] the Benjamin Rush Center for Problems in Living in Los Angeles,[27] the Emergency Psychiatric Service of Massachusetts General Hospital in Boston,[28] and the Madeline Borg Child Guidance Institute of the Jewish Board of Guardians in New York,[29] featured social workers as primary executors of the crisis approach.

Casework Theory on Stress and Crisis

Current practice theory in crisis situations is an amalgam of a number of theoretical approaches in social work with individuals, families, and groups which have evolved slowly over the years. As frequently happens, it took theoreticians some time to "tune in" on what practitioners in the field were already doing.

Functionalist Approach

The functionalist school was probably the first to place emphasis on the special needs of the client under pressure and to emphasize the importance of time as a factor in the casework relationship. Jessie Taft, in the early 1930s, felt that the short-contact case, to be meaningful, should encapsulate the whole therapy situation:

> Here for the first time in the history of casework . . . a few case-workers are struggling with the fundamental problem of therapy . . . . What happens, they ask themselves, to make a single or a short-contact meaningful, as it often is, for client and worker even if they never meet again? The fascination which the study of the short contact holds indicates that somehow it contains the whole problem of therapy, if it only can be mastered.[30]

Dawley noted that, when a client came to an agency for help, he had already taken the first step toward obtaining it. The caseworker's skill lay in her understanding of this and in the way she used the resources of the agency to keep alive the impulse that had brought the individual in. Thus the purpose of the first interview was to clarify immediately whether the client wanted what the agency had to offer, and to work on the way in which he could use what was available to him.[31]

Marcus pointed out that when we defined the aim of social work as "helping the client to help himself," we were expecting him to do so at the precise moment when he was least able to do so:

> The client with a problem he cannot meet without help is beset with crisis . . . . Because of some loss in his resources or some obstacle in himself or his circumstances . . . [he] cannot achieve the new organization of himself required to deal with his situation.

The task of the caseworker is to help him mobilize his inner and outer forces to handle his own problem.[32]

Lowry felt that, in carrying out short-contact casework, it was necessary to distinguish between those cases in which the request was precipitated by a crisis, whether immediate or the result of slowly accumulating pressures, and cases of "chronic crisis." She added that while the pressure of the time limitation in practice may generate anxiety in the worker, in short-contact casework, "just as time may be limited without being limiting, so . . . the limits of time need not limit our services."[33]

In a more recent statement of the functionalist position, Smalley emphasizes that understanding the nature of stress is basic to the casework process. She also reiterates the importance of time:

> The effectiveness of any social work process . . . is furthered by the worker's conscious, knowing use of time phases in the process (beginnings, middles, and endings) in order that the particular potential in each time phase may be fully exploited for the other's use.[34]

DIAGNOSTIC APPROACH

The early diagnostic theoreticians had a somewhat ambivalent view of what happens when an applicant comes in asking for help. In 1940, Hamilton, for example, said:

> The intuitive interviewer will recognize the feelings of insecurity, anxiety, and irritability. But most caseworkers have to learn the meaning of these attitudes and develop skill in reducing the fear, in restoring the damaged self-esteem, by giving the applicant undivided attention, privacy, and help in discussing the topic of greatest interest to him—namely his situation and request.[35]

She warned, however, that when a client comes to an agency for help, it is not always easy to discover what the real request is or what the client is suffering from. Real emergencies and cases of "psychological urgency" must be distinguished from the general run of applications and more prompt intervention must be attempted.

Even when emergencies do occur, she felt:

> It is possible to do too much and to act too quickly .... It is in so-called "emergencies" that the temptation to take the problem away from the client is greatest.... Yet the experienced caseworker who has not to "play providence" will be able to take responsibility for quick, decisive action or vigorous emotional support whenever necessary. When applicants are acutely ill or frightened or otherwise incapacitated, we must take active responsibility until they are well enough to take over the problem and themselves go on with it.[36]

As the differentiation between various levels of treatment became more emphasized, Austin spoke of *social therapy,* appropriate in situations where causation lies mainly in the external environment and treatment is aimed at preventing the bad effects of accumulated strains. (Presumably, crisis situations would fall into this category.) *Psychotherapy,* on the other hand, is designed to bring about some modification in behavior and attitudes, and rests on a diagnosis of the total personality.[37]

An even sharper distinction was drawn between "treatment aimed at maintaining adaptive patterns" and "treatment aimed at modifying adaptive patterns." The former was considered suitable for clients whose functioning was temporarily disabled as a result of a crisis in their lives.[38]

As the diagnostic school—or the psychosocial school, as it has come to be called—has drawn closer to other casework approaches, Hollis has picked up Hamilton's earlier person-in-a-social-situation configuration and speaks of "external pressure (press)" and "internal pressure (stress)" to describe forces within the individual and in his environment as they impinge upon and interact with each other.[39] In another context, she notes that crisis treatment is appropriate when a person has been thrown off balance by some hazardous external event of a time-limited nature, which touches off reactions within his personality with which he is unable to cope. In order to know what help is needed, a rapid diagnosis, well grounded in theory, must be made. Goals should be limited and well defined, treatment quite active, and pertinent interpretations made quickly.[40]

PROBLEM-SOLVING APPROACH

As a forerunner, during the 1940s, Towle emphasized the rehabilitative goal in social casework as a way of meeting common human needs. In her landmark volume, directed to workers in public assistance, she stressed that since we deal with people "in the midst of emotions that come from the major catastrophes of life," they must be allowed to relieve themselves of pressures and tensions which have made the problem disturbing.[41]

Shortly after the start of the Korean War, which disrupted many families, Towle pointed out:

> Social work has always served families whose individual worlds have been stressful. The noteworthy features today are the totality of life's uncertainty and the facts that parents and children have grown up during precarious times—war, inflation, depression, war, inflation, and now a defense economy. Many . . . are more vulnerable by reason of long-standing strain . . . . Stresses become more traumatic through repetition.[42]

Perlman described the person who comes to a social agency as being under a twofold stress: the problem itself, which is felt as a threat or as an actual attack, and his inability to cope with it, which increases his tension:

> The greater the client's sense of duress and tension, the more overwhelmed and helpless he may feel. The problem-solving functions of his ego are likely to be at least temporarily disabled or constricted. . . . Relief from stress in one aspect of living may lighten the burden in another.[43]

The problem, said Perlman, may be one of some unmet need or of stress—psychological, social, or physical—which causes the

person to be ineffective or disturbed in carrying his social roles. Whether such needs and stresses occur singly or in combination, the person's inability to "muster the means by which to maintain or achieve social comfort and adequacy" brings the problem within the locus of casework's concern. Typically, the client seeks help for some readjustment of himself or of some part of his social situation so that he can maintain or achieve the equilibrium needed for his daily pursuits.[44]

She pointed out that not all problems brought to an agency may be actual crises; nevertheless, at the point of calling or walking into an agency, the applicant *feels* that his problem is a crisis. He is keyed up and his energies are mobilized to cope with it. Thus the opportunity to provide the "little help at the strategic time" is missed if the applicant is assigned to a waiting list.[45]

In a recent statement of the problem-solving approach, Perlman sees as the goal of treatment "to help a person cope as effectively as possible with such problems in carrying social tasks and relationships which he now perceives, feels as stressful, and finds insuperable without outside help." To her, both crisis intervention and short-term treatment models are consistent outgrowths of the problem-solving model of practice.[46]

CRISIS INTERVENTION APPROACH

Howard Parad was one of the first social work theoreticians to recognize the potential in the Harvard public health model and did much to introduce the crisis-intervention approach into social work practice. He offered an ego psychology framework as an additional tool to the "medical social worker who deals with the crisis of illness, to the court worker who deals with the crisis of an antisocial act, and to the family, child welfare, and psychiatric worker who constantly deal with crises in personal and family function."[47]

Parad maintained that, at intake, most cases could be treated *either* on a short-term or long-term basis and that treatment arrangements are often influenced by expediency. Choosing cases in which a crisis has recently developed and disequilibrium still exists can be the key to successful short-term intervention. The caseworker, as an actively involved participant, observer, and change agent,

> mediates between the precipitating stress and the underlying problems it evokes, thereby attempting to engage and mobilize the client's untapped ego forces and those within his "current ego span" . . . as well as the larger forces in the relevant family and social environment.[48]

Activity is carried out simultaneously on two fronts: precisely articulated diagnostic formulation and immediate therapeutic contact. Differential techniques of support, on-the-spot clarification, and the use of environmental aids within the context of an empathic relationship become basic and can do much to eliminate waiting lists, avoid prolonged diagnostic investigations "that leave the worker with all the information and the client with all the problems," and provide economic, constructive service.

The late Lydia Rapoport, one of the most articulate and creative thinkers in the crisis-intervention area, pointed out that, in order to help people in a state of crisis, social workers and clients must have rapid and ready access to each other. This entails a structure in agencies and services that makes it possible to meet requests for help within a few days. Crisis intervention presupposes no intake or waiting list and no separation between the study, diagnosis, and treatment aspects of the case. The same worker maintains continuing contact throughout the length of service.[49]

Rapoport saw this type of intervention as requiring some important modifications in casework practice. It does not lend itself to systematic history taking, with its vertical and horizontal scanning of development, emotional, and social functioning, manifestations of psychopathology, and consideration of both genetic and dynamic factors.

Although she regarded some appraisal of basic personality structure and identification of basic defenses and habitual adaptive patterns as important, she felt that the worker has to operate quickly, out of past clinical experience, knowledge of personality organization, and ability to appraise the significance of the client's behavior on the basis of both overt communication and marginal clues.[50]

Goals of treatment, according to Rapoport, rest on the concept of restoration and enhancement of functioning rather than on cure. In view of the built-in time limits, intervention must start immediately, in the initial interview, to enable the client to experience reduction of tension and anxiety. The tidy dichotomization of treatment measures into maintaining or modifying modes is not characteristic of actual practice in either crisis or non-crisis situations. Treatment is primarily present-oriented, with the worker maintaining an active and directive stance.[51]

The concept of client-worker relationship in crisis intervention assumes a new dimension, according to Rapoport. She saw the worker's authority, derived from competence and expertness, as the significant aspects of the relationship which can be used to capitalize on the client's readiness to trust during this period of confusion, helplessness, and anxiety. The degree of worker-client *involvement* in the process rather than their mutual attachment becomes crucial.[52]

Strickler and Bonnefil see similarities between crisis intervention and traditional casework as it is currently practiced. In both instances treatment goals are aimed at enhancing the client's ability to cope with current problems in living. Treatment is focused on specific problems of interpersonal conflicts and role dysfunctioning; it is concentrated on the problem to be solved and geared largely to the conscious and near-conscious level of emotional conflicts. The practitioner recognizes transference impulses but moves to replace them with analogous feelings related to the client's current external situation and relationships. He must be able to formulate diagnostic evaluations in terms of the client's position in his intrafamilial and extended social relationships.

Nevertheless, these authors see significant differences between the two approaches. In the traditional psychosocial approach, the practitioner seeks to help the client gradually to sort out and clarify his feelings; in the crisis approach, the worker is uniquely active, working at an intense pace, sharing the client's sense of urgency. There is an implicit as well as explicit expectation on the client's part that his problem will be resolved as quickly as possible. Treatment is based on the unique readiness of the client to risk himself in order to gain a sense of mastery. The worker is constantly alert to forestall or minimize the client's dependent or regressive fantasies toward him.[53]

In view of these differences, it is not surprising that some practitioners still regard the crisis approach somewhat uneasily, seeing it largely in terms of symptom relief and "plastering over," without producing lasting change or cure. The need for quick, independent decisions and the activist approach tend to make them nervous and wary of making mistakes and inviting criticism.

In a review of emerging trends in social treatment, Gelfand observes that since the development and application of the crisis concept, a host of situations have developed that require brief, skillful intervention to provide clients with relief from stress and the possibility for growth.[54] Nevertheless, my own observations during visits to a number of social work, medical, and mental health facilities in the summer of 1976, revealed that, almost twenty years after crisis intervention was first introduced as a practice modality, many practitioners still use it only selectively and in a pro forma way.

However, in those settings where the crisis approach has been adopted fully, one outstanding characteristic was noted that deserves mention: the worker's consistently high level of enthusiasm and personal commitment to treatment goals and strategies.

Perhaps this can be attributed to the professional staff's comparative youth and lack of investment in the more traditional forms of casework or intensive psychotherapy; perhaps it lies in their recognition that the crisis approach engenders active involvement with accompanying feelings of hope and expectation of change. The facts stands out that participants in crisis programs or users of the crisis approach invariably voiced their conviction that they were indeed helping clients make significant changes in their coping styles, which, in turn, positively affected their overall levels of social functioning.

Notes

1. Margaret E. Rich, *A Belief in People* (New York: Family Service Association of America, 1956), p. 21.
2. Bertha C. Reynolds, *An Uncharted Journey* (New York: Citadel Press, 1963), pp. 54–62.
3. Rich, 1956, pp. 100–102.
4. See Libbie G. Parad, "Short-Term Treatment: An Overview of Historical Trends, Issues, and Potentials," *Smith College Studies* 41 (February 1971): 121–125, for a fuller discussion of this issue.
5. Wendell F. Johnson, "How Case Working Agencies Have Met Unemployment," *Proceedings, National Conference of Social Welfare,* 1931; quoted in Rich, 1956, p. 118.
6. Rich, 1956, pp. 129–130.
7. Robert S. Wilson, *The Short Contact in Social Case Work,* vol. 1 (New York: National Association for Travelers Aid and Transient Service, 1937), p. 64.
8. Nathan E. Cohen, *Social Work in the American Tradition* (New York: Holt, Rinehart, and Winston, 1958), p. 235.
9. Rich, 1956, p. 146.
10. Cohen, 1958, pp. 238–239.

11. Dorothy V. Thomas, "The Relationship Between Diagnostic Services and Short Contact Cases," *Social Casework* 32 (February 1951). Reprinted in *The Intake Process,* (New York: FSAA, n. d.), p. 32.

12. Catherine M. Bittermann, "Serving Applicants When There Is a Waiting List," *Social Casework* 39 (June 1958): 356–360.

13. Miriam Jolesch, "Strengthening Intake Practice Through Group Discussion," *Social Casework* 40, (November 1959): 504–510.

14. Helen LaMar, "The Intake Process in a Growing Community," *Social Casework* 34 (April 1953). Reprinted in *The Intake Process,* pp. 8–15.

15. Dorothy F. Beck, *Patterns in Use of Family Agency Service* (New York: FSAA, 1962).

16. Lilian Ripple et al., *Motivation, Capacity, and Opportunity,* Social Service Monographs, Second Series, School of Social Service Administration (Chicago: University of Chicago, 1964).

17. Grace L. Duckworth, "A Project in Crisis Intervention," *Social Casework* 48 (April 1967): 227–231.

18. Rachel A. Levine, "A Short Story on the Long Waiting List," *Social Work* 8 (January 1963): 20–22.

19. Howard J. Parad and Libbie G. Parad, "A Study of Crisis-Oriented Planned Short-Term Treatment," Part I, *Social Casework* 49, (June 1968): 346–355; Part II, *Social Casework* 49 (July 1968): 418–426.

20. Robert Leopold, "Crisis Intervention: Some Notes on Practice and Theory," in Gertrude Einstein, ed., *Learning to Apply New Concepts to Casework Practice* (New York: FSAA, 1968), pp. 9–33.

21. Kathryn Rummel, "Helping the Older Client Involve His Family in Future Plans," *Social Casework* 39 (November 1958): 508–512; Helen Lampe, "Diagnostic Considerations in Casework with Aged Clients," *Social Casework* 42 (May–June 1961): 241–244.

22. Edna Wasser, *Creative Approaches in Casework with the Aged* (New York: FSAA, 1966), p. 35.

23. Jeanette C. Oppenheimer, "Use of Crisis Intervention in Casework with the Client and His Family," *Social Work* 12 (April 1967): 44–52.

24. Alice Ichikawa, "Observations of College Students in Acute Distress," *Student Medicine* 10, no. 2 (1961). Reprinted in Parad, 1965, pp. 167-173.

25. Berta Fantl, "Preventive Intervention," *Social Work* 7 (July 1960): 41–48.

26. Betty L. Kalis, M. R. Harris, A. R. Prestwood, and E. H. Freeman, "Precipitating Stress as a Focus in Psychotherapy," *Archives of General Psychiatry* 5 (September 1961): 219–226.

27. Martin Strickler, Ellen G. Bassin, Virginia Malbin, and Gerald F. Jacobson, "The Community-based Walk-in Center: A New Resource for Groups Underrepresented in Outpatient Treatment Facilities," *American Journal of Public Health* 55 (May 1965): 377–384.

28. Eleanor Clark, "Round the Clock Emergency Psychiatric Services," *Social Work Practice, 1963* (New York: Columbia University Press, 1963). Reprinted in Parad, 1965, pp. 261–273.

29. Elise Fell, "An Experiment in Short-Term Treatment in a Child Guidance Clinic," *Journal of Jewish Communal Service* 36 (Winter 1959): 144–149.

30. Jessie Taft, *Dynamics of Therapy in a Controlled Relationship* (New York: Macmillan, 1933), pp. 10–11.

31. Almena Dawley, "Professional Skills Requisite to a Good Intake Service," in *Proceedings of the National Council of Social Welfare,* 1937 (Chicago: University of Chicago Press, 1937), p. 259.

32. Grace F. Marcus, "Helping the Client to Use His Capacities and Resources," *Proceedings of the National Conference of Social Welfare,* 1948 (New York: Columbia University Press, 1948), p. 254.

33. Fern Lowry, "The Caseworker in Short-Contact Services, *Social Work* 2 (January 1957): 53.

34. Ruth E. Smalley, "The Functional Approach to Casework Practice," in R. W. Roberts and R. H. Nee, eds., *Theories of Social Casework* (Chicago: University of Chicago Press, 1970), p. 81.

35. Gordon Hamilton, *Theory and Practice of Social Work* (New York: Columbia University Press, 1940), 2nd ed., 1951, p. 152.

36. Ibid., pp. 177–179.

37. Lucille N. Austin, "Trends in Differential Treatment in Social Casework," *Journal of Social Casework* (June 1948). Reprinted in C. Kasius, ed., *Principles and Techniques in Social Casework* (New York: FSAA, 1950), pp. 324–338.

38. *Scope and Method of Family Service* (New York: FSAA, 1953), pp. 18–19.

39. Florence Hollis, *Casework: A Psychosocial Therapy* (New York: Random House, 1964), p. 10.

40. Florence Hollis, *Casework: A Psychosocial Therapy,* 2nd ed. (New York: Random House, 1972), p. 324.

41. Charlotte Towle, *Common Human Needs* (Washington, D. C.: Federal Security Agency, 1945). Reissued (New York: NASW, 1957).

42. Charlotte Towle, "Reinforcing Family Security Today," *Social Casework* 32 (February 1951). Quoted in Rich, 1956, p. 163.

43. Helen H. Perlman, *Social Casework: A Problem-Solving Process* (Chicago: University of Chicago Press, 1957), pp. 25–26.

44. Ibid., p. 28.

45. Helen H. Perlman, "Some Notes on the Waiting List," *Social Casework* 44 (April 1963): 203–204.

46. Helen H. Perlman, "The Problem-Solving Model in Social Casework," in Roberts and Nee, 1970, pp. 139, 173–175.

47. Howard J. Parad, "Brief Ego-Oriented Casework with Families in Crisis," in H. J. Parad and R. R. Miller, eds., *Ego-Oriented Casework: Problems and Perspectives* (New York: FSAA, 1963), p. 146.

48. Ibid., p. 149.

49. Lydia Rapoport, "The State of Crisis: Some Theoretical Considerations," *Social Service Review* 36 (June 1962). Reprinted in Parad, 1965, pp. 22–31.

50. Lydia Rapoport, "Crisis Intervention as a Mode of Brief Treatment," in Roberts and Nee, 1970, p. 280.

51. Ibid., pp. 294–301.

52. In discussing transference in brief psychotherapy, Malan makes a similar observation that one factor making for success in treatment appears to be the "successful dynamic interaction" between

therapist and patient. See David H. Malan, *The Frontier of Brief Psychotherapy* (New York: Plenum, 1976), p. 54.

53. Martin Strickler and Margaret Bonnefil, "Crisis Intervention and Social Casework: Similarities and Differences in Problem Solving," *Clinical Social Work Journal* 2 (Spring 1974): 36–44.

54. Bernard Gelfand, "Emerging Trends in Social Treatment," *Social Casework* 53 (March 1972): 161.

Part 2

The
Basic
Practice
Model

Introduction

As CRISIS INTERVENTION has become part of the treatment repertoire of the helping professional, a number of models for practice in
stressful situations have been developed. Within the past few years,
detailed blueprints have been drawn up for psychiatric residents
in admission services,[1] for nonprofessional workers in psychiatric
emergency centers,[2] for mental health professionals on crisis-
intervention units for hospitals,[3] for staff members of suicide-
prevention programs,[4] and for crisis counselors in special crisis
services.[5]

In this section we shall offer a basic model for social work
practice using the crisis approach. It has much in common with
other models of practice in stressful situations in that it takes the
basic principles of crisis theory as its frame of reference. It is
different in that it is intended for use in a wide variety of settings
in which social workers operate and can be adapted for the broad
range of crisis-inducing problems which they can expect to encounter in their practice.

In Chapter 4, we shall present an overall view of the elements
of the crisis situation which the worker needs to evaluate in order
to assess where the client is and why he is asking for help at this
time.[6] Then we shall suggest various goals which can be set for
treatment. Finally, we shall discuss the nature and progression of
tasks which must be engaged in in order to effect reorganization.

Chapter 5 will deal in a chronological way with the three
phases of the practice model, the beginning, the middle, and the
end stages. In Chapter 6, we shall consider various treatment
techniques and strategies that can be used and determinants for

59

implementation of this model. Finally, we shall discuss special issues concerning work with families and groups.

Notes

1. C. Peter Rosenbaum and John E. Beebe III, *Psychiatric Treatment: Crisis, Clinic, Consultation* (New York: McGraw-Hill, 1975), pp. 19–41.

2. H. L. P. Resnik and Harvey L. Ruben, éds., *Emergency Psychiatric Care* (Bowie, Md.: Charles Press, 1975), pp. 28–34.

3. Julian Lieb, Ian I. Lipsitch, and Andrew E. Slaby, *The Crisis Team* (New York: Harper and Row, 1973), pp. 33–86.

4. Richard K. McGee, *Crisis Intervention in the Community* (Baltimore: University Park Press, 1974), pp. 200–208.

5. William Getz, Allen E. Wiesen, Stan Sue, and Amy Ayers, *Fundamentals of Crisis Counseling* (Lexington, Mass.: D.C. Heath, 1974), pp. 47–87.

6. For the sake of simplicity, we shall speak of the "individual" or the "client." Unless otherwise specified, this may be taken to apply to families, groups, and in some cases, communities as well.

Chapter 4

Identifying and Defining the Crisis Situation

The Nature of Crisis

Most simply put, a crisis is an "upset in a steady state."[1] In an attempt to pin it down more firmly, a number of writers have pointed out that the word *crisis* is derived from the Greek word for "decision," or, more broadly, a "turning point." The most frequently used dictionary definition is some version of "a vitally important or decisive stage in the progress of anything; . . . a state of affairs in which a decisive change for better or worse is imminent" or "an emotionally significant event or radical change of status in a person's life."[2]

It has also been pointed out that the Chinese ideograph for crisis can be interpreted both as a "danger," in the sense that it threatens to overwhelm the individual and may result in serious consequences, and as an "opportunity," since during such periods he tends to be more amenable to outside influences.[3]

Without going into the complex differentiations and nuances in the uses of such overlapping terms as *stress, crisis,* and *emer-*

gency,[4] we would accept as a working definition Caplan's statement that "a crisis occurs when a person faces an obstacle to important life goals that is, for a time, insurmountable through the utilization of his customary methods of problem-solving."[5]

Our formulation of the crisis approach and its application is based on certain assumptions regarding individuals in difficulties, some of which have already been stated in the basic theoretical points in Chapter 1 but which deserve repeating here. First, a crisis is *not* a pathological state; it may occur to anyone at any stage in his life span. Its occurrence and development are independent of but interwoven with the person's basic personality patterns, his relationship with significant others with whom he is involved, and the resources and supports available to him at the time.

Moreover, different persons faced with the same situation, or the same person at different stages of life or in other sets of interacting circumstances, may not necessarily display the same reactions or be similarly affected. An a priori assumption that a crisis exists may be unwarranted. A careful, individualized evaluation of the total field of social forces is the first stage in any type of intervention but becomes an immediate necessity if a crisis is involved.[6]

Sometimes the problem situation is so acutely stressful that the existence of a crisis can be considered highly probable, as in the case of a train crash or a serious heart attack. Sometimes the choice of setting to which the person comes or is brought—the emergency room of a general hospital or a suicide-prevention center—determines the nature of the approach. And sometimes the person's behavior seems so at variance with his or her current life situation that investigation into the possibility of a recent crisis becomes imperative: for example, if a "contented" housewife abruptly deserts her family or a college senior on the Dean's List fails to appear for his final exams.

When a practitioner in any type of setting is first faced with an individual, alone or with some part of his significant network, and learns that a stress-producing situation exists, he may find it productive to use the crisis approach. To do this, he must quickly make several sets of judgments and arrive at a tentative assessment of the person-in-his-social-situation on the basis of what Rapoport calls "marginal clues."

In order to understand more clearly what is often a highly volatile and emotionally charged picture and to take advantage of the client's high motivation for relief of discomfort, the worker should seek answers to the following questions as early as possible:

1. Does a crisis situation exist?
2. At what point in the process are we entering? (Why is he asking for help now?)
3. What should be the goals of intervention?
4. What tasks have to be carried out in order to achieve these goals?

Several sets of mental maps may be usefully kept in mind, not only at the start of the case, when the first decision to use the crisis approach is made, but periodically, throughout the treatment process, to help the practitioner check whether his earlier judgments still hold, whether the case is progressing satisfactorily, or whether a shift should be made in the approach, the focus, or the person being treated.

Elements in the Crisis Situation

To answer the first two questions, we must examine the aspects leading up to and involving the request for help and learn what has to be done in order to bring about change.

Building on the work of earlier crisis theoreticians,[7] we have called the total sequence of events, from equilibrium to disequilibrium and back again, the *crisis situation* (a simpler term than Klein and Lindemann's "emotional predicament"). Its five components are: the *hazardous event,* the *vulnerable state,* the *precipitating factor,* the *state of active crisis,* and the stage of *reintegration* or crisis resolution. It should be emphasized that these are diagnostic abstractions; the phases to which they refer overlap and cannot actually be isolated. Nevertheless, for evaluative clarity, they should be examined independently.

HAZARDOUS EVENT

The hazardous event is a specific stressful occurrence, either an external blow or an internal change, which occurs to an individual in a state of relative stability with his biopsychosocial situation and which initiates a chain of reverberating actions and reactions. It is the starting point that marks a change in the ecological balance and can usually be found by probing the person's relatively recent past. Such events can be classified as anticipated and predictable, or unanticipated and accidental.

An anticipated event often occurs during a developmental life stage, such as adolescence or old age, when a person may be particularly vulnerable to stress,[8] or during transitional phases as the person passes from one condition to another: from being single to being married or from being employed to being retired. It may involve a geographic place change: moving from a Mississippi farm to a Chicago slum or from a secluded small town to the nation's capital. In any of these situations, even expected changes in role and status and adjustments to new circumstances may have an unsettling effect.

An unanticipated event refers to the nonpredictable happenings which can occur to any person or group of persons with little or no overt warning. For individuals or families, the event may involve some actual or threatened loss of a person, a capacity, or a function—such as the sudden death of a child, loss of eyesight in an accident, or dismissal from a job without notice.[9] On the other hand, it may mark the unheralded entrance of a new person onto the scene: the sudden reappearance of a husband long presumed dead, the unannounced visit of a government inspector, the unforeseen pregnancy of a presumed menopausal woman. The event may have been totally unpredictable, as an auto accident on a clear, uncrowded highway, or may have merely been unexpected at this time, like the premature birth of a child. The unheralded event may involve an entire neighborhood, a community, or even a country. It may have been due to natural causes, as in the case of tornadoes, floods, and earthquakes, or be manmade, as in sociopolitical disasters such as civil wars and atomic bombings or economic-environmental catastrophes such as a bank failure or the gutting of a neighborhood by fire. Although a client being seen for the first time may not be able to state "when it all started," it is important to determine this information at some point in order to provide a baseline for gauging subsequent changes in the person and the situation.

VULNERABLE STATE

The vulnerable or upset state is the subjective reaction of the individual to the initial blow, both at the time it occurs and later. We have noted that, according to Rapoport, each person tends to respond to the hazardous event in his own way, depending on his perception of it. He may experience it as a *threat* to his instinctual needs or to his sense of integrity or autonomy. He may see it as a *loss* of a person or of an ability. Or he may feel it as a *challenge* to survival, growth, mastery, or self expression.[10] Each of these reactions is accompanied by a major characteristic affect: threat usually calls forth a high level of anxiety; loss brings with it depression and mourning; challenge may stimulate a moderate degree of anxiety plus elements of hope, excitement, and positive expectations. Intermingled with these, we find elements of shame, guilt, anger, and hostility, as well as some cognitive and even perceptual confusion.

During the vulnerable state, the individual usually goes through a series of predictable phases. First, he experiences an initial rise in tension and responds with one or more of his usual problem-solving measures. If these do not work, he feels an increase in tension and a sense of ineffectiveness; he then mobilizes his "reserve troops" of external and internal resources and tries out new, emergency coping devices which he does not ordinarily employ or may never have used before. If this further activity does not succeed in solving, mitigating, or even redefining the problem in a more acceptable way (to the individual and those around him), tension will continue to rise to a peak with an increasing disorganization in functioning.[11] Feelings of depression, helplessness, and hopelessness may set in, with some regression of ego functions to a more primitive level and to more childlike types of behavior.

PRECIPITATING FACTOR

The precipitating factor or event is the link in the chain of stress-provoking events that converts the vulnerable state into the state of disequilibrium. It is the "straw that breaks the camel's back," bringing tension and anxiety to a peak. The event may coincide with the initial hazardous blow; that is, the initial event may be of sufficient force to overpower immediately the person's homeostatic balance and send him into a state of active crisis. Or it may be a negligible incident in itself, not even directly or consciously linked to the hazardous event, which overloads the system and serves to tip the balance so that the person's self-regulating gyroscope no longer operates.

Obviously not every hazardous or precipitating event carries the same stress potential. Some blows are so overpowering that they immediately produce the maximal disequilibrating effect. Others appear to be handled initially with relative equanimity by the person and his immediate social network but have a cumulative effect when one pressureful event or situation is piled on top of another, with a consequent weakening of defense mechanisms and coping abilities and increased susceptibility to assault.

Holmes and Rahe have developed an interesting scale to evaluate the stress potential for a number of common life events (see Table 1).[12] While we may question the values attributed,[13] we can see that, as the scores mount, the likelihood of crisis in-

TABLE 1. The Social Readjustment Rating Scale

LIFE EVENT	MEAN VALUE
1. Death of spouse	100
2. Divorce	73
3. Marital separation	65
4. Jail term	63
5. Death of close family member	63
6. Personal injury or illness	53
7. Marriage	50
8. Fired at work	47
9. Marital reconciliation	45
10. Retirement	45
11. Change in health of family member	44
12. Pregnancy	40
13. Sex difficulties	39
14. Gain of new family member	39
15. Business readjustment	39
16. Change in financial state	38
17. Death of close friend	37
18. Change to different line of work	36
19. Change in number of arguments with spouse	35
20. Mortgage over $10,000	31
21. Foreclosure of mortgage or loan	30
22. Change in responsibilities at work	29
23. Son or daughter leaving home	29
24. Trouble with in-laws	29
25. Outstanding personal achievement	28
26. Wife begin or stop work	26
27. Begin or end school	26
28. Change in living conditions	25
29. Revision of personal habits	24
30. Trouble with boss	23
31. Change in work hours or conditions	20
32. Change in residence	20
33. Change in schools	20
34. Change in recreation	19
35. Change in church activities	19
36. Change in social activities	18
37. Mortgage or loan less than $10,000	17
38. Change in sleeping habits	16
39. Change in number of family get-togethers	15
40. Change in eating habits	15
41. Vacation	13
42. Christmas	12
43. Minor violations of the law	11

SOURCE: T. H. Holmes and R. H. Rahe, "The Social Readjustment Rating Scale." *Journal of Psychosomatic Research* 11(1967):213–218. See original for complete wording of the items.

creases. In one situation, the death of a husband might be shattering enough in its effect to send the wife into disequilibrium at once; in another set of circumstances, we might find a series of stresses: the husband's being fired from his job, followed by his wife's getting ill, followed by trouble with his in-laws, followed by the adolescent son's leaving home. While any one of these events might have been handled with relative adequacy, together they form a chain of debilitating blows that finally brings the husband to the social agency, apparently in a state of active crisis.

Sifneos sees the precipitating factor as initiating an emotional crisis, signaling the beginning of a psychotic break, or even acting as the crowning blow that may lead to a suicide attempt. Most often, it motivates the individual to seek some form of help.[14]

Frequently the precipitating factor is stated in terms of the presenting problem ("My husband left me last night"). Thus it can act as the entering wedge into the situation and becomes the focus for immediate engagement. According to some practitioners, there is little need to go beyond working on the precipitating event and the thoughts and feelings behind it in order to restore equilibrium. To Hoffman and Remmel, these thoughts and feelings, which they call the *precipitant*, are connected with an earlier unresolved core conflict and become the focus in their system of crisis psychotherapy.[15]

ACTIVE CRISIS STATE

The state of active or acute crisis describes the individual's subjective condition, once his homeostatic mechanisms have broken down, tension has topped, and disequilibrium has set in. This is the key aspect in crisis theory and should be the determining factor in the decision whether or not to use the crisis approach as the treatment of choice.

At one point in this theory-building, Caplan estimated that the actual stage of imbalance could last for only four to six weeks at the most. During this period, the person passes through a series of predictable reactions. First occurs psychological and physical turmoil, including aimless activity or even immobilization, disturbances in body functions, mood, mental content, and intellectual functioning. This upset is followed and accompanied by painful preoccupation with events leading up to the state of crisis. Finally comes a period of gradual readjustment and remobilization as the individual becomes attuned to the altered situation.[16]

Korner points out that, in a crisis, coping ability is reduced severely and habitual methods for dealing with discomfort, feelings of insecurity, anxiety, and fear have become inoperable. Actually two different etiological processes precipitate crises. In the *exhaustion crisis,* the individual may have coped effectively for some time under prolonged conditions of emergency but suddenly reaches the point of exhaustion; he no longer has enough strength, and the result is a "quasi-ungluing" of the total coping structure. In the *shock crisis,* a sudden change in the social environment creates an explosive release of emotions which overwhelms the available coping mechanisms. Without forewarning, which would have given the individual time to assimilate the impact, he goes into emotional shock.[17]

Since, as stated earlier, the individual's customary defense mechanisms during this stage have become weakened or have even disintegrated, his usual coping patterns have proved inadequate, and emotional discomfort and psychic pain are great, he is usually highly motivated to accept and use help. The chance that minimal effort at this time can produce a maximal effect— that a relative small amount of aid, focused appropriately, can achieve greater results than more extensive help during periods of less emotional accessibility—becomes a major consideration in the choice of treatment.

REINTEGRATION

The stage of reintegration or restoration of equilibrium is actually an extension of the state of active crisis, as the tension and anxiety gradually subside and some form of reorganization of the individual's ability to function takes place. Since the state of imbalance cannot continue for long, some new form of adjustment, either adaptive and integrative or maladaptive and even destructive, has to be found.

According to Hill's roller-coaster diagram,[18] the component parts of the process to be examined are crisis-disorganization-recovery-reorganization. The final level of readjustment may be lower than, equal to, or higher than the precrisis state.

The reintegration stage has been found to consist of several clearly identifiable steps. In the initial phase, *correct cognitive perception*, the problem is maintained at a conscious level as the person struggles to fill in the gaps in his knowledge and understanding of what has happened, both objectively and subjectively. In the second phase, *management of affect*, appropriate acceptance and release of feelings associated with the elements in the crisis situation take place. Finally, *development of new behavioral patterns of coping* occurs, including the appropriate seeking out and using of help. The individual begins to adopt constructive means for dealing with the problems which arise and utilizes other persons and organizations to aid him in carrying out the tasks to be done.[19]

An interesting aspect of correct cognitive perception of the stressful event and subsequent developments has been pointed out by Hooker. She observes that, if the individual believes that action and outcome are independent and that he has no control over the unfolding of events, whether or not this is objectively true, then he will cease his frantic responding. Instead of learning to resolve the crisis, he will lapse into a state of "learned helplessness," the belief that nothing he can do makes a difference.[20]

Jacobson points out that factors affecting crisis outcome include social and cultural prescriptions of behavior; the influence of family, friends, and community caregivers; and, of course, treatment. When a maladaptive outcome occurs, we find the increased use of such defense mechanisms as projection, introjection, and denial. Hostility may be thrust onto others, provoking reactive hostility on their part which is fed back to the individual, bringing about lowered self-esteem, which in turn brings forth further projection—and a vicious cycle is set in motion.

On the other hand, adaptive resolution of the crisis produces a benign cycle. The individual experiences feelings of mastery and increased self-esteem which he projects outward to others, resulting in positive reactions and feedback, leading to a heightened feeling of self-worth, which brings forth greater efforts to cope.[21]

Crisis Resolution

GOALS OF TREATMENT

Treatment goals in crisis intervention are usually relatively limited and related to the immediate crisis situation. Howard Parad suggests that the worker's interventive efforts should be designed to cushion the impact of the stressful event by offering immediate emotional-environmental first aid and to strengthen the person in his coping and integrative struggles through on-the-spot clarification and guidance throughout the crisis period.[22]

More specifically, Rapoport sees two levels of crisis-oriented treatment goals. At the minimal level, she suggests the following operational objectives:

1. Relief of symptoms.
2. Restoration to precrisis level of functioning.
3. Some understanding of the relevant precipitating events which led up to the state of disequilibrium.
4. Identification of remedial measures which the client or family can take or that are available through community resources.

In addition, where the personality and social situation are favorable and the opportunity presents itself or can be created, she recommends two additional goals:

5. Connecting the current stresses with past life experiences and conflicts.

6. Initiating new modes of perceiving, thinking, and feeling and developing new adaptive and coping responses which can be useful beyond the immediate crisis situation.[23]

TREATMENT APPROACHES

These two levels of treatment goals appear to be related to the two treatment approaches described by Jacobson and his associates, the generic and the individual.[24]

The *generic* approach emphasizes specific situational and maturational crises occurring to significant population groups, with no attempt made to assess the particular psychodynamics of the individuals involved. Intervention, often carried out by a paraprofessional, a non-mental health professional, or a community caregiver, focuses on the characteristic course that a crisis situation, such as bereavement or retirement, takes as it unfolds. (The underlying premise is that each crisis pursues its own identifiable patterns, some of which will result in adaptive and some in maladaptive outcomes.) Treatment consists of specific measures designed for the target group as a whole, largely disregarding individual differences.

The *individual* approach, on the other hand, emphasizes assessment of the client's specific intrapsychic and interpersonal processes, with special attention to the unique aspects of the particular situation. Jacobson feels this approach can be carried out most effectively by persons skilled in one of the mental health disciplines. However, he differentiates clearly between the individual approach to crisis and more extended psychotherapy in that the former focuses on why and how the precrisis equilibrium was upset and on the processes involved in reaching a new steady state.

The generic approach, says Jacobson, can be considered analogous to the public health method of immunization, which can be broadly applied to large population groups. Conversely, the individual approach is similar to diagnosis and treatment of a specific disorder and should be used selectively in those cases which do not appear to respond to generic treatment.

Other writers draw different distinctions between the aims of treatment, based not on the nature of the crisis situation or on the practitioner's expertise but on the level of functioning of the patient or client. For example, Langsley and Kaplan suggest two models of crisis treatment.[25] The *recompensation* model sees the person in crisis as "falling apart"; treatment consists of putting him back together again by helping him recompensate and return to his prestress level of functioning. The *limited psychotherapy* model assumes that the crisis is related not only to the fact that the person is decompensating but to the fact that the recent stress has reactivated old conflicts. Treatment consists of interpreting and understanding some of these earlier conflicts.

Sifneos, too, refers to two different kinds of treatment for crisis situation: *anxiety suppressive* and *anxiety provoking*.[26] The first, for disturbed patients with weakened egos, provides "crisis support" which aims to decrease or eliminate anxiety through the use of supportive techniques such as reassurance and environmental manipulation to help him overcome the acutely traumatic situation in which he finds himself. The second can be used with patients who have some ego strengths and capacities and can make use of rapport and the transformation of therapy into a learning experience. It utilizes the steps leading up to the current crisis, challenges actions taken in the past which the therapist considers to have been antitherapeutic, and teaches the patient to anticipate situations likely to produce unpleasant consequences. By stimulating a certain degree of anxiety, the therapist motivates the patient to understand his emotional conflicts, recognize and deal with his reactions, and engage in a corrective emotional experience. Anxiety thus becomes the tool to help the patient give up his maladaptive behavior and improve his affective functioning.

CLIENT TASKS

Bartlett, as mentioned in Chapter 1, suggests that problems presented by crucial life situations can be conceived in terms of tasks which must be met and dealt with. She defines the *task* as:

a way of describing the demands made upon people by various life situations. These have to do with daily living, such as growing up in the family, learning in school, entering the world of work, marrying and rearing a family, and also with the common traumatic situations of life such as bereavement, separation, illness, or financial difficulties. The task calls for responses in the form of attitudes or actions from the people involved in the situation.[27]

In a somewhat different context, Studt sees the task as the "common goal for worker and client," the way to cope with problems in social functioning.[28] Perhaps the simplest way to operationalize the task concept is to take Reid and Epstein's definition, "what the client agrees to attempt to do to alleviate a problem."[29]

Earlier, David Kaplan, as part of the work done at the Harvard School of Public Health, suggested that crisis treatment should be guided by knowledge of the psychological tasks that must be accomplished in order to master each stress situation. He feels it is possible to specify clearly what the person must do, psychologically and behaviorally, to achieve this mastery.[30]

This concept of task, which has become very prevalent in current social work practice, opens up many possibilities.[31] In crisis intervention, it allows us to think clearly about what must be done so that re-equilibrium will be achieved and who is in the best position to do it. The nature of the tasks to be accomplished can serve as the guideline to determine the kind of action to be taken. It might be considered equivalent to Rapoport's "useful next step."[32]

In 1971, in viewing immigration as a transitional stage, Gruschka and I tried to work out an operational model of the tasks which would have to be carried out in order to bring about successful integration into a community.[33] Somewhat later, part of the same basic model was used to examine the transitional process of widowhood.[34] I now suggest that developing similar series of tasks might be a useful way of resolving other types of crisis situations, whatever their nature or point of origin.

Intervention in a particular predicament involves, as part of our initial diagnosis, consideration of the following questions: What is the extent of disturbance in the current life situation brought about by the hazardous event and/or the precipitating factor? What problem areas have been affected?

In looking at immigration, for example, we checked six potential problem areas: income management, health, housing, education, leisure-time activities, and citizenship. In widowhood, where I viewed the situation in terms of both interpersonal and intrapersonal change, I considered disturbances in five significant role networks: marital, familial, occupational, leisure time, and institutional, as well as losses and threats to self.

Once the area of disturbance has been fixed, treatment can be conceptualized in terms of tasks which have to be accomplished so that the client can begin to cope successfully with these disturbances.[35] We suggest ordering these tasks along two parallel and complementary axes: *material-arrangemental* and *psychosocial*.

Material-arrangemental tasks[36] entail the providing of material assistance and the carrying out of substantive arrangements and service provisions (often erroneously dismissed as "environmental manipulation"). The point has been raised, though not yet sufficiently tested, that much of the activity carried out at Jacobson's generic level of treatment might fall into this category.

When faced with a crisis situation, the person must carry out the following sequence of material-arrangemental tasks for each problem area affected:

1. Explore available solutions, resources, and possible roles.
2. Choose an appropriate solution, resource, and/or role and prepare himself for it.
3. Apply formally for the solution or resource; take on the new role.
4. Begin to use the new solution or resource; function in the new role.
5. Go through a period of adaptation and development of increasing competence until performance rises to acceptable norms.

Supportive casework in many agencies is often carried out at exactly this level: helping the person explore his needs in terms of his altered situation, considering with him alternative solutions, informing him of resources, and mobilizing support in the community to develop new opportunities for him to use.

At the same time, because individuals (as well as families and groups) tend to react in complex, nonrational, and unpredictable ways, particularly during periods of stress, the person may have to engage in the following psychosocial tasks[37] as well:

1. Cope with the threat to his past security and sense of competence and esteem; deal with his feelings of loss and longing.
2. Grapple with the anxieties and frustrations in making decisions or choosing new solutions, resources, or roles.
3. Handle the stress generated in applying for the selected solution or resource and in taking on the new role.
4. Adjust to the new solution, resource, or role with all it implies in terms of shift in position and status in the family and community.
5. Develop new standards of well-being, agree to diminished gratification, and be able to delay satisfaction until able to function according to acceptable norms of behavior.

Work with persons at this level, which would probably fall into Jacobson's category of the individual approach, to a large extent involves dealing with their feelings—the doubts, ambivalences, anxieties, and despairs—which arise while trying to carry out what both client and worker agree needs to be done. Focusing on such tasks is an expeditious way to bring forward adaptive resolution of the predicament.

With this background and several sets of mental maps to be kept in mind, we can now present our model for practice in crisis situations.

Notes

1. Howard J. Parad, "Crisis Intervention," in Robert Morris, ed., *Encyclopedia of Social Work*, 16th issue, 1 (New York: NASW, 1971), p. 197.

2. *Oxford English Dictionary,* quoted in Getz et al., 1974, p. 16; *Webster's Seventh New College Dictionary* (Springfield, Mass.: G. & C. Merriam, 1965), p. 197.

3. Merle M. Foeckler, "Dynamics of Coping with a Medical Crisis," *Public Welfare* 23 (January 1965): 41.

4. For further discussion, see Rosemary Lukton, "Crisis Theory: Review and Critique," *Social Service Review* 48 (September 1974): pp. 385–391; Getz, 1974, pp. 16–18; Bernard L. Bloom, "Definitional Aspects of the Crisis Concept," *Journal of Consulting Psychology* 27 (1963), reprinted in Howard J. Parad, ed. *Crisis Intervention: Selected Readings* (New York: FSAA, 1965), pp 303–311.

5. Gerald Caplan, *An Approach to Community Mental Health* (New York: Grune and Stratton, 1961), p. 18.

6. Naomi Golan, "When Is a Client in Crisis?", *Social Casework* 50 (July 1969): 389–394.

7. See Donald C. Klein and Erich Lindemann, "Preventive Intervention in Individual and Family Crisis Situations," in G. Caplan, ed., *Prevention of Mental Disorders in Children* (New York: Basic Books, 1961), pp. 283–293; G. Caplan, *Principles of Preventive Psychiatry* (New York: Basic Books, 1964), pp. 40–41; Peter E. Sifneos, "A Concept of Emotional Crisis," *Mental Hygiene* 44 (April 1960): 169–179.

8. For an excellent summarization of developmental and transitional crises, see chart in Carol Meyer, *Social Work Practice,* 2nd ed., (New York: Free Press, 1976), pp. 72–74. This is reprinted and discussed in greater detail in Chapter 8 of this volume.

9. Martin Strickler and Betsy LeSor, "The Concept of Loss in Crisis Intervention," *Mental Hygiene* 54 (April 1970): 301–305.

10. Lydia Rapoport, "Crisis Intervention as a Mode of Brief Treatment," in R. W. Roberts and R. H Nee, eds., *Theories of Social Casework* (Chicago: University of Chicago Press, 1970), p. 277.

11. Caplan, 1964, pp. 40–41.

12. Thomas H. Holmes and Richard H. Rahe, "The Social Readjustment Rating Scale," *Journal of Psychosomatic Research* 11 (1967): 213–218.

13. Obviously the values would have different weighting for different individuals at different times in their life cycles and would probably

be influenced by a large number of extraneous and intervening variables.

14. Peter E. Sifneos, *Short-Term Psychotherapy and Emotional Crisis* (Cambridge: Harvard University Press, 1972), pp. 34–35.

15. David L. Hoffman and Mary L. Remmel, "Uncovering the Precipitant in Crisis Intervention," *Social Casework* 56 (May 1975): 260.

16. Caplan, 1964, pp. 39–48.

17. I. N. Korner, "Crisis Reduction and the Psychological Consultant," in Gerald A. Specter and William L. Claiborn, eds., *Crisis Intervention* (New York: Behavioral Publications, 1973), pp. 31–32.

18. Reuben Hill, "Generic Features of Families Under Stress," *Social Casework* 39 (February–March 1958). Reprinted in Parad, 1965, p. 46. Also in Resnik and Ruben, 1975, p. 7.

19. Richard. A. Pasewark and Dale A. Albers, "Crisis Intervention: Theory in Search of a Program," *Social Work* 17 (March 1972): 73–74. Also in Rapoport, 1970, p. 282.

20. Carol E. Hooker, "Learned Helplessness," *Social Work* 21 (May 1976): 194–198.

21. Gerald F. Jacobson, "Programs and Techniques of Crisis Intervention," in Silvano Arieti, ed., *American Handbook of Psychiatry*, 2nd ed., 2 (New York: Basic Books, 1974), p. 816.

22. Parad, 1971, p. 201.

23. Rapoport, 1970, pp. 297–298.

24. Gerald F. Jacobson, Martin Strickler, and Wilbur E. Morley, "Generic and Individual Approaches to Crisis Intervention," *American Journal of Public Health* 58 (February 1968): 338–343.

25. Donald G. Langsley and David M. Kaplan, *The Treatment of Families in Crisis* (New York: Grune and Stratton, 1968), pp. 4–5.

26. Peter E. Sifneos, "Two Different Kinds of Psychotherapy of Short Duration," *American Journal of Psychiatry* 123 (March 1967): 1069–1073. Also in Sifneos, 1972, pp. 44–71.

27. Harriett M. Bartlett, *The Common Base of Social Work Practice* (New York: NASW, 1970), p. 96.

28. Elliot Studt, "Social Work Theory and Implications for the Practice of Methods," *Social Work Education Reporter* 16 (June 1968): 22–24, 42–46.

29. William J. Reid and Laura Epstein, *Task-Centered Casework* (New York: Columbia University Press, 1972), p. 96.

30. David M. Kaplan, "Observations on Crisis Theory and Practice," *Social Casework* 49 (March 1968): 151–155.

31. See Frances H. Scherz, "Maturational Crises and Parent-Child Interaction," *Social Casework* 52 (June 1971): 362–369, for another use of tasks.

32. Rapoport, 1970, p. 291. She also speaks of problem-solving tasks in developing adaptive coping patterns and suggests as a priority for further research the identification of specific problem-solving tasks needed to achieve a healthy resolution of a specific crisis. See pp. 281–282.

33. Naomi Golan and Ruth Gruschka, "Integrating the New Immigrant: A Model for Social Work Practice in Transitional States," *Social Work* 16 (April 1971): 82–87.

34. Naomi Golan, "Wife to Widow to Woman," *Social Work* 20 (September 1975): 369–374.

35. Note the similarity between our use of the term *task* and Hollis's phrase, "intermediate goals," which she defines as the "way-stations on the road to the ultimate aim; the means by which it is hoped the final goal will be achieved." Florence Hollis, *Casework: A Psychosocial Therapy*, 2nd ed. (New York: Random House, 1972), p. 286.

36. I find the term *material-arrangemental* awkward, but more descriptive than the usual *instrumental*.

37. I prefer the broader term *psychosocial tasks* to the *psychological tasks* used by Kaplan and by Rapoport, although they refer to the same type of activity. When talking of interpersonal relations and role transactions, the former phrase appears to be more appropriate.

Chapter 5

Professional Intervention: Steps in the Model

Purpose of Model

This chapter presents a working model for treatment in crisis situations which can be used by professional practitioners in a number of primary and secondary settings. It is placed in the framework of social work practice, although other helping professionals can and do carry out similar activities. Part of the model is based on my own and others' practice and supervisory experience;[1] part was developed in a series of seminar-practicums during which advanced student-workers tested out the Reid-Epstein model of task-centered treatment[2] on a wide variety of cases, some of which involved crisis situations.[3] Some additional material has been supplied to provide greater strength and depth to the framework.

It should be kept in mind that this is a basic, all-purpose model to be used flexibly and differentially as the particular situation requires. Obviously there is no single, blanket "crisis situation." In Part III, we shall see how the model can be adapted differentially to various types of problems, clients, and settings.

As he gains experience in its application, the worker learns to be constantly alert for opportunities to use elements of the model in his current contact with his clients,[4] whether during the initial interview or as part of an ongoing case in which some aspect has suddenly changed.[5] Its appropriate usage is determined not only by the timing—at which point in the situation help is asked for—but also by who is applying for service and who, in the total interacting complex, is prepared to use what the practitioner has to offer.

Crisis intervention does not lend itself to neat marking off into the study, diagnosis, treatment planning, treatment, and termination/evaluation steps of the casework process. Instead we speak simply of beginning, middle, and ending phases. They may all take place within a single three-hour interview or may be spaced out over several months.

The division is based on the nature of client-worker interaction. The beginning phase is concerned with *formulation:* establishing contact, finding out what is going on, determining whether a crisis exists and what its current status is, and setting up a working contract for future activity.

The middle phase concentrates on *implementation:* the identifying and carrying out of tasks (by the client, the worker, and/or significant others) designed to solve specific problems in the current life situation, to modify previous inadequate or inappropriate ways of functioning, and to learn new coping patterns. Treatment is geared to achievement of limited goals already specifically decided upon or implied by the nature of the contract. It may simply be relief from the pressures built up during the generation of the crisis and promotion of a clearer understanding of what has been going on and what the available options are.

Elements in the total crisis predicament are reviewed and reworked, including affective ties (where appropriate) to previous unresolved conflicts and similar crises in the past. Emphasis in the latter situation is on recognition of recurrent patterns of feeling, thinking, and behaving, on the linkages, similarities, and differences between the past and the present, and on the severing of inappropriate connections so that the person may feel once more in control of his life and free to respond to the present reality. Specific aspects of the current situation are the primary focus, and the immediate aim is to help the panicked, pressured client regain his sense of ego autonomy.

The ending phase dealing with *termination* involves reviewing the intervention from the start of the case to the present, with emphasis on the tasks accomplished and the coping patterns developed or the building of new ties with persons and resources, and the planning for the near future when the client will be on his own.

Throughout the case, the crisis approach emphasizes a broad-spectrum viewpoint, making use of all possible resources and support systems in the community.[6] Wherever possible, significant others and social networks are actively involved and even built up anew.[7]

Time limits may be set, but generally the three dimensions of time—the number of interviews, the total length of time involved, and the spacing of intervals between interviews—are used flexibly as the situation requires. In the beginning, the worker may set up daily or even twice-daily interviews; as the situation progresses, he may stretch out direct contacts to once a week or less until the client is on his own. Often the case ends on an "as needed" or "patient will return when necessary" basis. (The administrative and logistic issues of the open door or revolving door have been discussed elsewhere and need not be dealt with here.[8])

The worker's overall stance is active, purposive, and committed. He immediately conveys the message to the individual and/or family that he knows what he is doing and is willing to take risks. In psychodynamic terms, he stands ready to lend his own ego strength to the client who has become temporarily immobilized or regressed until the latter has recovered sufficiently to function appropriately.[9] As Jacobson has indicated, although the practitioner formulates the dynamics of the situation in his own mind according to his own theoretical frame of reference, he does not necessarily share this with his client.[10] Instead, he conveys the message that the situation is a normal one that could have happened to anyone, that the client has functioned adequately in the past and will again in the future, and that their common purpose is to help the client "get back on the track."

By concentrating on the "glass half full"—on what the client has accomplished in the past and what is positive in the current situation—rather than on the "glass half empty"—on his lacks, damages to self-esteem, and other negative aspects—the worker conveys a sense of optimism and hope that things will change for the better. This is an integral part of the crisis approach and, when used appropriately, can be the key to promoting effective involvement and early reintegration.

We now present a step-by-step breakdown of the model. The left-hand column lists what may take place in the interview, including typical remarks made by the worker to illustrate his intervention. The right-hand column offers guidelines, including explanations of why the activity is being carried out. Once more it should be emphasized that practitioners attempting to use the model must be flexible, selective, and guided by the specifics of the situation.

MODEL FOR TREATMENT IN CRISIS SITUATIONS
I. BEGINNING PHASE: FORMULATION (USUALLY COMPLETED IN FIRST INTERVIEW)

WORKER'S ACTIVITY	GUIDELINES

A. *Immediate Focus on Crisis Situation*

1. Start with the "here and the now" Focus on the *precipitating factor,* the incident or event that prompted the client's referral or appearance: scope, persons involved, outcome, severity of effect, time event occurred.

   "What happened, what brings you in here now?"

   "I understand you were in an accident last night; can you tell me about it?"

By making the client focus on what happened in the recent past, try to help him gain *cognitive* awareness of the immediate situation through verbalization and ordering of all the aspects, including bringing into full consciousness those elements which may have been repressed or denied. Try to get as many facts as possible; make *him* tell you rather than rely on others who accompany and may be trying to shield him. Exact accuracy is not needed at this stage; the telling is the important feature.

2. Elicit subjective reactions to the event; try to get his affective responses to what happened and to the part he and others played in it.

   "You must have felt terrible about it!"

   "No wonder you sound so upset."

The client may engage in a good deal of ventilation with crying, anger, blaming, expressions of guilt feelings. It is important to listen attentively and quietly but to pay close attention to any discrepancies, particularly between *what* is being said and *how* it is being told. Note the appropriateness of affect, amount of anxiety, degree of tension, and lability of emotions. The aim here is to free and bring out reactions to the current situation.[11]

3. As the emotional pitch is lowered, try to place the client within the context of the crisis situation: find out the original *hazardous event,* and subsequent blows that started off and aggravated change. If unable to pinpoint, at least try to find

Here we get a weaving back and forth between the objective and subjective aspects of the situation. Be aware of recent losses, threats, challenges, even if not consciously tied to the present situation. Look for connecting themes, repetitive

Model for Treatment in Crisis Situations, *continued*

WORKER'S ACTIVITY	GUIDELINES
out when things began to go wrong.	patterns, actual or symbolic links to earlier crises and conflictual events. Do not attempt interpretations or confrontations at this point.[12] Also avoid getting caught up in chronic pathology or in long-standing situation problems.
"Sounds as if, after your father died, everything began to go badly."	
"Can you put your finger on what started this off?"	
"Things really began to change after you came to college."	
4. Ascertain the nature and duration of the *vulnerable state*, including changes in ability to manage, earlier attempts to cope with problems raised by initial and subsequent events, and previous efforts to obtain help.	Try to build up an orderly sequence of events. Keep the client focused on "So what happened then?" Try to bring out what worked and what didn't and other persons influencing the situation. Be alert to contributing factors behind differences between the client's responses and those of others involved.
"I suppose in the beginning you were in a state of shock."	
"How were you able to handle all this with your husband in the hospital?"	Begin to build up your diagnostic assessment of what is going on: client's anxiety and discomfort levels; extent of guilt, fear, anger, depression, despair, hope; his appropriateness of affect and realistic appraisal of elements in the situation; his motivation to invest himself in change; his capacities in the thinking, feeling, behavioral, and physiological areas; his ability to function at an acceptable level and to engage in a working relationship; his defense structure and previous problem-solving patterns.
"I guess, of the whole family, you took it the hardest."	

(continued)

Model for Treatment in Crisis Situations, *continued*

WORKER'S ACTIVITY	GUIDELINES
5. Assess the present situation, the *state of active crisis:* is he completely disequilibrated or is the area of dysfunction limited to specific areas? Has the situation stabilized, or are changes still taking place?	Do a horizontal scan of the client's current functioning in vital role networks, the extent to which his coping mechanisms are operating adaptively, the support systems and resources which can be called upon.
"I know you had a terrible time, but how are you getting along now?" "What's happening right now between you and your wife?"	Formulate within your own mind the dynamics of the situation and decide whether to use the crisis approach or to try another form of intervention.

B. *Evaluation of Current Predicament*

1. Make a "decision statement" as to what you think is currently going on and what you see as the most pressing problem and the area on which to concentrate.	Here an attempt is made to partialize the "tangled ball" of problems and complexities and to decide at which level you are going to direct your intervention: generic or individual, material-arrangemental or psychosocial, etc.
"It sounds to me as if you feel at the end of your rope and don't know where to turn." "Let's see first that you get the proper medical attention."	Sometimes the problem as you see it can be phrased in terms of the "core dilemma" or quandary with which you see the client is struggling.
"You're in a real dilemma; I guess the most important thing is to come to a decision as to whether or not to leave your husband."	
2. Ask the client how he sees the situation and what he regards as the most pressing problem, or the one he wants to work on first.	At this point, the client may be too emotionally drained or in shock to respond actively with a problem-for-work. In this case you may

Model for Treatment in Crisis Situations, *continued*

WORKER'S ACTIVITY	GUIDELINES

3. Together with the client, settle on one target problem upon which to focus. Occasionally two allied problems can be worked on simultaneously.

   "We've agreed, then, that the most pressing problem is your feeling of loneliness, of emptiness, now that your husband is gone."

have to take the initiative, postpone active intervention, or else work out plans with some significant other in picture. On the other hand, this "cutting the problem down to size" may give him hope and strength to bounce back with very definite views on what he wants to do.

C. *Development of Contract for Further Activity*
   1. Work out a tentative agreement on joint activity: specific goals at which to aim, tasks on which to focus. Set up a working plan of what the client will do, what you will do, and what others involved will contribute. Be as specific and concrete as possible.

      "In view of this, I'd say that the most important thing is to get you a proper place to live so that you can be on your own. Now, you'll get in touch with your mother, and I'll speak to this landlord I know. And I'll see you here in the office at two o'clock tomorrow afternoon so that we can compare notes and decide what to do next."

      "Let's concentrate on helping you and Jim decide whether or not you want to get married. Will you talk to him and have him call me at this number? I want to speak with him alone

Coming to an explicit agreement on mutual goals and expectations is an integral part of the crisis approach, whether expressly put in the terms of a contractual arrangement or not. Its main purpose is to treat the client as a mature, functioning adult who is expected to carry out his part in the agreement. This is definitely an egosyntonic approach that evokes a positive response. (See Nelson and Mowry for further views on this.[13])

(*continued*)

Model for Treatment in Crisis Situations, *continued*

WORKER'S ACTIVITY   GUIDELINES

and then we'll meet together
for, say, six sessions, to see how
you can work things out between you. Please call me after
he sees me."

II. MIDDLE PHASE: IMPLEMENTATION (FROM FIRST TO FOURTH INTERVIEW)

A. *Organizing and Working over Data*
1. Obtain missing background and
   face sheet data, particularly around
   the current life situation and recent
   past since the hazardous event. Try
   to get a clearer, more coherent picture of what has been going on and
   is still happening.

   "Before we go any further, can
   you tell me something more
   about your family?"

   "Did I understand that you have
   a law degree but you've always
   worked as a shoe salesman?"

   "Do you mean to say that, since
   the accident, your mother-in-
   law hasn't come to visit you
   once?"

This is aiming at further cognitive
awareness, started in I-A1. Now,
however, the tone is different.
Once the decision to become involved has been made and the
promise of help given, the client's
reaction and level of participation
often change dramatically. He begins to talk more rationally and
connectedly; he becomes more in-
formative and less guarded, more
willing to cooperate actively so
that greater detail and accuracy can
now be achieved.

Be particularly aware of gaps and
discrepancies and either bring
them up or file them away for
future reference.

The order of steps here is a matter
of worker style. Some find it helpful to reverse A1 and A2.

2. Select from what you have heard
   several central themes which have
   come out, e.g., losses or assaults
   to self-esteem. Ask about them,
   both in the present and—if appropriate or the client has brought it
   up—in the past.

This can be the heart of the intervention. As you "hit a nerve,"
you often may get a flood of emotions, with all sorts of ties and
associations. Much of the material
brought out in I-A3 comes up
again. This time, however, do go

Model for Treatment in Crisis Situations, *continued*

WORKER'S ACTIVITY	GUIDELINES
"Seems as though, whenever you get close to someone, they desert you."	into it, offer interpretations, bring up connections and recurring motifs.
"I don't know how much is the Lord's fault, but it sounds as though the Housing Authority also had a hand in the matter. You ought to be angry at them."	If the client's affect is appropriate, you can share his indignation and anger or empathize with his grief and sorrow. If the feeling is appropriate but the object is not, point that out and help channel anger or guilt into more reality-oriented directions. If the feeling is appropriate, but the client's time sense is wrong, be the "voice of reality" and point out the discrepancy and try to get an unlinking. And if the feeling is not appropriate, that too should be questioned.
"You remind me of a little girl who hides her head under the pillow during a thunderstorm. Were you always afraid of storms at home?"	
"I don't understand; your wife makes a reasonable request and you hit the roof. You know, you're not a kid anymore and your wife isn't your mother. Aren't you confusing the two?"	
	Keep interpretations relatively close to the surface and emphasize reality factors and ego functioning. Sometimes the focus can be put on role change and the difference between "what is" and "what ought to be," on role discrepancies and differences in role expectations.[14]

B. *Bringing about Behavior Change*
1. Go back to I-C1, to the area for action agreed upon. Identify how the client has coped with the situation in the past, what was the outcome, how effective or ineffective it was in dealing with the crisis situation and restoring balance.

This is your primary area of intervention during this period: helping the client identify what worked didn't work; what are his alternative ways of action; what are the resources, in himself, out in the community, and in his life networks, which can be utilized in his learning to cope effectively; and how to get him started in making changes.

"I gather that every time Bonnie asked about her daddy, you went into the bedroom and began to cry. Didn't this upset her?"

The client's high anxiety and dis-

(*continued*)

Model for Treatment in Crisis Situations, *continued*

WORKER'S ACTIVITY	GUIDELINES
"Well, going to the corner bar was one way to get your wife off your back. Did it work?"	comfort may become vital forces here in speeding up the tempo of action. However, anxiety can reach the point where it may become paralyzing.
2. Set up some overall task areas or intermediate goals which can be aimed at and realistically achieved in a short period of time.	It should be kept in mind that the client is the primary executor of tasks to be set. If you participate, your purpose is to act on his behalf or jointly with him until he is able to carry on alone.[15]
"The important thing seems to be to get you started on doing something to fill up those empty hours during the day until your husband comes home."	
"I understand the first priority is to have you pass your final exams so you can stay on in college."	
3. Work out a series of specific *tasks* together, designed to help client reach the goals set. These tasks can be *action* oriented and geared to bring about change in performance.	Giving the client "homework assignments" is a useful device to get him started; it also gives you a good starting point at which to open the next interview.
"If you want to do something about Joey's being kicked out of school, the first thing to do is to speak with his home-room teacher. Then you can talk to the principal, and after that I can arrange for some tutoring."	Interspaced between task arrangements, give the client support and encouragement, particularly around a new activity in which he has not engaged in before or one that recalls old memories and unhappy associations. If obstacles arise or if he becomes upset or discouraged, discuss alternate ways to carry out tasks and arrive at goals.
"If this happened to me, I'd find out exactly what my rights are under the law."	Act as a role model to indicate positive ways of handling the problem situation.

Model for Treatment in Crisis Situations, *continued*

WORKER'S ACTIVITY	GUIDELINES
4. Tasks can also be *thinking* oriented, to help the client decide on a course of action or ways to implement it.	A difficult problem for practitioners during this phase of crisis treatment is what to do when clients begin to regain their independence of action. While we see this as the end goal, it often results in a rapid change in plans and a shift in direction that make it hard for the worker to "keep on top" of what is going on. It involves a shift in worker role from engaging in a good deal of direction and activity at the start of the case to becoming more passive and retiring to the sidelines as the client regains his autonomy and fills up his lifespace with new relationships.
"I'd like you to think about what you really value in your relationship with your daughter. Then we can talk about how you can help her come home."	
"Why don't you try to figure out what you can do to attract girls more? Let's start out with this next time."	

III. ENDING PHASE: TERMINATION (LAST ONE OR TWO INTERVIEWS)

A. *Arriving at the Decision to Terminate*

1. Keep track of passage of time; remind the client how much time or how many interviews are left, according to the original agreement.	The time factor assumes particular importance in the last phase of treatment.[16] Since crisis situations are often transitory and provide their own solutions, termination in some cases is predetermined.
"Remember, next week is our last meeting, according to the plan we set up."	If tasks have been carried out successfully, the client may begin to feel restless and want to be on his own by now. Frequently a client will call after several sessions to say, "I've been thinking about what you said and I've decided to . . ."
2. If no overt agreement was made, suggest a spacing out of contacts, with a view toward termination.	
"You sound as though you're doing pretty well on your own.	

(continued)

Model for Treatment in Crisis Situations, *continued*

WORKER'S ACTIVITY   GUIDELINES

Why don't we skip a week and
see how things go by then?
Maybe you'll feel ready to
manage by yourself."

3. Deal with resistance to terminate, on both your and the client's part.

"We went through a lot together and it's hard to break it up. I feel the same way."

In intensive crisis treatment, three kinds of termination reactions can be found: clients who realistically wish to terminate upon completion of the contract; those who request ongoing therapy as a defense against termination; and those for whom ongoing treatment is both wanted and appropriate.[17] These must be dealt with individually in each situation; if the worker is uncertain or feels too involved, it helps to consult with other professionals at this point. A key factor is the client's current level of functioning.

B. *Reviewing Progress in Case*
  1. In the last or next-to-last interview, suggest summarizing the progress in the case since the start of intervention.

"Since this is our last time together, why don't we take a look at all that has happened since you first came to see me. Remember how you felt that first evening?"

  2. Review progress in terms of key themes, basic affective issues.

"Loneliness has always been a hardship for you, hasn't it? But at least this time you were able to do something about it."

While evaluation of progress is an important aspect in any case, in crisis situations it becomes an integral part which serves to tie together loose ends and make the treatment experience a positive one, stressing and building of feelings of efficacy and competence.

Because clients come in originally at moments of high tension and upset, they are often unable, or too embarrassed, to recall now how things were then. The emphasis here should be on recognizing the difficulty imposed by the initial event, the extent of the client's early disequilibrium, and the rapidity of his reintegration—the distance traveled.

Model for Treatment in Crisis Situations, *continued*

Worker's Activity	Guidelines
"Remember you told me how difficult it was for you to handle authority? Is it coming any easier for you by now?"	This can be a very moving mutual experience and requires a good deal of skill to handle the transference elements in the situation, ranging from excessive gratitude to anger at being deserted. A frequent reaction is "You didn't do anything for me; I would have gotten over it by myself!"
3. Go over tasks covered, goals reached, changes in direction taken, and work not completed.	
"We had set out to improve communication between the two of you. Well, at least you're talking things over as far as handling the checkbook and where to go on weekends. Now, how about the problem of who puts the children to bed?"	A helpful device here is to refer back to your own notes and written record of how the tasks have progressed and review them together.

C. *Planning Future Activity*

1. Discuss current status and what are the client's plans for the future, when he will be on his own.	Here the emotional tone is lowered and you resort to working out practical, reality-oriented details and specific arrangements regarding persons to contact in the community and what the client can expect to happen. Writing down names, addresses, and directions is helpful for anxious clients who are apprehensive of going out on their own.
"I understand the doctor has signed your discharge and you're going to the nursing home this afternoon. Here is the name of the woman in charge. I told her about your coming."	
"Now let's see if I have it straight. The plan is for you to move in with your sister and have her take care of the children during the day, while you go back to finish your secretarial course."	
2. Close the door, but leave a crack open; set the tone for the client's feeling that treatment in the crisis situation was a complete experience in itself.	This is a very delicate line that in crisis treatment requires skill in handling: on the one hand, you want to emphasize the client's independence; on the other, you

(continued)

Model for Treatment in Crisis Situations, *continued*

WORKER'S ACTIVITY	GUIDELINES
"Good-by and good luck; you're all set to manage on your own. Remember, if you need help again, I'm always here and you can call at any time. But I hope you try it on your own for a while."	want him to feel free to return in case of need. In the event that further treatment on a more extended basis is planned, it may be advisable that it *not* be with the same worker or at least that a time gap be inserted so that it becomes a "different ball game."

Notes

1. See Golan, 1969, p. 392, for model for intake interview.
2. See Reid and Epstein, 1972, for the original model. This has subsequently undergone a number of changes and adaptations.
3. Naomi Golan, "A Field Study of the Task-Centered Model of Short-Term Treatment: Final Research Report," (School of Social Work, University of Haifa, April 1976), mimeo. Also, "Work With Young Adults in Israel," in William J. Reid and Laura Epstein, eds., *Task-Centered Practice* (New York: Columbia University Press, 1976), pp. 270–284.
4. For simplicity's sake, we shall use the term *client* throughout the model, although in some settings, the expression commonly used may be *patient, counselee,* or *parolee.* The whole discussion of when an applicant becomes a client is also being sidestepped.
5. Theoretically the crisis approach can be used for nonplanned short-term treatment, as seen in the paradigm in Howard J. Parad, Lola Selby, and James Quinlan, "Crisis Intervention with Families and Groups," in Robert W. Roberts and Helen Northen, eds., *Theories of Social Work with Groups* (New York: Columbia University Press, 1976), p. 308. Ruefully, however, we must recognize that few workers appear capable of shifting their gears in mid-trip in this fashion.

6. Gerald Caplan, *Support Systems and Community Mental Health* (New York: Behavioral Publications, 1974), pp. 1–40, should be reviewed in this connection. Also, Alice H. Collins and Diane L. Panncoast, *Natural Helping Networks* (Washington, D. C.: NASW, 1976).

7. Ross V. Speck and Carolyn L. Attneave, in *Family Networks* (New York: Pantheon Books, 1973), offer an innovative approach to involving natural support systems and building new ones.

8. Naomi Golan, "Crisis Theory," in F. J. Turner, ed., *Social Work Treatment* (New York: Free Press, 1974), p. 441.

9. The temporary aspect of the crisis situation should be emphasized. Korner, 1973, p. 31, makes a good point when he notes that, if behavior control has been permanently lost, the outcome is collapse rather than crisis.

10. Jacobson, 1974, p. 819.

11. Howard J. Parad and H. L. P. Resnik, "The Practice of Crisis Intervention in Emergency Care" in Resnik and Ruben, 1975, p. 28, list "senses" which are used in this connection at the Rush Centers in Los Angeles during the initial interview: bewilderment, danger, confusion, impasse, desperation, apathy, helplessness, urgency, and discomfort.

12. Hoffman and Remmel would bear down at this point on the *precipitant*, the feelings and thoughts which led up to the call for help. Personal communication. Also found in Hoffman and Remmel, 1975, p. 264.

13. Zane P. Nelson and Dwight D. Mowry, "Contracting in Crisis Intervention," *Community Mental Health Journal* 12 (Spring 1976): 37–43.

14. Jacobson, 1974, pp. 819–820.

15. For further use of tasks, see Reid and Epstein, 1976. Also Charles D. Garvin, William J. Reid, and Laura Epstein, "A Task-Centered Approach," in Roberts and Northen, 1976, pp. 239–267.

16. Robert L. Leopold, "Crisis Intervention: Some Notes on Practice and Theory," in Gertrude Einstein, ed., *Learning to Apply New Concepts to Casework Practice* (New York: FSAA, 1968), p. 26.

17. Hoffman and Remmel, 1975, pp. 266–267.

Chapter 6

Treatment Methods, Strategies, and Techniques

Levels of Intervention

Once our basic treatment model has been set up, we can begin to consider how to implement it and what basic tools we have at our disposal. In recent years a valiant attempt has been made to clarify some of the ambiguity in social work terminology. Without entering into the discussion itself, it might be well to try to anchor our use of terms. The following are based on Siporin's definitions,[1] which are compatible with our own line of thinking:

> *Intervention* (or treatment) refers to the application of a helping repertoire, of the methods and processes of differential, influential, planned action taken by a social worker to attain selected helping purposes.... They are change-inducing, resource-providing actions.
> *Method* refers to the how of helping, to purposeful, planned, instrumental activity through which tasks are accomplished and goals achieved.... In social work practice, method denotes an

96

orderly use of means, resources, and procedures through the performance of helping roles.

Strategy is a set of procedures involving a planned line of action and the employment of resources.

Procedure refers to a course and set of task-oriented interventive actions that are role patterned . . . . [It] may take the form of verbal or non-verbal communications or . . . transactions in which instruments and facilities are utilized. *Technique* or tactic is a specific, limited behavioral form of intervention. [Synonymous with "procedure," in our usage]

Using this vocabulary, we can see that in crisis treatment the worker intervenes by engaging in direct work with clients, indirect work on behalf of clients, and a combination of the two, depending on the professional role he fills at the time. Since crisis intervention is considered part of the problem-solving process, Siporin notes appropriate roles for the worker—for example, counselor, adviser, enabler, expert problem solver, troubleshooter, broker, referrer, expediter, arbitrator, discussion leader, gatekeeper, resource person, coordinator, administrator, work manager, and consultant.[2] The list is varied enough to encompass almost every type of activity engaged in by the crisis practitioner.

In terms of helping methods of intervention, the worker primarily moves in at the system level of the individual, the family, or the group to engage the client in direct interaction. Strategies of intervention, along one dimension, would be to use either the generic or individual approach described in Chapter 4. Along another dimension, they would be concerned with carrying out the material-arrangemental tasks and/or the psychosocial tasks also described in Chapter 4.

These strategies are determined at the close of the beginning phase of treatment, when specific goals are set up and a working plan is developed. They must be explicit in terms of tasks and intermediate goals, although the worker has to be flexible enough to take advantage of every nuance of change in the situation.

Specific procedures and techniques for effecting these changes become the major concern at this time. The choice depends to a large extent on the practitioner's frame of reference and professional background. (Frequently the same procedure may be called by different names by different disciplines—e.g., "catharsis" and "ventilation."). Moreover, the kind of technique considered appropriate will vary with the stage of intervention and the particular demands of the situation. Although techniques used in face-to-face engagement with a client and in negotiations with others on his behalf may differ in emphasis and intensity, the nature of the communication has been found to be basically similar.[3]

Direct Procedures: Hollis Classification

Hollis' treatment typology is probably the most widely known among social work practitioners. The following discussion relies to a large extent on her classification of techniques and procedures, which is concerned with the dynamics of the interaction between worker and client.[4] Treatment procedures are clustered around a series of nuclei of worker-client communications.

SUSTAINMENT, VENTILATION

During the initial phase of treatment of a crisis situation, the use of *sustainment techniques,* designed to lower anxiety, guilt, and tension and to provide emotional support, is an important aspect of the development of the client-worker relationship aimed at restoring equilibrium. The techniques range along a continuum of increasing activity on the part of the worker. Toward the more active end, *reassurance*—particularly that anxiety is normal in a crisis and that others frequently experience similar reactions—can be very supportive to a client worried about going crazy or seeing his particular world fall apart. Care must be taken, however, not to be inappropriately reassuring or to use this technique to the point where all anxiety disappears. Anxiety, as we have seen, can become a catalyst for change.

Encouragement is used in the initial stage to counteract the client's sense of helplessness and hopelessness and, later on, to give him confidence to engage in new forms of coping. *Offering "gifts of love"* can take the form of interceding directly on the client's behalf "beyond the call of duty," making home visits, or seeing him at unscheduled times or during afternoon and evening hours. This is intended to demonstrate the worker's active concern and to sustain the client's feeling of being cared for and about.

At the other end of the sustainment continuum, *sympathetic listening* on the worker's part, particularly at the start of the case, is often coupled with encouragment of *ventilation* on the client's part. "Getting it off one's chest" is a basic procedure in the early stages of crisis intervention and becomes helpful in working through bottled-up feelings of anger, frustration, grief, and loss. Often, however, the use of ventilation needs to be curbed sharply in the latter phases of treatment, when attention centers more on effecting cognitive and behavioral changes than on airing feelings.

DIRECT INFLUENCE

Procedures of direct influence, designed to promote specific kinds of changes in the client's behavior, are probably used more often in crisis intervention than in other types of direct treatment. They range along a continuum of increasing activity by the worker from emphasizing what the client is already contemplating doing to intervening directly.

Of these techniques, *advice giving* is frequently and appropriately used during periods of active crisis, particularly when the client is feeling overwhelmed by what has happened and needs guidance in choosing a course of action and assuming unaccustomed roles. Both Ewalt[5] and Davis[6] found that parents who received advice used it and felt it to be helpful in resolving specific parent-child problems. Barten and Barten also found this to be true in brief therapy with children and their families, particularly around the educative aspects of treatment.[7]

The worker, out of his own practice experience with similar situations and his knowledge of community resources, can offer appropriate replies to the often-posed question, "What do I do now?" Later on, however, as noted in the guidelines to the model in Chapter 5, advice giving can become a source of professional frustration, as clients regain their feelings of being in control over their lives and begin to make decisions on their own, ignoring or outstripping the worker's offerings.

Advocating a particular course of action and *warning* clients *of consequences,* two more forceful techniques along the continuum of direct influence, can be very effective with confused, bewildered, or depressed clients when the practitioner is concerned about their own or others' safety, as, for example, with a mother too sunk in grief to take notice of her children's frightened reactions.

In the extreme conditions where suicide may have been threatened or even attempted, or where community caregivers have informed the agency of a deteriorating situation, the worker may have to use the technique of *direct intervention,* either with the authority of his own position or in conjunction with other community facilities, such as the police or the courts. The roving "Car 201" unit of the Erie, Pennsylvania, Family Crisis Intervention Program is a prime example of the implementation of this technique.[8]

Similarly, with children brought into hospital emergency rooms in suspected neglect or abuse situations, the social worker's direct intervention, based on his professional authority and competence, can be a decisive factor in reducing tension and arresting the disequilibrating process on the part of family, hospital personnel, and community caregivers.[9]

PERSON-SITUATION REFLECTION

As the client's anxiety level becomes reduced and he begins to view the picture more objectively, the worker engages him in reflective discussion of his current situation and of his recent past since the advent of the hazardous event.

Three particular aspects can be focused on. First, the *information* he has on the objective reality: Does he see the picture clearly and realistically? Does he have all the facts (as in the case of a complicated surgical procedure)? Does he see the entire picture or only selected aspects of it (as when a child tells his parents he has been expelled from school)? Is his grasp of the situation distorted by his own emotions or prejudices (as in parents' reactions to their son's interfaith marriage)? Does he know that certain reactions can normally be expected in, say, a critical developmental stage (such as adolescence)?

The worker's asking appropriate questions and giving correct answers to fill the gaps in the client's perception of the situation and to replace his forebodings and fantasies with more accurate information may be prime features in reversing the disequilibrating process. Informing clients of their social and legal rights and interceding with medical and judicial authorities to have them explain complex technical procedures in lay terms can be helpful at such times.

The second aspect deals with the person's *interaction* with the objective situation. Does he grasp what his choices of action are in view of his recently changed situation (as after the death of a spouse)? What are the options open to him (in the case of responsibility for children in an impending divorce)? The consequences to himself and to others of the decisions and actions he might take at this time are the gist of worker-client discussions in this area. Helping the client examine the alternatives, make a choice, and embark on an appropriate course of activity can set a new pattern for constructive coping with similar difficulties in the future.

Finally, the worker can help the client examine introspectively *his own part in the situation,* to help him gain awareness of his own emotional reactions to the total crisis complex. It may be that the client is truly unaware of his or her own feelings (for example, a woman's ambivalence about having an abortion). He may be aware of them but too embarrassed to bring them out in the open because of fear of censure (unwillingness to participate in a group sexual experience). Or he may be aware of his feelings but unaware of their relevance (admitting his dependence on his mother, but not connecting this with the chest pains he experienced before taking on a new job). Helping the client "get in touch with himself" and bringing such feelings out into the open for joint examination can be a critical factor in crisis intervention.

A technique that Hollis does not mention specifically in this context but which is implied and elaborated elsewhere is *confrontation*. Getz defines this as "helping the client come face to face with some of his difficulties," pointing out discrepancies between feelings and behaviors, and confronting him with the use of inappropriate defenses.[10] Small describes it as a "mirroring technique" in which the person is confronted with his actual behavior and, in some cases, with the secondary gains derived from his symptoms. He points out that potential dangers in the use of confrontation may be the substitution of denial and repression for previous defenses or the eruption of a panic state during which the client flees from treatment.[11] Gelb and Ullman nevertheless feel that "immediate, active, empathic, and accurate confrontation of the patient with examples of his neurotic functioning is more effective than passive working through."[12]

DYNAMIC AND DEVELOPMENTAL UNDERSTANDING

Using the techniques described above may be as far as the worker chooses to carry the uncovering aspects of treatment. However, with those clients whose intellectual and emotional capabilities permit, it may sometimes be helpful to use Hollis's techniques of examining the underlying personality dynamics which make the person's reaction to the crisis situation unique. *Reflective consideration of life experiences* which have influenced the client in the past and are still affecting him in the present is usually undertaken in an episodic way. Specific themes, such as loss, loneliness, or fear of authority, can be explored in terms of how they have shaped current reactions. This is the prelude to breaking the inappropriate linkages between past and present which may be a prominent feature of active crisis states.

In looking at the dynamics of the individual, the worker helps him examine broader patterns of behavior which cause him to react in a specific way, not only to the crisis situation, but to other areas of his life as well. He helps him see some of the intrapsychic bases for his feelings, attitudes, and behavior and enables him to draw connections, to become aware of unrealistic or inappropriate responses ("How is it you get so angry at your son, no matter what he does?"). The client may not see his behavior as inappropriate. He may feel that something is wrong but be unable to talk about it ("You say that whenever you see a new baby you get this aching pain inside").

Looking at defense structures may be a useful way of interpreting personality dynamics ("Sometimes when people are very angry inside, they blame others instead of themselves"), even though it runs into the danger of setting up new defenses of denial and repression. Pointing out maladaptive coping patterns may produce better material for reflective consideration ("I gather that, whenever you get depressed, you shut yourself in your room and stop talking to the family, even about such an important matter as losing your job").

Even the most experienced crisis therapists engage in this search for understanding and insight selectively, keeping interpretations relatively close to the surface. It becomes a matter of letting the pieces fall into place so that the client can gain some understanding of the sources of his exaggerated or inappropriate reactions. Sometimes drawing parallels between earlier and current losses or threats and pointing out the differences between the two serves to reduce the affect and produce more appropriate reactions, ("Just because your mother fell apart after you were born doesn't mean that the same thing will necessarily happen to you").

Rapoport, however, points out that insight is sometimes no more than hindsight—interesting but not particularly relevant. In crisis-oriented short-term treatment, the goal is usually *foresight*, the enhancement of anticipatory awareness, to be used for action-oriented problem solving in the present and near future.[13]

Getz notes that considerable disagreement exists over the extent and depth of interpretation found fruitful in crisis treatment. He feels that interpretation should be geared to leaving a client with a minimal amount of anxiety at the close of an interview. He also suggests that material which is seriously disturbing to someone in severe crisis should not be introduced, particularly near the end of a session. When interpretations are made, they should be tentative and nonthreatening and certainly should not be presented in a way that is beyond the client's ability to grasp.[14]

Malan, among psychotherapists who employ interpretation in brief treatment, ties this in with the use of *focusing* as a technique in crisis therapy. By concentrating on selected aspects of the current situation and avoiding others, he feels he can bring about permanent change in the patient so that he can deal more constructively with similar conflicts in the future.[15] (This technique of focusing is close to the basic casework concept of partializing, the "carving out of some part of the identified problem for intensive consideration in relation to problem solving."[16])

Behavior-Changing Techniques

Since the goals of crisis treatment include the initiation of new modes of perceiving, thinking, and feeling and the development of adaptive coping responses which can help the client handle the current situation and can also be applied in the future, techniques geared to learning how to change behavior become important tools. Several of them are part of the social worker's daily repertoire. *Anticipatory guidance, role rehearsal,* and *rehearsal for reality* are three closely allied procedures which emphasize the learning component in crisis treatment, in which worker and client together prepare for new types of grappling experiences, such as looking for a job, handling one's children more adeptly, or facing up to a supervisor.

Psychologists and, more recently, social workers have introduced a long series of elaborate behavioral modification techniques into practice repertoires. Among the techniques listed by Fischer and Gochros,[17] those designed to increase the magnitude, frequency, or duration of desired behaviors appear to be most appropriate for use in crisis intervention. Several of the most frequently mentioned are discussed below.

Positive reinforcement is a technique by which the client learns to increase behavior which he already has learned and which both he and the social worker have agreed would be adaptive in overcoming the crisis situation. The worker, immediately after the act is carried out, presents a rewarding stimulus in the form of a smile, an expression of approval, or even a concrete token reward. (Note the similarity to some of the sustainment and direct-influence procedures.)

Negative reinforcement or *avoidance* is a procedure by which the client learns to stop engaging in undesirable behaviors through seeking to avoid aversive consequences (for example, a mother stops crying so that the children will not be upset; a husband stops shouting at his wife so as not to provoke an argument). The worker can reinforce this by warning the client of consequences, threatening punishment, or even engaging in actual intervention (such as removing the children from the home).

Shaping is action in which the client learns new behavior which either has been missing completely from his repertoire or heretofore has appeared only in rudimentary form. It is carried out with the worker's help in a series of step-by-step reinforcements of successfully closer approximations of action until the desired behavior has been reached. (For example, a man whose wife has been hospitalized learns first to give the new baby a bottle, then to change his diapers, then to give him a bath, and finally to take over his care completely.)

Modeling, teaching, coaching, and *prompting* are all self-explanatory techniques which have long been part of the social worker's armamentarium of services. Other techniques such as *assertive training* and *desensitization* have not yet been reported on sufficiently in crisis situations to determine whether they can be used appropriately or systematically in these pressureful circumstances.

Other Techniques

In the past few years Gestalt therapists, under the leadership of Fritz Perls, and client-centered practitioners, influenced by Carl Rogers, have added an array of new techniques and a whole new vocabulary to direct treatment. Their concern is to help the client develop awareness of himself and of the world around him and to engage him in a personal growth experience. The worker, rather than remaining objective and detached, becomes actively involved with his client in a personal encounter.[18] This stance, often used in crisis situations without being labeled, is a natural one in view of the high level of mutual involvement and commitment, although the extent to which these treatment techniques fit in with the overall goal of crisis resolution remains to be seen.

Similarly, the transactional-analysis approach favored by followers of Berne, Satir, and others[19] has been applied in crisis situations, particularly by specially trained counselors.[20] Terms such as "feedback," "game playing," "life script," and "self-worth" have become widely incorporated into crisis-team vocabularies.

Other new and innovative techniques have been emerging with considerable rapidity as practitioners continue their search for sharper tools. Thus we get "paradoxical instructions,"[21] "screening-linking-planning conference,"[22] and "social-network therapy."[23] All of these have been reported as effective in crisis intervention and tend to reflect the particular investment of their originators.

Indirect Procedures: Environmental Work

Environmental manipulation, milieu therapy, indirect treatment, and *work with collaterals* are all expressions for activity carried out by social workers on their clients' behalf, rather than directly with them. Such activity becomes an essential ingredient in crisis intervention where time is at a premium and a variety of tasks must be carried out at the same time, both directly with clients and indirectly with collaterals.

Treatment thus becomes a blend of "strengthening the back and lightening the load." Hollis suggests that the worker is always confronted with the dilemma of whether to intervene on the client's behalf or to encourage him to tackle the milieu on his own.[24] In crisis situations, particularly during the earlier phases, when the client is immobilized by depression or overwhelmed by anxiety, the worker often needs to take the initiative to activate speedily the network of resources at his disposal. Later, through the techniques of anticipatory guidance and role rehearsal, he can prepare the client to seek out his own community resources and opportunity.

BUILDING A REFERRAL SYSTEM

Much of the practitioner's work with community resources is carried out before a crisis actually occurs. Building up a two-directional network of referral sources is an integral part of any social worker's practice expertise; it becomes a vital element in crisis-intervention services. A continuous investment of time and effort in interpreting the nature of his own agency's role, learning about other resources in the community, and laying the groundwork for collaborative effort is a tremendous advantage once a crisis erupts. Not only does it serve to ensure appropriate referrals *to* the agency but it paves the way for appropriate joint efforts during the crisis and a smooth referral to other services once the emergency aspects of the crisis are over. A complete, up-to-date resource file, with personal ties to "opposite numbers," is an invaluable asset in dealing with particular stressful situations (for example, in finding temporary shelters for the aged or indigent or in locating foster homes for neglected infants).

In mobilizing community resources to meet the needs of the client in crisis, the worker must take on a number of new roles: *provider* of his own agency's facilities, *locater* of existing resources elsewhere in the community, *creator* of new resources and opportunities by working with other community groups and with service organizations, *interpreter* of his client's needs before civic and governmental bodies, *mediator* between groups of clients competing for the same scarce resource or between client and staff as to eligibility, and *aggressive intervener* when he believes his client's needs and rights may have been ignored or violated.[25]

The sensitive nature of some hazardous events tends to build up a high level of community reaction, particularly when communication media are involved. If the climate is sympathetic, as in the case of a family's being involved in a tragic accident, the worker may try to take advantage of this to mobilize ameliorative action on behalf of the client and preventive measures for others like him. If public opinion is adverse, as in situations of rape or child abuse, he may have to work to counteract this by acting as a buffer between his client and community forces.

WORKING WITH COLLATERALS

The social worker in crisis services learns to cooperate with all types of collaterals: with other social workers in different agencies; with other professionals from collaborative disciplines; with community caregivers such as the police, school personnel, and health authorities; with religious, service, and volunteer organizations; with mutual[26] and self-help groups;[27] with natural support systems of relatives, friends, neighbors, and interested others;[28] and with the client's family network.

Using essentially the same techniques of intervention as in direct work with clients (with the possible exception, says Hollis, of discussion of dynamic and developmental material), the practitioner carries on continuous communication with collaterals and resource persons in formal conferences, informal meetings, individual discussions, and frequent telephone calls and written reports throughout the duration of the crisis.

Where more than one agency is providing service to the client, a key issue is that of keeping communication channels open so that each collaborator becomes aware of what the others are doing in order to eliminate duplication and working at cross-purposes. An important decision in such situations is to choose the worker (and the agency) who will accept primary responsibility for the case, so that all information on activities and decisions can be passed on to him.

ACTING AS A CONSULTANT

Much of the work with collaterals can be carried out by volunteers and nonprofessionals, either as part of the agency staff or outside of it, leaving the professional free to concentrate on direct work with clients and to act as a consultant at times of need, providing his special expertise and experience to help them function better.[29]

Rosenbaum and Beebe make the important point that the emergency therapist often serves as a consultant to a *system in crisis,* the ecological group made up of the patient and all those people in his social environment with whom he has major dynamic relationships. As such the therapist must first clarify in his own mind and then make clear to the others involved whether he is acting as the agent of a special-interest group (for example, city officials) or as consultant to the situation as a whole. The latter position need not mean that he does not become an involved participant; it enables him, however, to view the situation in broad perspective.[30]

Intervention by Using Families and Groups

Many of the examples given throughout this discussion have shown that family interaction is a central factor in crisis situations. In Part 3, as we consider various specific crises, this should become even more evident. However, using the family as a treatment strategy deserves some mention at this point.

It has been said, only partly facetiously, that families are either part of the problem or part of the solution in crisis situations. Many crises experienced by individuals are the direct outcome of family friction: for example, the teenager who runs away because of parental strictures[31] or the wife who is beaten during a violent argument with her husband.[32] In other situations the hazardous event involves one member but the rest of the family experiences the crisis: for example, the family's reaction to the mental illness of one of its members[33] or their collective response to the sudden death of a child.[34]

Part of established casework practice involves seeing couples together about a marital problem, or parents and children about a specific school difficulty. In fact, considering their strong feelings of guilt and desperation, it is hard *not* to involve family members in crisis treatment. Much of the initial activity in such cases centers on ventilation of their feelings of self-blame and anger, which usually starts out with, "If only we had realized . . ." or "If only he had told us. . . . "

THE FAMILY AS THE TREATMENT UNIT

Work with the family unit has been part of crisis intervention since the early work at Harvard in the effort to resolve the crisis situation adaptively and constructively.[35] Langsley, Kaplan, and their associates have reported using family treatment as the means of avoiding psychiatric hospitalization of one of the family members. They start out with the hypothesis that a family crisis results when an important family role is not being filled adequately or at all. When communication of the role assignment is unclear or lacking, pressures build up within the family, and the susceptible member uses psychotic or suicidal behavior as an attempt to escape or to express his desperation.

In such situations, the entire family is seen together immediately in a home visit. The nature of the crisis situation is interpreted in terms of the faulty communication, family cooperation is enlisted, and each member is assigned specific tasks to improve the situation. Whether the tasks are individual or collective, they tend to be family oriented and usually result in rapid improvement in the functioning of the whole unit. To buttress the treatment plan, differential use is made of psychotropic drugs, emergency services, and brief hospitalization for the decompensating member. Community resources are extensively involved in both the planning and treatment phases.[36]

Jacobson points out that family crisis intervention is technically harder than individual treatment. How each member views the crisis situation and how he has attempted to cope with it must be elicited individually. Among the risks involved are the tendencies to take sides in family disputes and to become enmeshed in chronic problems rather than focus on current issues.[37]

Nevertheless, Parad, Selby, and Quinlan report in a recent review that family therapy is becoming an established strategy in the practice of social workers and other mental health professionals during periods of high stress.[38]

USE OF SMALL GROUPS

The crisis approach is being used, not only with nuclear and extended families, which are natural small groups, but with friendship and common-interest groups, such as gangs and clubs.[39]

Crisis groups have been used extensively at the Benjamin Rush Centers in Los Angeles since the 1960s. Their groups are usually open-ended in that members rotate in and out at different times, each person being limited to six weekly sessions. After an initial individual interview in which the hazardous event and crisis situation are evaluated, the person is assigned to an ongoing group whose members explore ways in which each of them can cope with his own problems. The one criterion for inclusion is that each member must be in a crisis or be connected with an individual who is. The only persons excluded are those who appear to be suicidal or homicidal risks, are psychotic to a degree that would be disruptive to the group, or are unable to speak English.[40]

Opinions about the value of using groups for crisis resolution are mixed. The advantages, as reported by Morley and Brown, seem to be that people are willing to accept help in a group who would not otherwise do so. Group support, particularly for disadvantaged persons, is significant, and social relationships often grow out of group contacts. The group provides a means for encouraging expression of significant feelings and developing desensitization to disturbing topics. Members often suggest alternative coping mechanisms which help others overcome their own crises.

The disadvantages, however, are that an individual may find it difficult to focus on resolution of his particular difficulty in a heterogeneous group whose other members are in different stages of struggling with their own crisis situations. Moreover, members may suggest coping mechanisms that can be more maladaptive than adaptive, and the therapist must be alert to try to change these into more helpful solutions. It is hard to fill groups and keep them going with persons who can work together, and much time is spent in matching and sorting out membership. Finally, little saving in terms of professional treatment time appears to be gained by using groups.[41]

Nevertheless, groups continue to be used as the treatment of choice in various types of crisis situations. Sometimes, following a community disaster, the group provides a quick, economical way to reach large numbers of victims to provide psychological first aid and to inform them of the nature of the catastrophe, the resources at hand, and ways to minimize disruptive aftereffects. After the disastrous elevated train crash in Chicago in 1972, group sessions of survivors were found helpful in working out feelings of mourning and grief and sharing their reactions with others who had passed through the same experience.[42] The same held true for victims of the San Fernando Valley earthquake.[43]

In Israel, widows of soldiers who were killed in the Yom Kippur War of 1973 met in social interest groups to share their experiences in learning to overcome the transitional stage of widowhood and to explore their feelings of "being different."[44] As a result of positive reactions to this strategy, groups are currently being formed as part of the social services of the Israeli National Insurance Institute to offer the same services to survivors of civilian accidents and sudden deaths.

Groups of patients and staff members are being used during periods of brief hospitalization with lower-status patients, using a specific inpatient crisis-intervention model of transactional analysis (IPCIM) geared to a here-and-now, problem-by-problem approach.[45] The number and range of these groups are increasing.

Whatever the context, say Parad, Selby, and Quinlan, four basic steps are utilized with crisis-intervention groups: (1) search for the precipitating event and its perceptual meaning to the client(s); (2) search for coping means which have been utilized by the client(s) in the past and appraisal of the extent to which these have or have not worked; (3) search for alternative ways of coping, with particular emphasis on suggestions from group members and for resources that might benefit the current situation; and (4) review and support of the family or group members' efforts to work in new ways. These writers hold that the crisis group's advantage over individual crisis intervention is that it offers group support, companionship, and shared information about community resources and problem-solving techniques.[46]

From the wide variety of techniques and strategies being offered it becomes apparent that the crisis-intervention practitioner tends to be eclectic, innovative, and responsive to the particular needs of the client and the situation of the moment. The success of these procedures appears to derive in large part from the increased willingness of professionals to employ non-traditional tactics and to take calculated risks to further resolution of the crisis. The extent to which these tactics can be considered truly helpful or remain mere stylistic gimmicks, we suspect, varies considerably with the personal style of the worker.

Notes

1. Max Siporin, *Introduction to Social Work Practice* (New York: MacMillan, 1975, pp. 43–44.
2. Ibid., p. 34.
3. Hollis, 1972, pp. 305–307.
4. For a full discussion of these techniques, see ibid., pp. 89–163.
5. Patricia L. Ewalt, "An Examination of Advice Giving as a Therapeutic Intervention," paper presented at the Annual Meeting of the American Association of Psychiatric Services for Children, November 1975, mimeo.
6. Inger P. Davis, "Advice Giving in Parent Counseling," *Social Casework* 56 (June 1975): 343–347.
7. Harvey H. Barten and Sybil S. Barten, "New Perspectives on Child Mental Health," in Barten and Barten, eds., *Children and Their Parents in Brief Therapy* (New York: Behavioral Publications, 1973), pp. 8–9.
8. Howard E. Henderson, "Helping Families in Crisis: Police and Social Work Intervention," *Social Work* 21 (July 1974): 314–315.
9. Anne Bergman, "Emergency Room: A Role for Social Workers," *Health and Social Work* 1 (February 1976): 38–40.
10. Getz et al., 1974, pp. 34–35.
11. Leonard Small, *The Briefer Psychotherapies* (New York: Brunner/ Mazel, 1971), pp. 98–99.
12. L. A. Gelb and M. Ullman, "Instant Psychotherapy Offered at an Outpatient Psychiatric Clinic," *Frontiers of Hospital Psychiatry* 4 (August 1967); quoted in Small, 1971, p. 98. See Hoffman and

Remmel, 1975, for an example of how this is carried through in practice.

13. Lydia Rapoport, "Crisis-Oriented Short-Term Casework," *Social Service Review* 41 (March 1967): 43.

14. Getz et al., 1974, pp. 36–37.

15. David H. Malan, *The Frontier of Brief Psychotherapy* (New York: Plenum, 1976), p. 29.

16. Helen H. Perlman, *Social Casework: A Problem-Solving Process* (Chicago: University of Chicago Press, 1957), p. 147.

17. Joel Fischer and Harvey L. Gochros, *Planned Behavioral Change: Behavior Modification in Social Work* (New York: Free Press, 1975). See table on pp. 238–240.

18. Getz et al., 1974, p. 7; James K. Whittaker, *Social Treatment: An Approach to Interpersonal Helping* (Chicago: Aldine, 1974), pp. 215–216; Rosenbaum and Beebe, 1975, pp. 239–240.

19. Eric Berne, *Games People Play* (New York: Grove Press, 1964); Virginia Satir, *Peoplemaking* (Palo Alto, Cal.: Science and Behavior Books, 1972); Donn Brechenser, "Brief Psychotherapy Using Transactional Analysis," *Social Casework* 53 (March 1972): 173–176.

20. Kathryn Hallett, *A Guide for Single Parents: Transactional Analysis for People in Crisis* (Millbrae, Cal.: Celestial Arts, 1974).

21. John H. Weakland, Richard Fisch, Paul Watzlawick, and Arthur M. Bodin, "Brief Therapy: Focused Problem Resolution," *Family Process* 13 (June 1974): 156.

22. John Garrison, "Network Techniques: Case Studies in the Screening-Linking-Planning Conference Method," *Family Process* 13 (September 1974): 337–353.

23. Speck and Attneave, 1973.

24. Hollis, 1972, pp. 302–305.

25. Hollis, 1972, pp. 155–161.

26. This issue is gone into in greater detail in Collins and Pancoast, 1976.

27. Joanne E. Mantell, Esther S. Alexander, and Mark A. Kleiman, "Social Work and Self-Help Groups," *Health and Social Work* 1 (February 1976): 86–100.

28. Naomi Golan and Shlomo Sharlin, "Using Natural Helping Systems to Intervene," paper presented at the American Orthopsychiatric Association Annual Meeting, March 1975, mimeo.

29. For a full discussion of the role of the consultant, see Lydia Rapoport, "Mental Health Consultation," published originally in Leopold Bellak, ed., *Handbook in Community Psychiatry* (New York: Grune and Stratton, 1963) and reproduced in commemorative volume to her, Sanford N. Katz, ed., *Creativity in Social Work: Selected Writings of Lydia Rapoport* (Philadelphia: Temple University Press, 1975), pp. 141–167.

30. Rosenbaum and Beebe, 1975, pp. 14–15.

31. Charles Zastrow and Ralph Navarre, "Help for Runaways and Their Parents," *Social Casework* 56 (February 1975): 74–78.

32. Beverly B. Nichols, "The Abused Wife Problem," *Social Casework* 57 (January 1976): 27–32.

33. Margaret Raymond, Andrew E. Slaby, and Julian Lieb, "Familial Responses to Mental Illness," *Social Casework* 56 (October 1975): 492–498.

34. Rita R. Vollman, Amy Ganzert, Lewis Picher, and W. Vail Williams, "The Reactions of Family Systems to Sudden and Unexpected Death," *Omega* 2 (May 1971): 101–106.

35. Lydia Rapoport, "Working with Families in Crisis: An Exploration in Preventive Intervention," *Social Work* 7 (July 1962). Reprinted in Katz, 1975, pp. 125–138.

36. Langsley and Kaplan, 1968.

37. Jacobson, 1974, p. 821.

38. Parad, Selby, and Quinlan, 1976, p. 311.

39. Ibid., p. 316.

40. Martin Strickler and Jean Allgeyer, "The Crisis Group: A New Application of Crisis Theory," *Social Work* 12 (July 1967): 28–32.

41. Wilbur E. Morley and Vivian B. Brown, "The Crisis Intervention Group: A Natural Mating or a Marriage of Convenience," *Psychotherapy: Theory, Research, and Practice* 6 (Winter 1969): 30–36.

42. Leona Grossman, "Train Crash: Social Work and Disaster Services." *Social Work* 18 (September 1973): 42–43.

43. Herbert Blaufarb and Jules Levine, "Crisis Intervention in an Earthquake," *Social Work* 17 (July 1972): 16–19.

44. Golan, 1975, pp. 372–373.

45. Edwin L. Rabiner, Carl F. Wells, and Joel Yager, "A Model for the Brief Hospitalization Treatment of the Disadvantaged Psychiatrically Ill," *American Journal of Orthopsychiatry* 43 (October 1973): 774–782.

46. Parad, Selby, and Quinlan, 1976, p. 322.

Part 3

Intervention in Typical Crisis Situations

Introduction

ONCE A BASIC MODEL for crisis intervention has been developed, the question arises: how can it be applied? Obviously it must be adapted and shaped to suit each situation or complex of conditions.

In this section we examine three groups of stressful events: natural and man-made disasters, developmental and transitional crisis states, and acute, situational crises. They are presented as separate entities, although in actuality we find an overlapping and mutual exacerbation brought about by a convergence of different types of initial and subsequent hazardous events and precipitating factors. Thus, for example, we find a family in which the mother has become depressed by the approaching departure of her last child for college, the father feels threatened by the announcement that a recent company takeover has put his "secure" job in jeopardy, the oldest daughter has returned to the parental home with her two small children after a series of marital clashes, and the second son has smashed up the family car and is hospitalized with head and internal injuries.[1] The difficulties of unraveling such a complex family picture are manifest.

This type of situation, reflected in such folk sayings as "It never rains but it pours" and "Troubles always come in threes," is being examined more closely. Researchers at the Rush Centers are considering the concept of a "crisis matrix," as opposed to a single hazardous event, as describing many stress-laden situations in which a number of persons and networks are involved.[2]

When examining a particular predicament, it becomes apparent that two separate processes are being dealt with. First is the *objective* unfolding of the effects of the hazardous event(s) on the persons, families, and groups involved. As mentioned in Chapter 4, each type of stressful event seems to produce a characteristic progression of time-linked phases in returning the situation to a precrisis level of equilibrium. These phases are governed by the nature of the stressful event itself—for example the tornado which strikes the area or the climacteric which comes at a particular life stage—and evidently can be generalized to all those who undergo this type of crisis.

Intertwined with this process but by no means identical to it is the *subjective* process going on within the particular persons, families, or groups struck by the event, each of whom may be struggling separately with other stressful situations at the same time and who are at a different stage of crisis-proneness. Here, too, we find a progression of phases which can and should be identified and which is probably quite different for each person concerned. (Jacobson's differentiation between generic and individual treatment, discussed in Chapter 4, is pertinent here.)

Schulberg points out that a major gap in the conceptualization of crisis is the failure to specify the association between risk events and personal situations. He suggests that three factors come into play: the probability that a hazardous event will occur, the probability that an individual will be exposed to the event, and the vulnerability of the individual, should he be so exposed. Assessing each of these elements has definite implications for intervention strategies.[3]

The focus in this section will be on attempting to plot the life cycle of some specific types of crisis situations, with case material used as illustration. No attempt will be made to be all-inclusive or definitive; this thinking is still at the exploratory level and needs much further testing in the field before we have explicit blueprints.

Notes

1. See Naomi Golan, "Short-Term Crisis Intervention: An Approach to Serving Children and their Families," *Child Welfare* 50 (February 1971): 101–107.
2. Howard J. Parad, Lola Selby, and James Quinlan, "Crisis Intervention with Families and Groups," in Robert W. Roberts and Helen Northern, eds., *Theories of Social Work with Groups* (New York: Columbia University Press, 1976), pp. 327–328.
3. Herbert C. Schulberg, "Disaster, Crisis Theory, and Intervention Strategies," *Omega* 5 (1974): 79–80.

Chapter 7

Natural and Man-made Disasters

The Nature of Disasters

Disasters can happen to all of us. They occur frequently, cause a great deal of public concern, and their effects have been chronicled faithfully since the time of the Flood. They can range in extent from a local power failure, which may inconvenience a neighborhood for a few hours, to the Hiroshima bombing, which had long-lasting, world-wide repercussions.

Probably the simplest definition of a disaster is that it is a collective stress situation in which many members of a social system fail to receive expected conditions of life, such as safety of the physical environment, protection from attack, provision of food, shelter, and income, and the guidance and information necessary to carry on normal activities.[1]

The collective stress can arise from sources *external* to the system, including large, unfavorable changes in the environment such as droughts, floods, and earthquakes, or from sources *internal* to the system, such as economic breakdowns (depressions or strikes) or political breakdowns (riots, civil wars, purges).[2]

Siporin points out that a disaster can engender severe crisis in that it threatens self-images and identities, life goals and values, and the structure of social systems. It calls for greatly extended or restricted functioning for which customary coping patterns are, for the most part, inadequate. Both individuals and systems become disequilibrated and dysfunctional.[3]

Disasters are unique among hazardous events in that they involve collective as well as individual hardship, loss, and suffering. Since these are public rather than private, a "community of sufferers" comes into being during the acute phase. Survivors rescue each other, provide mutual physical and emotional support, and develop an altruistic community which helps heal the wounds of the individuals, adds to their resources, and ultimately contributes to the community's survival.[4]

In examining disasters, one must look at the interactions of three sets of variables: the characteristics of the disaster agent (the hazardous event), the coping resources available, and the perception of the disaster as a stressful event by those involved.

Phases in the Disaster Process

During the 1950s and 1960s, sociologists made extensive and detailed studies of a wide range of disasters, both natural and man-made. One of the most frequently applied analyses, developed initially by Powell and Rayner and augmented by others, divides the sequence into seven phases: warning, threat, impact, inventory, rescue, remedy, and recovery.[5] The following explication, based on this division, separates the process into three periods: before, during, and after the disaster strikes.

PRE-IMPACT PHASES

1. WARNING OR ALARM

Awareness develops that a potential danger exists. The mass media begin to broadcast warnings that a hurricane is building up, the river is rising, or the enemy is massing at the borders. Individuals and communities begin to gird themselves, both physically and emotionally, for the impending blow. Families gather and debate alternative ways to deal with the danger: to put up the storm shutters, to retire to the bomb shelter, to flee from the area, and so forth.

This period is usually marked by heightened anxiety and gradually increasing apprehension. Most people carry on their essential activities but keep an eye on the barometer and an ear glued to the radio. They take reasonable precautions, such as stocking up provisions and packing emergency kits, but for the most part are not yet ready to drop everything and run. It has been observed that the majority tend to handle their anxiety with reasonable courage and prudence since the danger is still probabilistic; after all, the hurricane *may* veer out to sea; the approaching forest fire *may* be arrested; the stock market *may* stop dropping. However, some extreme cases of uncontrolled terror or complete denial of danger and feelings of personal immunity ("It can't happen to us!") do occur.[6]

Reality-oriented or reflective fear usually evokes some increased attention to environmental clues, an aroused feeling of vigilance, and a greater need for reassurance. Some optimal level of stress at this stage seems necessary to prepare communities, groups, and families to cope with the disaster. A moderate amount of anxiety plus some previous experience in dealing with danger tend to make for effective behavior at this stage.[7]

2. THREAT

This phase may be almost simultaneous with the warning and/or impact. Now the danger is imminent and inevitable. It is perceived as specific, local, and personal ("It *can* and *will* happen to us!"). It may vary in length, may occur in diverse ways for different individuals, may be cumulative or occur in a wave pattern.

People tend to react individualistically in the action they take to ward off the blow: they may run for safety, panic and run around in circles, or simply hide their heads under the bedclothes and hold their breath. Family members hurry to join one another; parents run to protect their children. Those who respond with definite action usually feel less impotent than those who simply wait passively for the blow.[8]

The question of manning an official warning system assumes vital importance. It has been found that, where danger signs are ambiguous or fragmentary, people tend to develop their own interpretations. Attention paid to official announcements often depends on the timing. If these warnings are couched in terms of "low probability" and issued slowly, over time, people often ignore them. However, if an emergency warning is issued sharply about an imminent, high-probability danger, the public tends to heed it and take defensive action. False alarms will increase vigilance for a short period but lose their effectiveness in time (the "cry wolf" phenomenon).

IMPACT PHASE

3. IMPACT OR ISOLATION

Persons and families huddle together to protect themselves and each other from the blow and its concomitant injury, death, and destruction. Families suffer, persons are killed or wounded, possessions are lost. Activities are reduced to withstanding the onslaught with whatever self-protection is possible. The boundaries of the system have been invaded; internal and external communications have been disrupted; and persons and groups are more or less isolated until the danger has abated. The usual community structure is fragmented as coordination and controls disappear.

At the moment of impact, each individual tends to think that only he and his house were hit. The illusion of *centrality,* the feeling that the blow was focused particularly on himself, springs up. He feels alone and isolated: only *his* family suffered, and the rest of the world *must* come to his aid. As he begins to realize the extent of the damage, he feels abandoned and helpless.[9]

A frequent set of reactions in this and in the next phase (depending on whether the blow was of short or continuing duration) has been called the "disaster syndrome": absence of emotion, lack of response to present stimuli, inhibition of outward activity, docility, undemandingness. Persons are described as "stunned," "dazed," "shocked." Panic is frequently anticipated at this stage but actually has been found to occur rarely, except in situations of extreme and continued danger, where the victims feel trapped and unable to escape.[10]

During this phase, people tend to react in terms of extremes. After their first sharp constriction of feelings and concern about themselves and those dearest to them, impulses of generosity and concern for others emerge. The sense of helplessness is replaced by the desire to help others. Occasionally, however, one finds the urge for self-survival taking precedence (for example, pushing others off the life raft, eating human flesh). During disasters involving devastation and injury, people seem capable of incredible physical effort and endurance, working for long periods of time with an indifference to their own discomfort that would seem almost impossible under normal conditions.[11]

When people are caught in groups during the impact period, they tend to experience a sense of cohesiveness, of togetherness and "shared fate"; at the same time they feel isolated from the rest of the world. Morale is high, and ad hoc leadership, with little relationship to official roles, soon develops.[12]

POST-IMPACT PHASES

4. INVENTORY

As the debris settles, the bombers fly off, or the earth stops quaking, the stunned survivors emerge from their shelters and begin to take stock.[13] The first effect of the impact is a momentary fragmentation of the social scene into isolated individuals, each one reacting to the event and checking on his own personal injuries and those of his immediate companions. Then slowly each begins to rove about, to search for his loved ones and to examine the extent of the physical destruction in his immediate area.

First reactions range from dazed bewilderment, disbelief, and a sense of catastrophic loss to profound relief and gratitude for having passed through the worst and still being alive. Recent research has shown that the apparent mass confusion is not really so disoriented as it appears. Most individuals are engaged in highly purposive individual and small-unit activity at the survival level, which simply is not socially coordinated.[14]

Emotional ties to others in the immediate proximity are rapidly established, with feelings of concern, warmth, and mutual helpfulness, regardless of social, racial, or economic status. Those who are unhurt or only slightly wounded begin to rescue the trapped victims and administer first aid to the badly injured, sometimes performing superhuman feats of strength and perseverance. For some survivors, the same disaster syndrome of shock, passivity, and withdrawal noted during the impact phase continues for hours and sometimes days afterwards.

During this period of fragmentation, the importance of the family as the basic social unit becomes emphasized. Family roles are intensified and internal rifts and differences forgotten in the new sense of concern for family survival. Family loyalty becomes a potent force in guiding individual behavior and decision making.[15]

On the other hand, official and professional roles, especially if the community was unprepared for the disaster, tend to be confused, lost, and inappropriate during this phase. Official structures and procedures (for example, hospital admission regulations) frequently cannot accommodate themselves easily to the changed situation.[16]

At this stage the social scene is marked by disequilibrium and lack of coordination. Ties to and from the outside world are usually disrupted and communication media weakened or not functioning. Information on the extent of the destruction is absent or very fragmentary and rumors spread like wildfire through the community as each unit tries to "put together the pieces." Gradually communication becomes resumed and requests for help trickle out. The greater the disaster and the more extensive the disruption, the harder it is and the longer it takes to reestablish ties to the outside.

5. RESCUE

This phase is often indistinct from and coexistent with the previous phase. The people in the impact zone continue to organize and cooperate in rescuing themselves and each other. They begin to clear away the worst of the debris, administer first aid to the injured, and erect temporary shelters, sometimes evacuating survivors to some central, destruction-free point such as a school, city hall, or park. Rescue work is still informal and spontaneous but soon develops a structure as basic supplies of water, food, and shelter are shared impartially. The general emotional tone is one of goodwill and elation, sometimes even euphoria—the phenomenon of the "altruistic community."

The areas surrounding the impact zone usually provide the earliest aid from the outside as people from nearby begin to pour in, despite the difficulty of access and the lack of accommodations. This convergence toward the center of impact brings not only official rescue teams but crowds of persons anxious to find out the fate of friends and relatives, volunteers eager to help in the rescue work, and tourists who are simply curious or seeking thrills. Frequently severe traffic problems are created which hamper and prevent relief efforts. Roadblocks set up to permit the inflow of needed goods and services while keeping out the avid and self-interested are not always efficient or appropriately placed.

The public in the rest of the country or the "suprasystem" frequently responds generously to requests for help, and immediate rescue supplies begin to pour in, but often they are not of the right type, or the efforts to distribute them are uncoordinated. Disruption of the communications and transportation networks may prevent an accurate survey of the extent of the damage and may result in inaccurate predictions about needs based on rumors and false estimates of damages. This may mean a waste of valuable time, effort, and supplies.[17]

6. REMEDY

Once the immediate rescue efforts are completed, the extent of the damage is inventoried, and the first needs are met, more permanent efforts to remedy and rebuild what was destroyed by the catastrophe are begun. People now start to restore their own homes and move out of their temporary tents or barracks. The dead are buried, the injured are sent for healing and recuperation, and the period of mourning begins—not only for the persons who died but for the old ways and landmarks that have been obliterated.

The earlier informal, voluntary means of helping of the altruistic-community period, with its strong community identity and unity, based on common dangers and losses, shared objectives, and cooperative self-help experiences,[18] are now replaced by more established, formalized patterns of help-giving. Outside relief agencies with their experienced fieldworkers set up operations. Requesting and providing assistance now mean filling out forms and proving eligibility requirements to banks, lending institutions, and federal and state bureaucracies.

According to Siporin, the convergence of informal and organizational helping efforts appears to be initially effective but operates under great strain. Gradually, bureaucratic perspectives and standardized policies and procedures gain ascendance over informal victim- and volunteer-based activities.

Gradually, individuals resume their previous roles, volunteers go back to their regular jobs, and the early mutual-aid banding-together gives way to more formal means of communication and relationships. Social distinctions, submerged during the inventory and rescue phases, begin to reappear as the community returns to its predisaster pattern of social and economic stratification.

In time, the community becomes fully organized for reconstruction. Long-term plans are made, funds allocated under disaster relief programs, and bids solicited for the repairing of roads, buildings, and other damaged elements of the infrastructure. Community action groups are formed by citizens eager to become involved in the reconstruction in order to remedy some of the earlier mistakes in planning and building the community. The atmosphere, at least initially, is one of high morale and collective good-will.[19]

During this period, some of the emotional and psychological damage to individuals and families wrought by the disaster becomes apparent. Depression, agitation, nightmares, excessive fears, dependency, and regression to more childlike behavior are some of the symptoms reported at this time. Another syndrome is the emergence of various somatic symptoms: shivering, trembling, dizziness, nausea, vomiting, diarrhea, and insomnia. At times parent and child roles in the family become reversed in the effort to master the situation and provide reassurance and emotional support for the remaining members.

7. RECOVERY AND RESTORATION

The degree and extent of final recovery from the effects of disaster are governed by a number of factors: the nature and severity of the damage, the individual's proximity (physical and emotional) to it, the death and destruction witnessed, and his own personality. Some classes of survivors, such as the aged, the bedridden, pregnant women, and small children, tend to be more vulnerable than others. The person's position in his family and in other primary groups, his sense of social responsibility, and his occupational skills are all important factors which can aid in recovery but can also produce significant role conflicts in determining priorities.

Sometimes effects of the trauma wrought by the disaster show up long after apparent equilibrium has been regained. While for most victims overt symptoms disappear relatively quickly and are integrated into the personality structure, for a certain number, the effects are long-lasting and even irreversible.[20] In extreme cases, such as the survivors of concentration camps, symptoms may even be passed on to the second generation through distortions in intrafamilial relations.[21]

It is difficult to measure the long-range effects of a disaster and to determine when the system finally recovers. Basic changes in individual performance, family role patterns, and community structure have taken place in the process and the clock can never be turned back. Even after a new equilibrium is reached, the disaster remains a significant milestone in the survivors' life history—a turning point for better or worse.

Intervention in Disaster Crises

THE PROFESSIONAL'S ROLE

The role of the professional in disaster situations is often ambiguous and marked with feelings of frustration and helplessness. It differs according to the extent and timing of his involvement. If he himself is a member of the system struck by disaster, his participation from the beginning becomes legitimated by that very fact. He sees himself, and is seen by the rest of the community, as operating in a dual capacity, as both a fellow victim and a professional helper.[22]

On the other hand, if he comes in after the event, either as part of a rescue team or as a personally motivated volunteer, he may not find the same degree of acceptance by the local population. Although they may have called for help from the outside, once he arrives, his credentials are not always recognized (at least until he proves himself) by the local service structure. He often is viewed as an interloper, a threat to their own power base, and more of a hindrance than a help, regardless of his expertise.[23] Moreover, even if he is a "local," his effectiveness may depend on whether he functions during the period of the disaster in his regular position or away from his accepted network, in a strange setting, without knowing its pattern of operation and resources.

Sometimes the worker's own involvement in the disaster blurs his perspective so that he can no longer weigh matters objectively. Role conflicts and opposing priorities (for example, should he continue at his post or flee to safety with his family?) may further complicate the picture. In time, his continued exposure to the demanding, emotionally draining situation may result in his entering into a serious emotional crisis.

Schulberg makes an important distinction between *anticipatory intervention* in disasters which can be predicted with a high degree of probability and *participatory intervention* in low probability disasters. In the former, efforts can be made in advance to prepare individuals psychologically for what will probably happen, to organize and train caregiving networks, and to establish public policy to minimize the risks of ecological imbalance which might occur. In the latter, efforts can be directed only after the disaster has occurred to deal with the tensions and stresses generated: to pay particular attention to high-risk groups such as welfare recipients or the chronically ill, to organize ad hoc support systems, and to set up priorities and public policy for the distribution of scarce or unavailable resources.[24]

Anticipatory intervention, analogous to the primary prevention level in the public health model, has been receiving increasing attention in recent years. Spurred by the disaster research studies of the past twenty years, considerable effort has gone into drawing up detailed contingency plans by local, state, and federal authorities, sometimes based on game-theory planning. Legislation has been broadened and a range of public and private programs for disaster relief and assistance have been developed.[25]

TREATMENT OBJECTIVES

Since disasters are, by definition, nondiscriminatory in their effects, crisis intervention must usually begin at the generic level. Minimal goals are to provide relief from immediate tension and pressures, to help participants understand fully what has happened and what lies ahead, to help them decide what to do and identify the tasks that must be carried out to implement their decisions, and to mobilize scarce resources to help them return to some degree of equilibrium.

Two guiding principles should be kept in mind. First, the role of the professional in disasters is usually "ephemeral"; he serves primarily as a temporary bridge to help the victim connect with the needed services and supplies and to rebuild a support system to take the place of the one that has been weakened or lost. The family has already been identified as the most preferred source of support during disasters. Relatives, friends, neighbors, volunteers, other survivors, community caregivers ("gatekeepers"), mutual-help and special-interest groups can all be enlisted in the "broad push" approach which is basic to rapid reintegration.[26]

Second, interventive tasks will largely lie along the material-arrangemental axis. Only in cases of persons too shocked or overwhelmed to participate actively in the rehabilitation process, or where the disaster serves to exacerbate precrisis conditions, need a more individual approach be used.

PRE-IMPACT PHASES

During the warning and threat phases, the practitioner has little direct contact with potential victims, although he may have been included in anticipatory intervention planning in the event of high-probability dangers. In Israel, for example, social workers now function as active members of local and national Psychological and Social Service Emergency Committees (PESACH), which are automatically activated when disasters are threatened. The aim here is to exchange information and supplies, coordinate activities, and make maximal use of scarce resources during the course of the catastrophe.[27]

The worker can also take part in staffing information centers and hot lines, to see that accurate, up-to-the-minute information is made available on the imminence and extent of the threat. Often, strategic position and access to accurate sources, rather than professional preparation, are the vital key. During the height of the street fighting in Beirut during the 1976 civil war, a middle-aged Lebanese schoolteacher became a folk hero by manning the local radio station almost single-handedly and acting as the clearing house for detailed information about where the fighting was going on, who was involved, what neighborhoods were safe, who was searching for whom, and so on. Involved concern marked his effectiveness.

Other functions during the pre-impact period might be to help local authorities see to it that shelters are properly prepared and stocked, that first-aid stations are staffed and ready, and that evacuation centers are available in case of need. Finally, as the danger approaches, the professional can serve as the ''voice of reason'' to counteract the rising anxiety and tension among the other inhabitants braced for the blow. This emotional support can be a vital factor before and during the hazardous event.

IMPACT

During this phase the professional role gives way to that of the involved member of the community who does as all other citizens do: protects his head, takes all precautions possible, follows instructions, and waits for the danger to pass.

POST-IMPACT PHASES

INVENTORY

The worker now has an important task: to recover from the effects of the impact as quickly as possible in order to begin to carry out rescue plans, either preplanned or spontaneous, based on his past background and training. It has been found that persons with previous experience in disaster work or with special preparation in crisis intervention start to act more quickly and productively than others at such a time.

As the shock waves recede, the trained professional has two primary jobs: (1) to help assess the extent of physical damage and to get word to the outside about what has happened, and (2) to provide immediate first aid to the injured and keep an eye on the vulnerable elements in the population. The focus is on the primary level of attending to survival needs.

RESCUE

As the inventory phase merges into the rescue period, the practitioner begins to function intensively. At this stage, his work is still largely concerned with the distribution and provision of basic needs such as food, shelter, and medical care. Scattered family members must be reunited, supplies distributed, debris cleared, sanitation facilities provided, and communications reestablished. The social worker's professional obligation to extend himself to help others, despite his own personal discomfort, may help him remain calm as he reassures survivors and provides emotional support.[28]

This intense involvement can be both an exhilarating and a profoundly humbling experience. At this time the altruistic community in effect operates on an egalitarian, first-name, sleeves-rolled-up basis, paying little attention to precrisis rank or status. The worker may have to lend a hand in a dozen short-term projects in rapid succession, shifting and adapting his role to meet the needs of the moment. Because of his knowledge of community resources, his chief concern may be to help persons in need of specific items to obtain them from whatever pool of resources and supplies is available.

This concentration on immediate needs, however, means that the professional may have to shift his entire perspective and order of priorities. Whether he is locally based or is brought in from the outside, Barton warns:

> Professionals, however expert in meeting emergency needs of one client at a time, do not necessarily have the training and experience for coping with a massive overload of clients. Their sense of ''godlike'' abilities in the normal situation may actually make them overconfident about what they can accomplish in disaster. The problem of *to whom* they should provide service, of how rationally to schedule different degrees of treatment to many clients all seeking help at once, is crucial to an effective professional role in disaster.[29]

REMEDY

Once the acute phase of the emergency is over, the social worker may have to give up his temporary job on the ''front line'' and return to his previous professional framework. As survivors start to repair or rebuild their homes, shops, schools, and other community structures which have been damaged or destroyed, he concentrates on helping them make important decisions in daily life situations and work out rehabilitation plans. His expertise in finding his way through the bureaucratic maze, unraveling the complex regulations on licensing, funding, and eligibility requirements, and his linkages with the power structure can be extremely significant for his clients at this crucial time.

Equally important, he can help them come to other significant decisions as they struggle to adjust to the changes in their shattered lives brought on by the disaster. The calamity may have been the precipitating factor which brought to a head other doubts and pressures they were previously struggling with: whether to give up a failing business, to move from a large, no-longer-needed family home to a small, utilitarian apartment, to get into a less demanding line of work.

The worker can make use of the opportunity within the tragic circumstances to help clients review alternatives, cut their losses, make new adaptations, and embark on new directions. Often a routine request for financial assistance or practical aid can be turned by the experienced, alert worker, sensitive to the underlying pain, sorrow, and doubt, into an intense, drama-packed helping experience which alters the whole course of the client's life.[30] And above all, he can help them begin or continue their grief work—whether for a beloved person, a cherished home, or a way of life now forever lost.

Helping families adjust to the death or disability of one or more members can become an extremely significant part of the worker's activity during this phase.[31] Hill and Hansen point out that community disasters bring about a sharp rise in family functioning and solidarity following the initial drop brought about by the impact.[32] The worker can use this intense feeling of mutual goodwill to help the family shift and reapportion roles, to have members take on new responsibilities, and to develop new patterns of communication.

If, however, the family conceals or postpones dealing with the hardships engendered at this time, or if the worker is not sufficiently perceptive to pick up the clues, the difficulties may well turn into festering, chronic problems of family malfunctioning. He will have failed to grasp that vital moment when, on the one hand, the family is highly motivated to effect change and, on the other, the community, out of its new-found awareness and group solidarity, can tolerate, condone, and accept new modes of adjustment.

Since survivors in disasters tend to cling together and share common experiences, the use of short-term, focused groups can be very productive during both the rescue and the remedy phases. When a severe earthquake shook the San Fernando Valley in 1971, workers at the local child-guidance clinic met with some three hundred families in groups for a five-week period to help them discuss their mutual reactions to the disaster and share their common fears and upsets. The workers' primary task was to help reduce the level of anxiety in both parents and children, often by suggesting concrete changes in role performance and family living arrangements. Children were encouraged to verbalize their feelings of fright and terror, while immobilized parents were firmly advised to resume their parental functions as quickly as possible and to re-establish normal family patterns.[33]

This use of groups to exchange common coping patterns and receive mutual support, an important technique in all crisis intervention, here "tunes in" on the post-disaster feelings of sharing and caring catalyzed by the survivors' participation in this shattering experience.[34]

RECOVERY

As the community gradually returns to its precrisis level of functioning, many of the scars left by the disaster on persons, as well as property, disappear or at least are no longer visible. For some survivors, however, the long-term effects of the catastrophe will occupy professional helpers for months and years. At times, long after apparent adjustment has been reached, some small event will trigger a series of past associations and significant material, long repressed, will surface.

For this type of client, the generic level of treatment will no longer suffice. Here the individual approach, with attention paid to the unique circumstances of the situation, is indicated. A close, careful examination of the client's involvement in the disaster, his attendant feelings and associations, and the subjective meanings he has attached to elements in the situation in terms of his total life process may be necessary. Difficult though this uncovering process may be, it can also be the key for the person to finally come to terms with the traumatic effect of the disaster on himself and result in a genuine growth experience for both helper and helped.

For other clients, irreparably damaged by the disaster yet still struggling with its long-lasting aftereffects, the worker has to continue to provide tangible assistance, emotional support, and help with adjustment problems, as in the case of families of American prisoners of war and soldiers missing in action[35] and with Holocaust survivors.[36]

CASE SUMMARY: TRAIN CRASH

The following report of a disastrous train crash, already reported in the literature,[37] is presented here in summary form to illustrate the role of social workers in the crisis situation which followed.

IMPACT

Early on Monday morning, October 30, 1972, as commuters were pouring into the Chicago Loop, a crash on a local railroad killed 45 passengers and injured more than 300. No advance warning was given, no pre-impact threat was felt, in this man-made, low probability disaster. Fortunately, the staff of Michael Reese Hospital had just completed and rehearsed disaster plans and, together with the city fire and police departments, immediately intervened to deal with the effects of the catastrophe.

The staff of social workers, most of whom did not hear of the accident until they arrived at work, quickly recovered from its initial shock and confusion and organized itself into a functioning unit at the nurses' residence where family members and friends were chaotically milling about, trying to learn the fate of their loved ones. Staff morale was high and an ad hoc structure was quickly developed in which roles were covertly defined and a rational leadership soon emerged. The spirit of cohesiveness and support among the professional groups provided the stability upon which the fragmented system of family and relatives could lean.

The social work staff provided the urgently needed comfort and help and, in turn, drew closer to the relatives and friends with whom it was in contact. Following the immediate immersion and initial shock, there was some recoil, some jockeying for power or status. Some of the staff felt pushed aside by their colleagues, but eventually each worker discovered some satisfying level of usefulness, accepted the leadership, and developed effective modes of rapid, nonverbal communication.

INVENTORY AND RESCUE

As they waited for news, survivors began to feel concern for each other and to reach out helpfully. While family and relatives searched desperately for survivors, the social work staff, later assisted by outside professionals, other hospital personnel, clergymen, and volunteers, was there to inform, guide, and offer them hope and comfort.

Lists of the injured and dead were relayed continuously to the social work staff from the hospital's public relations department, and the workers, supported by members of the clergy, acted to inform relatives and friends. Family members clung together and comforted one another. Strangers sat side by side, waiting, not speaking, but observant of each other. A few attached themselves to staff members and returned periodically for news; they seemed to feel reassured that someone was personally concerned about them. Volunteers stayed with people who seemed lost and confused or who wanted to talk or cry. Some needed someone to hold their hand or pat their shoulder. The function of touching became important, both for families and staff members. Serving of food, provided by the hospital, also played an important role in comforting.

As the day wore on, the tension and anxiety mounted. The fatigued staff, however, remained remarkably patient, and relatives and friends were encouraged to express their fears, to cry, and to talk endlessly. For those families who had to identify relatives in the morgue, emotional responses were extreme. Families turned to each other in their sorrow, and professionals seemed locked out or chose to remove themselves; one of the priests was left to deal with this.

REMEDY

Most of the staff members, despite their exhaustion, felt that they had accomplished something significant and had extended themselves fully.

Because the severe loss and grief they witnessed had aroused repressed memories of past personal loss, despite responses ranging from emotional outbursts to denial, a series of staff meetings, informal discussions, and group meetings was held over a period of several weeks following the disaster.

Groups of survivors, relatives, and staff members were notified of the opportunity to talk over what had happened; some persons attended a few times, others just once. Initially survivors tended to ruminate over the details of the crash in an attempt to develop cognitive awareness of what had happened. Most recalled what had been happening just before the crash; some had superstitious reasons why they had survived while others were killed. Some struggled with reactions of moral censure in the belief that they should have done more to help the others instead of fleeing to safety. Discussion about the range of panic reactions helped to restore participants' feelings of self-worth.

Somatic effects reported were headaches, sleep disturbances, startle reactions, gastric distress, temporary amnesia, and tremors, as well as phobias and fears. Survivors found that talking to one another had a cathartic effect and became a vital part of recovery. Relatives, listening to the survivors talk in the group sessions, were helped to understand and empathize with their experiences. In several instances, emotional reactions were linked to past events, real or vicarious, as, for example, army experiences. In other cases, the tendency to deprecate and embarrass others for not being more courageous was noted. Depression and outbursts of sudden anger were prevalent.

Social work staff members were totally engrossed in the sessions and were able to relate with empathy and reflect openly on their own reactions. Increased insight and closer relations with one another were gained from this intense involvement.

Although some effort was made to reach out to families of the deceased, the bereaved families did not appear to be interested in talking with others in the same situation and instead sought the intimacy of their own family group or the comfort of religion.

RECOVERY

Patients who had been injured enough to require hospitalization and their families also felt the urgent need to talk about the accident, to compare impressions, and to express their feelings of grief and anger. These were dealt with by the hospital social workers in their traditional roles.

Out of the total experience, it was found that the social work staff, through its commitment to the survivors, was able to permit mutual caring and helping involvement to take place. Crisis intervention provided a significant opportunity for growth through self-reflection and feedback and increased mutual respect. The total experience reconfirmed the effectiveness of the social worker's role in crisis intervention in which action, as well as a high level of empathy and respect for human dignity, is a major priority.

Notes

1. Allen Barton, *Communities in Disaster* (New York: Doubleday, 1969), p. 38.

2. Section III, "Disaster Aid Phenomena and Mental Health Emergencies," in Howard J. Parad, H. L. P. Resnik, and Libbie Y. Parad, eds., *Emergency and Disaster Management* (Bowie, Md.: Charles Press, 1976), pp. 209–391, offers graphic accounts of a wide range of disaster situations, both natural and manmade, and how communities coped with them.

3. Max Siporin, "Disaster Aid," in Robert Morris, ed., *Encyclopedia of Social Work*, Sixteenth Issue, 1 (New York: NASW, 1971), p. 246.

4. Charles E. Fritz, "Disaster," in R. K. Merton and R. A. Nisbet, eds., *Contemporary Social Problems* (New York: Harcourt, Brace, and World, 1961), p. 655.

5. J. W. Powell and J. Rayner, *Progress Notes: Disaster Investigations* (Edgewood, Md.: Chemical Corps Medical Laboratories, Army Chemical Center, 1952); J. W. Powell, J. E. Finesinger, and M. H. Greenhill, "An Introduction to the Natural History of Disaster," vol. 2, *Final Contract Report, Disaster Research Project* (Psychiatric Institute, University of Maryland, 1954); James G. Miller, "A Theoretical Review of Individual and Group Psychological Reactions to Stress," in George H. Grosser, Henry Wechsler, and Milton Greenblatt, eds., *The Threat of Impending Disaster*

(Cambridge: M.I.T. Press, 1964), pp. 11–33; Richard I. Shader and Alice J. Schwartz, "Management of Reactions to Disaster," *Social Work* 11 (April 1966): 99–105.

6. Dwight W. Chapman, "A Brief Introduction to Contemporary Disaster Research," in G. W. Baker and D. W. Chapman, eds., *Man and Society in Disaster* (New York: Basic Books, 1962), pp. 9–10.

7. Irving L. Janis, "Psychological Effects of Warnings," in Baker and Chapman, 1962, pp. 60–62.

8. Miller, 1964, p. 26.

9. Martha Wolfenstein, *Disaster: A Psychological Essay* (Glencoe, Ill.: Free Press, 1957), pp. 51–56.

10. Anthony F. Wallace, *Tornado in Worcester: An Exploratory Study of Individual and Community Behavior in an Extreme Situation*, Committee on Disaster Studies, No. 3 (Washington, D. C.: National Academy of Sciences—National Research Council, 1956). Quoted in Wolfenstein, 1957, pp. 72–84.

11. Sheila Tidmarsh, *Disaster* (Harmondsworth, Middlesex: Penguin, 1969), pp. 20–21.

12. Wolfenstein, 1957, pp. 91–31. Also see James B. Taylor, Louis A. Zuicher, and William H. Key, *Tornado: A Community Responds to Disaster* (Seattle: University of Washington Press, 1970).

13. It should be noted that many of the reactions noted in the impact phase merge into and are continued during the inventory period. This depends largely on whether the impact is sharp and quickly over, as in the case of a sudden explosion, or whether it continues and is repeated or drawn out over a period of time, as during a series of earthquakes or a week-long hijacking.

14. Steven Kafrissen, Edward S. Heffron, and Jack Zusman, "Mental Health Problems in Environmental Disasters," in H. L. P. Resnik and H. L. Ruben, eds. *Emergency Psychiatric Care: the Management of Mental Health Crises* (Bowie, Md.: Charles Press, 1975), p. 161.

15. Chapman, 1962, pp. 15–17.

16. Miller, 1964, p. 28.

17. Chapman, 1962, pp. 18–19; Miller, 1964, 28–31.

18. Siporin, 1971, p. 249. This point is further amplified in Max Siporin, "Altruism, Disaster, and Crisis Intervention," in Parad, Resnik, and Parad, 1976, pp. 217–219.

19. Chapman, 1962, pp. 19–22.

20. For a sensitive, detailed discussion of the aftermath phase of disaster, see Wolfenstein, 1957, pp. 135–221.

21. Kafrissen, Heffron, and Zusman, 1975, p. 161.

22. For two accounts of social workers participating in disasters, see Sylvia R. Jacobson, "Individual and Group Responses to Confinement in a Skyjacked Plane," *American Journal, of Orthopsychiatry* 43 (April 1973): 459–469; Allen Feld, "Reflections on the Agnes Flood," *Social Work* 18 (September 1974): 46–51.

23. See Fred Birnbaum, Jennifer Coplon, and Ira Scharff, "Crisis Intervention After a Natural Disaster," *Social Casework* 54 (November 1973): 545–551, for professionals' frustrations about the underutilization of social work expertise when they are brought in for short stints from the outside.

24. Schulberg, 1974, p. 81.

25. Richard K. McGee and Edward I. Heffron, "The Role of Crisis Intervention Services in Disaster Recovery," pp. 309–323, and Ann. S. Kliman, "The Corning Flood Project; Psychological First Aid Following a Natural Disaster," pp. 325–335, both in Parad, Resnik, and Parad, 1976, give examples of the type of imaginative programs set up in recent years.

26. Gerald Caplan's position, which has already been discused, should be reviewed in this connection. See Caplan, *Support Systems and Community Mental Health* (New York: Behavioral Publications, 1974), pp. 4–38. For social workers' activities with natural support systems, see Alice H. Collins and Diane L. Pancoast, *Natural Helping Networks* (Washington, D.C.: NASW, 1976), pp. 65–74.

27. For an example of this in action, see Naomi Golan and Batya Vashitz, "Social Services in a War Emergency," *Social Service Review* 48 (September 1974): 422–427.

28. Shader and Schwartz, 1966, p. 103.

29. Barton, 1969, pp. 100–101.

30. See Birnbaum, Coplon, and Scharff, 1973, 547–549, on help given survivors of the Wilkes-Barre flood.

31. Stanley B. Goldberg, "Family Tasks and Reactions in the Crisis of Death," *Social Casework* 54 (July 1973): 398–405.

32. Reuben Hill and Donald A. Hansen, "Families in Disaster," in Baker and Chapman, 1962, pp. 194–199.

33. See Herbert Blaufarb and Jules Levine, "Crisis Intervention in an Earthquake," *Social Work* (July 1972): 16–19, for an excellent example of brief, focused treatment at a time of group crisis.

34. See Naomi Golan, "Wife to Widow to Woman," *Social Work,* 20 (September 1975): 372–373, for the use of groups by widows during the remedy phase.

35. Hamilton I. McCubbin and Barbara B. Dahl, "Social and Mental Health Services to Families of Servicemen Missing in Action or Returned Prisoners of War," in H. I. McCubbin et al., *Family Separation and Reunion* (San Diego, Cal.: Center for Prisoner of War Studies, Naval Health Research Center, 1974), pp. 191–209.

36. Although a wealth of therapeutic data on work with survivors and families of concentration camp victims (both German and Russian) has been gathered in the United States and Israel, I have chosen not to discuss the issues here in view of the complexity in interpreting the situations as disasters or crises. See, for example, Bernard Trossman, "Adolescent Children of Concentration Camp Survivors," *Canadian Psychiatric Association Journal* 13 (April 1968): 121–123.

37. Leona Grossman, "Train Crash: Social Work and Disaster Services," *Social Work* 18 (September 1973): 38–44. Quoted with permission of the author and of the National Association of Social Workers (condensed).

Chapter 8

Developmental and Transitional Life Crises

Individual Developmental Crises

The application of the term *crisis* to the upsets which occur during developmental stages is usually traced to the work of Erik Erikson, who theorized that psychosocial crises can be internally as well as externally generated and that they may develop because a person is at a certain stage in the process of his ego formation when situations arise that force him to make radical selections. Erikson views the life cycle as a gradual unfolding of the personality through phase-specific core conflicts, precipitated both by the individual's readiness and by society's pressure.[1]

By now, the study of normative life crises from birth to death has become a recognized and significant area of academic and clinical interest.[2] Much of the recent research has centered on plotting stresses experienced at various stages in the life span, examining them for different population groups, and correlating

149

the results with other aspects of the persons' lives, using standardized instruments such as the Social Readjustment Rating Scale (SRRS), mentioned earlier.[3] While some of this research has proved to have direct application to practice,[4] much of the theoretical and research material requires careful weighing in terms of its relevance to the "real world" in which practitioners operate.

Broadening the term *crisis* to refer to a whole developmental stage[5] creates basic difficulties in conceptualization. While entire periods such as adolescence or middle age may meet our thumbnail definition of crisis as an upset in a steady state, the time span is too broad, too encompassing, and too multifaceted to be considered to have the same attributes as other crisis situations: starting with a defined hazardous event, experiencing a continuous rise in tension, being open and anxious for help, and so on.

It has been suggested that the term *critical condition* or *crucial situation* would be more appropriate, though less eye-catching, to describe the characteristics of certain stages in the normative life cycle which tend to make the individual more vulnerable to and less able to deal with the periodic stresses and pressures that arise, whether they are biophysiological, psychosocial, or situational in origin. This change in terminology would answer the practitioner's objection that we cannot "treat" adolescence as such; we can, however, recognize it as a contributing and complicating factor in situations presented to us for help. During such developmental periods, physiological processes plus their emotional accompaniments have the potential for turning otherwise workable situations into complex crisis states.[6]

Much current social work practice deals with cases in which developmental and situational aspects seem to blur and converge. The practitioner's diagnostic understanding of developmental processes can serve as a guide to help him determine when, where, and how to intervene. Often efforts are concentrated on helping a person achieve mastery of the particular problems encountered as he passes through stages in his life cycle. Bartlett sees these problems as specific life tasks that must be met and coped with.[7]

Meyer has managed to tie these aspects together very effectively in her chart on the normal individual transactions faced at different life stages (see Table 2). For each developmental level, she identifies age-specific tasks and needs that arise, expectable transitional crises and problems to be faced, and resources and services that have to be supplied in order to meet these needs.[8] This brings the social worker's role during crisis situations sharply into focus. It also raises broader policy issues on the provision of necessary community resources to service these needs.

Family Developmental Crises

Paralleling and dovetailing with the individual life stages are the life stages of the family as a unit.[9] Scherz conceptualizes certain *universal psychological tasks* which arise for the family and for the individual, which interrelate and influence one another. These tasks arise in different forms at each stage in the life cycle, depending on the age-phase of the individual family members and on the family's perception of its tasks at each developmental phase.[10]

For the family, these tasks are: (1) emotional separation versus interdependence or connectedness; (2) closeness or intimacy versus distance; and (3) self-autonomy versus other responsibility. For the individual, these tasks are: (1) separation and the working out of dependency needs; (2) closeness and the establishment of sexual identity; and (3) autonomy and the development of self-control and self-worth.

Scherz sees management of these tasks as involving growth-producing conflict which arises from the opposing needs of the family to regulate interaction and of the individual to assert his own developmental tasks. The degree to which the conflict is resolved successfully at each stage depends on whether a flexible

TABLE 2. Normal Individual Transactions*

Individual Developmental Age-Specific Tasks and Needs	Expectable Transitional Crises and Typical Problems	Available Institutions Providing Social Services

I. Infancy, 0–3
   Tasks:
   Basic trust vs. mistrust
   Autonomy vs. shame and doubt
   Needs:
   Mothering, care, learning, verbal and conceptual skills
	Role transition for parents, working mothers, absent fathers
	   Typical problems:
	   Inadequate parenting
	   Unwanted children
	   Neglect and abuse
	   Marital conflict
	   Physical handicaps
	   Mental retardation
		Income maintenance programs
		Prenatal care centers for medical care, advice, and parent education
		Hospitals, clinics
		Well-baby stations
		Family services
		Child welfare services
		   Homemakers
		   Home helps
		   Day care
		   Protection
		   Placement (foster care, adoption)

II. Preschool, 3–6
   Tasks:
   Initiative vs. guilt
   Needs:
   Learning, socialization, play
	Child's separation from home
	Changing tasks of child rearing
	   Typical problems:
	   Inadequate socialization
	   Lack of supervision
	   Behavioral reactions
		Nursery school care
		Group care services
		(And see above as appropriate)

III. Grade school, 6–13 *Tasks:* Industry vs. inferiority *Needs:* Intellectual and social stimulation	Expanding world and increasing stimuli to be coped with *Typical problems:* Social and learning failures	School guidance services Recreational services Developmental group services (And see above as appropriate)
IV. High school, 13–18 *Tasks:* Identity vs. identity diffusion *Needs:* Achievement, partial separation from parents	The time for decisions about sexual identity, work, and the future *Typical problems:* Identity crises Alienation Addictions Delinquency School maladjustment	Youth services, hotlines, crash pads, etc. Vocational counseling Correctional services Addiction services (And see above as appropriate)
V. Young adult, 18–21 *Tasks:* Intimacy vs. isolation *Needs:* Opportunities for self-fulfilment in adult roles	Leaving home Marriage Working *Typical problems:* Unwed parenthood School/work maladaptation Marital conflict Addictions Crime	Marital-conflict legal-aid services Probation services (And see above as appropriate)

(continued)

153

TABLE 2, *continued*

INDIVIDUAL DEVELOPMENTAL AGE-SPECIFIC TASKS AND NEEDS†	EXPECTABLE TRANSITIONAL CRISES AND TYPICAL PROBLEMS	AVAILABLE INSTITUTIONS PROVIDING SOCIAL SERVICES
VI. Mature adult, 21–65 *Tasks:* Generativity *vs.* stagnation *Needs:* Expanding opportunities for self-development in life roles	Household management and care *Typical Problems:* Family breakdown, divorce Financial needs or mismanagement Parent-child conflict Work, career failure Disability, personality disorganization Death of family and friends	Family court services Medical and mental health services (And see above as appropriate)
VII. Aged adult, 65 and over *Tasks:* Integrity *vs.* despair *Needs:* Living arrangements, physical care, continuing opportunities for self-development in roles of aged	Physical and mental depletion Loss of friends and separation from family Retirement *Typical problems:* Sickness Loneliness Social isolation Economic deprivation	Meals on wheels Centers for the aged Income-maintenance programs Foster grandparent programs Foster family care Institutional care (And above as appropriate)

*The author [C. Meyer] is grateful to Max Siporin, who, in correspondence, recommended some modifications of this chart.

†It is evident that the stages are cumulative. People do not develop in discrete stages; there is overlapping and always residue from previous stages. Thus "And see above" (in the third column) indicates that available services are applicable at all stages, whereas some are more prominent at certain times. [—C. Meyer]

SOURCE: Carol H. Meyer, *Social Work Practice,* 2nd ed. (New York: Free Press, 1976), pp. 72–74. Reproduced by permission of the author and The Free Press.

yet stable family system has been established which can permit individual growth while keeping within the bounds of its tasks and society's demands. As these tasks are reworked again and again, they are often accompanied by temporary regression to earlier modes of expression and behavior, as well as by mixed emotions of sorrow, depression, anger, and the wish to hold onto the old.

The family life cycle, according to Scherz, is divided into seven stages, each with its key crisis-tasks:

1. ESTABLISHMENT OF THE MARRIAGE

Prior to marriage, the couple does preliminary work during courtship. On the conscious level, they carry out the tasks of making decisions about designating and allocating role functions in the use of money, household management, relationships with others, and testing sexual compatibility. On the unconscious level, they begin to accommodate intrapsychically to each other's needs.

During the early period of the marriage, the partners carry out a number of tasks. One is to separate from their families of origin while still remaining connected in a new way. Another is to develop new modes of communication, particularly in how to express to each other their needs and wishes directly and openly. A third task is to work through the issues of separateness and connectedness, closeness and distance, and autonomy and responsibility in relation to each other.

2. BIRTH OF THE FIRST CHILD

Now the marriage must change to accommodate to the new family member and, at the same time, must retain the husband-wife bond. During pregnancy and afterward, the major task is to maintain emotional separation and connectedness between husband and wife in a new form, while mother and child are involved in a symbiotic relationship. The husband needs his wife's support to keep from unduly regressing as she temporarily denies his needs in the intensity of the mother-child interaction.

Once the child is born, specific parenting roles and new divisions of responsibility, with attendant normal anxieties, must be learned actively. The parents have to trust each other, to deepen their intimacy, and, at the same time, to provide room for distance so that the child's needs can be met. The father's support of the mother's competence as a mother enables the infant to develop a sense of trust.

3. CHILD'S DEVELOPMENT OF PHYSICAL MOBILITY

As the child develops independent movement, a transitional crisis develops between the parents and child. The child experiences conflict as his autonomous striving and need for emotional separateness clash with his inability to challenge their control over him for fear of losing their care. The parents are torn between their wish for the child to develop and their desire to have him remain emotionally close to and dependent upon them. Not only do they begin to doubt their roles as good parents, but they often disagree between themselves on management. The child may add to this disagreement by playing up the different roles of the two parents. At this stage, parents must reach basic agreement about permitting the child's autonomous strivings to proceed within bounds and must support each other against undue regression over their feelings of loss. When the parents can encompass the major tasks of emotional separation and autonomy, the child can develop self-control, self-esteem, and self-responsibility for his actions to others.

Often the issue of independence of movement is displaced onto the area of toileting. Here the battle of control also involves the parents' sense of responsibility as opposed to the child's wish to assert responsibility for himself. Where the battle is prolonged and intense, serious regression to earlier stages may occur in both parents and child. They may infantilize him so that he is overdependent and later becomes inhibited or uninterested in school learning tasks. On the other hand, he may win at the cost of the loss of some parental love or even emotional abandonment.

4. ENTRANCE OF FIRST CHILD INTO SCHOOL

Now the parents must release the child to a greater world. Since he is also likely to be involved at the same time in working through his sexual identity with both parents, intimacy versus distance becomes an additional task with which to cope.

In this phase the overlapping between these two universal tasks is so closely linked that both family and child may experience confusion and lack of differentiation between the tasks. In the usual family this does not cause a serious problem except for a certain rise in anxiety. The family grapples with the joys and conflicts over separation and tends to emphasize the differences between the sexes while preparing the child for school.

If the family seeks help at this stage, the worker should be clear as to whether the conflict is based largely on the separation or on the sexual-identity issue. School phobias, for example, which often develop at this time, may not necessarily indicate a hostile-dependent tie between mother and child; they might instead be part of the larger family problem of emotional separation. It may be helpful to differentiate between those families who may require long and complicated treatment at this stage and those who need only brief crisis intervention to deal with a developmental hurdle.

5. BEGINNING OF ADOLESCENCE

Adolescence brings the "identity crisis" not only for the adolescent but for his parents as well. This period is characterized by successive waves of turbulence and quiet and a series of transitional maturational crises, during which all the universal tasks are heightened for both the family and the adolescent.

Old quiescent conflicts within the parents may now emerge under the stress of the adolescent's struggles with himself and with them. Tasks from earlier stages which have not been successfully mastered now become more difficult for the whole family. Parents may experience difficulty in maintaining a supportive coalition under the impact of the adolescent's divisive tactics, not understanding that these are unconsciously designed to help him work out his sexual identity.

The adolescent's periodic regressive, dependent behavior frightens and angers the parents, who themselves are struggling over separating from him. His confusion over self-responsibility and his projection of responsibilities onto them are duplicated in their confusion, since they are torn between protecting and controlling him and permitting him to experiment in ways that are alien or repugnant to them.

The parents feel a threat to their integrity and self-esteem because the adolescent's attacks on them arouse residual conflicts of universal tasks. Thus they create situations in which they compete with him—over achievement, over sexual identity and abilities, and over separation.

Most often the competition and conflicts, part of the normal transitional crises, are expressed in terms of clashes over family values and behavior standards, school and work achievement, and sexual interests. These conflicts may intensify if the father's achievement status is either unsatisfying or on a plateau, if the parents' sexuality seems to be waning, or if they have undue fears of separation. In turn, the adolescent both desires and fears growth for himself and fans parental anxieties over it. At times during this transitional period, temporary marital disharmony may emerge as the parents project the arousal of their personal conflicts onto each other by accusing the other of failures in child-rearing.

6. ACHIEVEMENT OF ADULT STATUS

The next transitional crisis occurs when the last child leaves home for work, further education, or marriage. The young adult sees this transition as a final leap into adult self-identity in which the universal tasks merge, the conflicts become quiescent, and he feels himself to be a whole person in his own right, but still connected to the family on an equal footing.

Parents, however, must give permission for the child to achieve this state of individual growth. In some ways this transitional crisis is more difficult for them than for him. When the last child leaves home, they face the need for a marked change in their relations to each other, particularly in the task of closeness versus distance. They need to achieve a different marital equilibrium.

As the partners struggle to find new modes of communication, to change the patterns of intimacy established during the long child-rearing years, and to effect new divisions of responsibility, temporary marital disharmony may occur. There may also be regression in their efforts to hold onto the children, to involve them in inappropriate mediation between the parents, or to complain about the other partner. Gradually the crisis is resolved as the parents settle down into a new equilibrium, and a new relationship of nonpossessive warmth between parents and their adult children develops.

7. ARRIVING AT OLD AGE

This is the family's last great developmental crisis. It usually brings with it problems in separation for the older and younger family members. The older members inevitably suffer losses in work, in health, and in important people at this stage. They often become dependent on their children for money, for physical care, and for emotional needs that had been met by spouses or others.

Adult children often have to take care of parents in ways that arouse old conflicts about dependency, achievement, and separation.

The inevitability of death exacerbates these conflicts and fears over separation. The parents' demands and sometimes regressive behavior are frightening and embarrassing to the adult child. Remnants of old angers, old hurts, and guilt over these feelings come to the fore on both sides. Since both usually deny these feelings, it becomes difficult to work through the critical mourning process of separation that has to take place, for example, when the aged parent can no longer sustain himself independently and a change in living arrangements must be made.

Frequently both generations can be helped to manage separation and mourning when they understand the normality of their feelings and place them within the current context. It also helps the third generation when they hear parents and grandparents express their feelings rather than bury or conceal them.

At each transitional maturational crisis, changes must take place in family tasks that parallel individual developmental tasks in order to permit individual growth and facilitate the management of family tasks. The management of these universal tasks at any time in the life cycle will depend on how successfully the family has managed previous tasks, on what intrafamilial conditions prevail, and on situational factors.

Treatment in Maturational Crises

Treatment in situations involving developmental difficulties often starts with a presenting problem of an acute situational nature: a teen-ager is arrested for "borrowing" a neighbor's car; a bewildered young husband is left by his bride, who has returned to her parents following his all-night drinking bout with his pals; a fifty-year-old schoolteacher is caught slipping a cheese packet into her purse despite having a well-filled wallet.

While the practitioner may recognize, in his diagnostic evaluation, that inability to carry out maturational tasks (of identity, of intimacy, and of generativity) lies at the root of the three situations cited above, he may never allude to it directly, keeping his intervention geared to the practical remedial aspects of the crisis situation. On the other hand, he may find, underneath the anger, the depression, and the shock, real confusion on the part of the client network as to what is going on, the feeling that things are "different" from what they were last month or last year, and that processes seem to be taking place over which they have no control.

In such instances, treatment contains a large educational component. The worker can discuss how "most" teenagers behave or what older people "generally" feel when they face retirement. Often individuals do not know or cannot recognize age-stage normative behavior and particularly need help in grasping the emotional parallels of the physiological changes taking place within themselves and in those with whom they interact. Role shifts and role conflicts may be involved, requiring clarification in terms of mutual expectations and opposing values. Sometimes it may be useful to help the client trace his inappropriate feelings, thoughts, and behaviors back to conflicts in earlier stages of development which had never been completely resolved. And in some cases all that can be done is to provide support and reassurance that, in time, "This too shall pass."[11]

It may be that more than one developmental crisis is involved. Smith points out that, in parent-adolescent child conflicts, a two-sided reaction is involved. While much attention has been paid to adolescents' behavior and their developmental tasks, only recently has it been recognized that the parents, in addition to experiencing a reawakening of their own earlier adolescent conflicts, are concurrently struggling with the developmental tasks of their *current* middle-age period: the effort to value wisdom rather than physical powers, to learn to socialize rather than sexualize human relationships, to attain emotional flexibility rather than emotional impoverishment, and to maintain mental pliability instead of mental rigidity.[12]

The following case summary is presented in some detail in order to show the two sides of the developmental struggle as it emerges in the treatment process:

THE ANDREWS CASE

BEGINNING PHASE

After a distraught phone call, Dr. and Mrs. Andrews came in with their sixteen-year-old son, Jerry, to a private family counseling agency. They were seen together for an initial assessment interview. Dr. Andrews, a pediatrician in a prosperous group practice, was a blond, handsome, carefully groomed man of forty-four. He remained somewhat aloof and silent throughout the interview, thoughtfully sucking on his empty pipe. Betty Andrews, petite and vivacious, with a pixie hairdo and carefully casual clothes, looked younger than her forty years. Jerry, already taller than his father, wore a faded T-shirt and ragged jeans. He sat slumped in his chair, scowling at the floor, his tangled, long black hair almost covering his acne-scarred face.

Mrs. Andrews took the initiative. Last night Jerry disappeared before dinner and didn't come back till 3:00 A.M. Even then, he refused to tell her where he had been and just told her to "get off his back." She was sure something awful had happened to him, he looked so terrible, and she spent the rest of the night crying. This morning she told her husband that this was the end; they had to get help for Jerry, because he was going crazy and driving them crazy in the process.

She said that Jerry, the oldest of their three children, had been giving his parents a hard time ever since he came back from summer camp three months earlier to find that the family had moved into a new home in a different section of town. She had never had brothers of her own but she had heard about the "terrible teens" and had been braced for them. Jerry had been doing fine, however, until after the summer; he was one of the top students in his class, was captain of the tennis team at school, and had lots of friends. But he still liked her best, and they used to have lots of heart-to-heart talks; she felt she really understood him and tried to act like a friend and not a typical mother.

Suddenly everything began to go wrong. When the fall term started he refused to wear the new clothes she had prepared for him, fished out his old jeans from the ragbag, and wore them all the time, even to his new high school. He refused to get his hair trimmed and stopped combing it. He almost never ate meals with the rest of the family and wouldn't even answer her half the time. He refused to share his room with his fourteen-year-old brother Billy, and kept the door closed. Instead of making new friends in the neighborhood, he'd bicycle back to the old playground or just disappear for hours. Or else he'd lie on his bed, not bothering to read or turn on the stereo, just staring at the ceiling.

Once when she went into his room to check on his winter clothes, she found two new shirts slashed into ribbons and stuffed into a bag on his closet shelf. He became enraged when she asked him about it and since then has been locking his door. Mrs. Andrews said tearfully that Jerry was becoming a monster and she was sure something terrible was happening to him; maybe he was killing himself with drugs or getting into trouble they didn't even know about. She tried so hard to be a good mother but nobody would cooperate; her husband just kept telling her not to worry, that Jerry would get over it. But this was their *son,* not just another patient, so how could she help being frantic?

Dr. Andrews said, rather stiffly, that he kept telling Betty that she was acting hysterically, that Jerry would straighten out in time. True, he behaved pretty strangely at times, but so did many of the other youngsters the doctor saw. He remembers he used to do the same sort of things when he was a kid, but eventually he "took himself in hand." Betty always tended to exaggerate and to expect too much from the children. Jerry hadn't gotten into trouble until now, and there was no sense blowing this out of proportion. He'd had him checked medically a few weeks back and found him in pretty good physical shape, though he'd just had a growth spurt and was a little anemic and had some skin problems. His grades had dropped down a bit this term, but that was probably due to his having changed schools. He expected Jerry to apply to Yale, where he himself had gone, and then to his old medical school. But competition was pretty tough and he'd have to buckle down soon to make the grade.

Throughout all this, Jerry refused to take part in the discussion or even raise his eyes from the floor. When I asked what he saw as the problem, he shrugged and muttered, "Ask her; she knows it all!" When asked how he'd like to have the situation changed, he answered "Just get her off my back!"

To my mind, the key problem seemed to be the parent-adolescent conflict. I decided to concentrate intervention on the core issue of helping Jerry work on his own identity and achieve partial separation from his parents, on the one hand, and helping them understand some of the emotional aspects of their son's development and free him to grow up, on the other.

Because of the boy's overt hostility, it was agreed that I would see Jerry and his parents separately for several interviews and then we would reassess the situation. A secondary goal of improving communication patterns between Jerry and his parents and between Dr. and Mrs. Andrews was considered but left open.

MIDDLE PHASE: JERRY

Jerry was seen twice, once the following day and again six days later. He came in reluctantly to the first interview, looking more unkempt and bedraggled than before, morosely convinced that this was a put-up job between his parents and me to force him to conform.

When told that this was a chance for him to talk about himself and what *he* wanted, he became more animated and began to speak about the pressures his family was putting on him, just now when he had a lot on his mind. He had some important decisions to make but he couldn't talk about them to "her." His dad wasn't a bad guy but he was all wrapped up in his work and never had time for his family. He had promised they'd play golf together once a week last summer, but he never carried it out. He was also going to let Jerry use the family car, now that he'd got his driving license. But even though Jerry had passed his sixteenth birthday a month ago, nothing was mentioned about it, and he guessed "she" got his dad to punish him by not letting him have the car.

As for his mom, she used to be a pretty keen person, the sort who was interested in what went on at school and whom he could talk to. But ever since they moved to this fancy neighborhood, she was busy yakking with the new neighbors and comparing him with *their* sons. She kept trying to push him to be like them—or like what she thought they were like—even though T-shirts and jeans were all you ever saw the guys wear. He had come home from camp full of plans for the coming year, but suddenly things changed, "just went downhill all the way."

This last month was really the worst. She had bought him some fancy striped shirts some clerk told her were what kids were wearing and took away all his good old clothes, the ones he was used to and were right for him. He got so furious, he just tore them up into strips and stuck them away. Then she had to come snooping into his room and go through his private things. He came home from school to have her waiting to blast him for the shirts and for everything else he'd done wrong. She even accused him of being on drugs, even though he knew enough from reading his dad's medical journals to stay away from that, though there was plenty floating around school.

Jerry revealed that the other night, when he came home so late and she waited up for him, he had been working as a carhop at a drive-in. He had to earn some money because a couple of fellows were thinking of buying an old jalopy and driving down to the Everglades for Christmas vacation. He hadn't been sure he wanted to go because he liked being home at that time of year. But the way his mom was carrying on, maybe that was the best way out. He was even thinking of staying down there afterwards and getting a job as a busboy or locker boy at one of the clubs. At least he'd have some privacy and people would treat him with respect instead of pushing him around.

The tone in our second interview was much calmer. We focused on Jerry's plan to give up school and go down south. It turned out that he felt very ambivalent. On the one hand, he was anxious to get away from his mother's nagging and the bickering that went on about his long hair, his clothes, and his table manners. On the other hand, he didn't care too much for the other fellows going on the trip; one was a kook and the other two weren't really serious about it. He knew he'd end up having to do most of the driving and pay the major part of the expenses. Last week, after the blowup with his mom, he'd told the guys he'd definitely go; now he felt committed and unable to back out.

Closer examination, however, showed that they had not yet bought the jalopy and that the others were also beginning to have second thoughts about the whole idea. From this, the discussion turned to more general issues, particularly to his relations with his mother. What really bugged Jerry was the invasion of his privacy; every time he thought about her snooping through his private things, he felt outraged. He admitted he never told her she should keep out of his room, but he wasn't a kid anymore and she should know how important it was for him, he said with tears in his eyes.

When I asked about his plans for his future, Jerry rather self-consciously confided that they had a pretty good physics club in school and he had been fooling around with all sorts of new electronic gadgets. He had always been good at that sort of thing and his physics teacher had been talking to him about going to Cal Tech and majoring in electronic engineering, even though his dad wanted him to go to med school.

I agreed that it sounded like a sensible goal, but how did this jibe with his plans to become a busboy in Florida? Jerry then admitted that maybe the Florida trip wasn't such a good idea if it meant dropping the physics club. I suggested that it might be a good idea to talk this over with his father, but he felt sure his dad would never allow it; his father's whole family had been doctors and he had his heart set on Jerry's following suit. Jerry did agree that I might mention it when I talked to his parents. The last few days they had stopped pressuring him so much and things were easier at home.

MIDDLE PHASE: PARENTS

The first interview started with a discussion of normal adolescent behavior. I described some of the emotional upsets and unevenness that accompanied physiological changes during this period and listed some of the unexplicable ''schizy'' behavior that worried parents so much. Dr. Andrews, who had given up much of his defensiveness, became quite animated in describing similar instances he saw in his practice. He admitted that he had not thought of Jerry in this light since he conscientiously avoided ''bringing the office home with him.'' There he treated kids' illnesses and mothers' complaints all day, and when he got home he just didn't have the heart to face more of the same.

Mrs. Andrews, who was much more subdued this time, was relieved to hear that Jerry's behavior, though difficult to take, was well within normal limits for his age group. She really didn't know much about boys; she and her three sisters had grown up in a close, sheltered family atmosphere where they shared all their feelings and thoughts. Her parents were quite poor and, after her father died when she was ten, her mother went back to work and the girls "raised each other." She had never had a room of her own, or anything else either, and she couldn't understand Jerry's insistence on privacy. She had always done her own housework and prided herself on keeping a neat, well-managed house. She had always straightened up the boys' rooms because they were so messy, even though Susan, at twelve, was expected to keep her own room clean.

At this point she began to cry. She tried so hard to build a nice family life to make up for the one she never had, but no one seemed to want it except herself. Her husband, in building up his practice, kept spending more and more time at the office, and on weekends he went off to play golf and left her to drive the kids around and do all the shopping by herself. The boys—first Jerry, and now even Billy—dashed in and out of the house as if it were a hotel. No one cared what they ate or if the new house, on which she had worked so hard to make "right," was up to expectations. Their whole family life seemed to be falling apart since they moved out here. Susan was the only one who noticed if she made fancy meals or fixed up the family room. None of the men, neither her husband nor her sons, really cared about what was important to her.

At this point, Dr. Andrews moved over to where she was sitting on the sofa, put his arms around her, and held her while she cried. He told her he hadn't meant to neglect her; they had gone into a lot of extra expense in buying the new house and he had taken on additional work in order to pay for it without cutting down on his retirement plans. Part of the time on weekends, when he said he was playing golf, he was doing consultation at Children's Hospital. He hadn't wanted to worry her, so he kept it to himself; he guessed he was a workhorse, as his father had been.

He said he knew the family was very important to her, and it was for him too, but he seemed to have gotten his priorities mixed. With the kids growing up, he'd have to think about shifting some of his work to his partners so the family could spend more time together. Instead of a big family celebration at Christmas this year, maybe the kids could go to his parents' in Minnesota and they could go down to the Bahamas for a second honeymoon.

In our second interview, the Andrews told me that they had been trying to spend more time together; Dr. Andrews had finally gotten around to laying the foundation for the barbecue pit he had been promising her since they moved. When I told them about Jerry's feelings that neither of them took him seriously, they were quite shocked. Dr. Andrews was surprised to hear that Jerry was interested in electronics. He himself had always been interested in gadgets like that and once had thought of becoming an engineer. But his father, who was a general practitioner in upstate Minnesota, had pushed him into the family tradition of medicine instead. Now he was doing the same thing to his son.

This led to a discussion of the ties between fathers and sons and mothers and daughters. Mrs. Andrews felt very comfortable with Susan, whom she saw as being very much like herself, but who she hoped would have all the things she never had as a child: a comfortable home, lots of friends and pretty clothes, and the feeling of being watched over by her older brothers. Billy was always cheerful and good-tempered and never gave her any trouble; he had quickly made friends in the neighborhood and joined the Sea Scouts and now talked about going into the Navy. It was Jerry who worried her; he was so dark and intense and angry all the time. She knew she had made a lot of mistakes when he was a baby and she worried that maybe she had "warped" him so that he had become emotionally disturbed.

Again we went back to discuss normal expectations for boys of Jerry's age and the importance of his distancing himself from his mother at this stage. Dr. Andrews, who was very supportive of his wife, decided to work on ways he and Jerry could develop some mutual interests.

END PHASE

A joint meeting with Jerry and his parents was held to evaluate the situation and decide on future activity. The atmosphere in this interview was in marked contrast to the stormy first one. The parents sat together on the sofa, with Jerry, whose hair was still long but neatly combed, in a chair next to his father. Dr. Andrews opened by saying that they had had a family conference since we last met and had come to some decisions. First of all, they were getting a new family station wagon and, instead of selling the present car, they would let Jerry use it, provided that he kept up his work at school and helped his mother with the grocery shopping.

Mrs. Andrews added that she and Jerry had set up some rules about his room: once a week she'd let him know when she wanted to come in to clean it; the rest of the time, it would be out of bounds for everyone in the family without his express permission. He was giving Billy his fish tanks since they made quite a mess and he was really no longer interested in them.

Jerry had told his parents about working as a carhop and they agreed he could keep this up on weekends, since it was important for him to earn his own money, but on weekdays he had to be home by 10:30 P. M. Dr. Andrews and his associates had just bought a small portable computer and were in the process of putting their office records onto tape for easier accessibility. They were having trouble coding the data and Jerry, who was familiar with a similar computer setup from his physics lab at school, had offered to come down on Saturday mornings to help his father "get the bugs out of the system." This could turn into a regular job if he wanted it.

The family had talked about plans for the approaching winter vacation and had decided that, instead of having the children go to their grandparents and the parents go to the Bahamas, they would all break in the new car by taking a trip to California, stopping at Pasadena to check on Cal Tech and maybe getting to see the Navy installations at San Diego for Billy's sake.

When I asked them what they wanted to do here further, they looked at each other somewhat embarrassed. Dr. Andrews said it wasn't that they didn't appreciate my help, but it looked as if they had gotten back on the track and could manage by themselves. They would let me know if things "blew up" again. As the family left, Mrs. Andrews dropped behind her husband and son to thank me with tears in her eyes. "For a while things kept getting worse and worse and I felt as if everything I had wanted was slipping away from me; our whole family life was falling apart. I don't know what happened, but suddenly I feel hopeful again and as if we have a lot going for us."

Transitional Crises

Individuals and families, when faced with significant changes in their life situations, either during a particular developmental stage or when passing from one stage to another, often go through a period marked by affective and cognitive upsets, which sometimes reach crisis proportions. This can occur when the individual is moving from one occupation to another, from one role set to a new one, or even from one place to another.

Such a transition can be viewed in the Eriksonian sense of being a "turning point, a crucial period of increased vulnerability and heightened potential."[13] Rhona Rapoport notes that, within the normal, expectable processes in the life cycle, these critical points often provoke disequilibrium:

> If the crisis is handled advantageously, it is assumed that the result for the individual is some kind of maturation or development. If the stresses engendered by the crisis are not well coped with, it is assumed that old psychological conflicts may be involved or new conflicts may arise and a state of poorer mental health may be the result. Further, it is suggested that persons undergoing the crisis are amenable to influence when skilled intervention techniques of relatively brief duration are applied.[14]

Recent thinking has broadened this approach somewhat. Silverman emphasizes the concept of a transitional *period* as being more apt than that of a specific turning point. This can be defined as a series of events which can be disequilibrating and tax the individual's ability to cope, and as a finite time interval during which the individual carries out his "transition work." This usually involves a status change and often necessitates redefinition of the roles the person carries in his social network.

In such situations, notes Silverman, it should be possible for the person to prepare for and rehearse how to pass through the period adaptively (as in the engagement period prior to marriage). However, when the transition is unanticipated, or when no suitable rituals or societal practices are available to serve as a model (as in the period following the death of a spouse), he may not know how to cope and so may run into serious difficulties. At such times, preventive intervention can be carried out to help him pass through the transition adaptively.[15]

Within the past twenty years, a large number of transitional periods have been studied in detail, including marriage,[16] the birth of the first child,[17] the first child's entrance into kindergarten,[18] migration,[19] retirement,[20] and death.[21] A particularly intriguing study carried out by Lowenthal and her associates examined four groups of subjects facing transitional phases in their lives—high school seniors, young newlyweds, middle-aged parents, and older adults about to retire—for similarities and differences in the ways they passed through and coped with the stresses encountered during these periods.[22]

A common characteristic of transitional periods seems to be that each has a characteristic life of its own which can be differentiated into phases and plotted. Regardless of the particular aspects of the individual situation, each phase has its own specific attributes and an identifiable set of instrumental and affective tasks.[23] Unless the person is able to engage in his transition work by carrying out these tasks, he tends to remain disequilibrated and "stuck" at this particular phase.[24]

THE DIVORCE PROCESS

Typical of transitional periods frequently encountered is the process of divorce which involves a considerable number of persons and families in our society. Unlike bereavement, divorce does not suddenly happen to a couple; it is the termination of an interactional process that developed over a long period of time and usually has been preceded by an extended period of conflict.[25]

Bohannan views divorce as a complex procedure composed of at least six different interlocking and interacting experiences of separation:[26]

1. The *emotional divorce,* which centers around the problems of the deteriorating marriage and the chain of events and feelings which led up to the breakup. It starts when the spouses begin to withhold positive emotions from each other, and attraction and trust are replaced by mutual antagonism and conflict. Two of the issues most frequently fought over are sex and money,

though often they are used to mask more basic personal difficulties.

2. The *legal divorce,* which revolves around the judicial procedures for formalizing dissolution of the marriage and provision of the legal basis for remarriage. Divorce laws, says Bohannan, reflect the concept of "punishment of the guilty party" through the establishment of legal grounds. Part of the legal activity is concerned with the setting up of alimony and child-support payments, as set by a court order.

3. The *economic divorce,* which deals with the division of money and property and the separation of joint assets. This is sometimes governed by state laws of community property and sometimes by personal and legal negotiations. Many of the difficulties and recriminations arise around division of nonmonetary assets such as furniture, house, car, common gifts, etc.

4. The *co-parental divorce,* which deals with the custody of the children, single-parent homes, and visitation rights. Although parents divorce each other, both retain their relationship with their children, with one parent given legal custody and—but not always—physical custody. In our present society this is usually the mother, unless she is considered delinquent in her behavior as a mother. The father usually is allowed to see the children at established intervals. Such arrangements create many lasting problems in parent-child relationships, as well as between the parents themselves.

5. The *community divorce,* which concerns itself with the changes in friends and place of living. Problems of friends' taking sides and the divorced persons' need to find their own communities of persons with similar interests emerge and may last for a considerable time.

6. The *psychic divorce,* with its problem of regaining individual autonomy, is the most difficult aspect of the process since it involves the distancing of each spouse from the formerly loved person and the regaining of self-esteem. It is concerned with becoming a whole, complete, and autonomous individual

again, without someone to lean on and also without someone to support.

Against this complex background, the transitional period of divorce must be seen as a process that may take two years or even longer. Rather than view the total interval as a crisis situation, it appears to be much more useful to look at it as a series of overlapping stages, each concerned with its own goals and tasks. Wiseman divides the process into five phases:[27]

STAGE I: DENIAL

This phase begins long before the precipitating stress arises which throws the marriage into a state of crisis. Denial of difficulties is used to keep the marital relationship going; the spouses may even be aware of the liabilities but feel they can accommodate themselves to the discomforts involved or even prefer it the way it is. They may employ an external rationale such as finances or the children to keep from considering divorce and to justify their remaining together, sometimes indefinitely. Homeostasis, however, is so fragile and the system so inflexible that almost any stress can provoke a major marital crisis.

STAGE II: LOSS AND DEPRESSION

At this point the spouses find they can no longer cope with their problems together and begin to recognize that being together is, in itself, a problem. One spouse may seek help from the family physician or from a therapist for some form of depressive manifestation. Complaints may include fatigue or headaches, a series of minor accidents, or even the more overt expression of depression. Underneath this, the reactions are those of loss: grief, depression, isolation, and the inability to communicate. It may be possible and useful at this stage to help the person break through his sense of isolation and verbalize his fears that he is losing a spouse, a marriage, and a way of life.

STAGE III: ANGER AND AMBIVALENCE

As the ending of the marriage approaches, the previous depression lifts to uncover the underlying feeling—anger. Legal negotiations predominate at this point, as the couple begins to talk of separate maintenance, child support, and division of property. Often egged on by their lawyers, spouses haggle and feud over financial matters, living arrangements, visitation rights, and current expenditures. A resurgence of adolescent conflicts may occur, with one spouse behaving like a rebellious teen-ager and the other acting the role of the indignant parent.

Feelings of overt anger toward the other spouse, says Wiseman, alternate with intense ambivalence over terminating the marriage. Often a last attempt at marriage counseling may take place, though it quickly becomes evident that neither partner has a real interest in continuing the marriage. Sometimes efforts are made to compromise or overcompensate in financial questions and legal issues in the hope of maintaining peace. While momentarily softening the conflict, such compromises have a number of detrimental long-term effects. They tend to gloss over feelings of ambivalence which need to be recognized and dealt with. They often prevent the full declaration of independence from each other that is necessary if the couple is to go on to healthy postmarital adjustment.

STAGE IV: REORIENTATION OF LIFE STYLE AND IDENTITY

Gradually each spouse devotes less time to looking back in anger and more to focusing on present and future plans. The idea of divorce becomes a reality; ways to cope with it must be found. The primary task becomes the reworking of identity in all areas touched upon by the marriage: personal, vocational, sexual, and social. At this time, unresolved identity issues which may have been tabled during the marriage arise, and the whole issue of "Who am I?" comes up.

Concurrent with this renewed exploration of personal identity comes a reappraisal of the person's place in the world of work.

Older women particularly may need help in establishing their feelings of self-worth, purpose, and social status unlinked with those of their former husband. Younger women may find it easier to move into the academic or career world, although this process may be hampered by their need to provide physical care and emotional support for the children.

The sexual aspect of identity also needs reworking at this time. Most persons undergoing divorce find their confidence shaken in themselves as sexual and social beings. They feel sexually undesirable, unknowledgeable, or inadequate. Conflicts over having nonmarital sexual relationships arise. The need to experiment sexually at this time appears to be of vital importance to many divorcing persons, who seek a variety of sexual experiences with a series of short-term partners to whom they have little emotional commitment.

The reasons for this "candy-store phase" lie in the person's primary need to rebuild his or her damaged self-concept by seeing him- or herself as sexually desirable again, to avoid serious emotional commitments, and to compensate for previously limited extramarital sexual experience. Within a short time, however, most persons leave this phase of social and sexual exploration and are ready to move on to more intimate relationships.

STAGE V: ACCEPTANCE AND ACHIEVEMENT OF NEW LEVEL OF FUNCTIONING

As the divorced person begins to feel himself or herself socially, sexually, and vocationally adequate and as his depression and anxiety begin to abate, he moves from casual and transitory relationships to an intimate relationship involving one other person for a longer period of time and with a deeper degree of emotional commitment. Along with this improvement in self-concept, he may begin to accept his former partner and terminated marriage as they really are and to feel free to establish better relationships with his former spouse and in-laws.

By this phase, new patterns of interaction without the absent spouse become firmly established and the ex-spouse's role with the children has been well worked out. Some of the old social and family relationships are retained, others are discarded. New patterns, usually involving persons in the same situation, are established. In some instances there will be a new marriage; in others, adjustment to divorced life will be more or less permanent and comfortable.

Wiseman finds that persons who have become well adjusted to their divorced status show strong feelings of satisfaction with things as they are. While they may feel that a suitable spouse would be desirable, the search for a new mate is no longer constant. They find their lives balanced and enriched by work, family, and close friendships, and they can even accept forms of intimacy other than marriage. The result is a new social and personal identity, often more mature and satisfying than that which existed before the divorce.[28]

Treatment in Transitional Crises

Many persons succeed in passing through transitional crises alone or with the help of the natural support systems of family, friends, and relatives. Within the last few years, a wide range of mutual-help groups have arisen to provide advice, encouragement, and material assistance during these periods.[29] When people turn to professional help during the transitional process, they usually come with a specific complaint: depression over lost roles and statuses, psychosomatic manifestations of increased anxiety over what lies ahead, or inability to deal with the children who have become upset during the shift.[30]

Regardless of the particular point of entry, it is important to establish early in the case just where the client is in the total transitional process and what are the specific issues with which he is struggling. Hallett, for example, feels that the central issue in the process of divorce, separation, desertion, or death is the learning of "letting go" skills, especially when children are involved.[31]

Treatment may range from intensive reworking of earlier primary relationships in an effort to remove blocks in passing through the transition to providing advice and guidance on how to grapple with the numerous concrete problems that arise. Frequently it is focused on helping the client carry out the material-arrangemental and psychosocial tasks entailed, as well as providing emotional support and opportunities for ventilation of feelings of anger, despair, loneliness, and grief over what has been lost or given up. Anticipatory guidance over what lies ahead, improvement of communication patterns, and the teaching of new coping skills are all techniques found helpful in treating transitional situations.[32] These are particularly useful in helping parents help their children pass through the transition.[33] One of the most important aspects of treatment in transitional periods is helping the client build a new network of support systems to replace the ones left behind.

The following case summary illustrates crisis intervention during the process of divorce. In it can be seen not only the separational aspects of the transition period, but also its maturational function in helping a woman achieve independence from her parents as well as from the husband she had outgrown. While worker-client contact was maintained for almost a year, active treatment consisted of several relatively short but intensive intervention episodes alternating with more attenuated supportive treatment.

THE CASE OF HELEN

BEGINNING PHASE: INTAKE

Helen, a college senior of twenty-six, with a piquant, pretty face and long blond ponytail, came into the university counseling center in a state of acute anxiety. She had been in the middle of writing a midyear exam when she suddenly felt "dizzy and confused." She burst into tears and rushed out of the room. One of the proctors stopped her at the door and, noting her upset, suggested that she go to the center. Helen said this was the first time this had happened, although she had been unable to concentrate for the past few weeks and had had frequent crying spells. She was seen on an emergency basis and accepted for crisis-oriented brief treatment.

Presenting Problem.   Speaking rapidly and with considerable affect, Helen said her seven-year-old marriage to her husband, Dan, was rapidly deteriorating. Her parents, for whom Dan worked, sided with him and were accusing her of seeking to destroy "everything they built for her." She felt deserted and betrayed, not so much by her husband, whom she described as a "nothing," as by her parents, particularly her father. She had expected that they would want her to be happy; instead they accused her of shaming them and breaking up her marriage to spite them. They threatened to cut off financial support and take away the car they had given her unless she agreed to stay home and be a good wife and a proper mother to Timmy, age five, and Suzy, age three.

Background Information.   The marriage, Helen related, had been in difficulties almost from the start. She was an only child and had been raised as a "latchkey child" because her parents were so immersed in running their small factory and store that they had no time for her. She spent most of her time alone, was repeatedly called "fat and stupid," and had never been shown any real affection for as long as she could remember; the important thing to her parents was for her not to give them trouble. She grew up shy and timid, engrossed in books and in fantasies. She said she resolved to marry the first man who would have her in order to escape from home.

Dan, an amiable, unexceptional young man two years her senior, began to work as a clerk in her parents' store. She deliberately encouraged him and, when she was nineteen, they were married with her parents' blessing. The parents gave the newlyweds a small share of the business, bought them a house and furnished it, and put them under obligation to them for all facets of their life.

In the beginning, Helen had no way of comparing Dan with other men, since he had been her first serious boyfriend. She soon realized, however, that something basic was missing in her marriage. He was, according to her, a passive, closed, conforming kid from a broken home who was completely under her parents' domination. He was non-intellectual, limited, and conventional in his points of view, and she found they had nothing to talk about except the store. He had very little active sex drive, and their sexual relations were rare and unsatisfying to her. She thought having children would give substance to the marriage and, upon her mother's advice, they had two. Dan was not interested in the children, and she had to care for them and take them to the park and the beach alone while he spent his nonworking hours watching sports on television. Helen tried taking out her frustration and anger in housework, but, "How long can you polish pots?"

Three years ago, her father, sensing her disillusionment and restlessness, suggested she enroll at the university. She discovered she was not stupid, as she had always been told. She "devoured" courses and did very well, carrying a full program of studies as well as doing all her own housework, caring for the children, and working parttime in the business.

Eighteen months ago a new element was introduced. She had gone to a doctor for some internal upset and, when she found him sympathetic, spilled out her whole story, including her disappointment in her marriage and her image of herself as unwanted and unloved. The doctor, "old enough to be my father," was himself going through a complicated and drawn-out divorce at the time and this struck a chord. He decided to take her in hand. Since then he had completely changed her: he persuaded her to change her hair color and style, lose thirty pounds, wear contact lenses instead of her ugly spectacles, and "become a new person." She, in turn, comforted him, and they became emotionally and physically involved. Although there had been no commitments on either side, he encouraged her to decide what she wanted to do about her marriage and her life.

Treatment Plan.   Because of Helen's acute anxiety, it was agreed to have her continue on a crisis-intervention basis in order to help her pass through this transitional state and come to decisions about her future direction. Treatment was focused on three areas: (1) to help her end her relationship with her husband amicably; (2) to clarify her feelings about her parents and to help her separate herself from them; and (3) to help her decide what she wanted for herself in the future, including her relationship with her "friend."

MIDDLE PHASE: TREATMENT

Helen was seen intensively for eight interviews; then she was seen on a less intensive level for four more months; then again intensively after her divorce was granted. Finally, after a break of two months, she was seen twice again to "wrap things up."

In the early phase of treatment, attention was directed to the first two areas of concern. It became quickly apparent that Helen had emotionally divorced Dan some time ago. By the end of the second week, she consulted a lawyer and learned what her rights were and what steps she would have to carry out. The same week, she asked her husband for a divorce. Although this came as no surprise to him, his main concern was what he stood to lose in terms of the family business and their common property. His chief weapon was passivity: she would ask him to carry out some action in the divorce process, and he would delay. As the price of his compliance, she had to make considerable concessions in terms of financial arrangements, property division, and visitation rights. Dan continued to live at home, and they carried on a semblance of married life while their lawyers slowly pushed them toward agreement on the legal issues. Helen needed a good deal of support to carry on consistently and not to explode as frustration and anger at her husband's obstructionism replaced her earlier depression.

Far more emotionally wearing, however, were Helen's relations with her parents during this period. They became furious at the news that she was divorcing Dan and reacted characteristically. Her mother stormed that Helen was bringing disgrace to the family and demanded that she retain the façade of a happy marriage as the mother herself had done for the past thirty years. When this had no effect, she began to rush about in a frenzy, consulting psychiatrists to demand that they restrain her daughter forcibly from ruining her life and their parents' and children's. She developed symptoms of acute disturbance herself: paranoidal outbursts alternated with attacks of severe depression. Helen learned painfully that the only way to deal with her mother's accusations of disloyalty and threats of reprisal was to distance herself, physically and emotionally.

Helen's separation from her father was even more emotionally taxing. A handsome, imposing man whose extramarital exploits were well known in the community, he had seductively shared the details of his affairs with Helen. Now he alternated between accusing her of bringing about her mother's emotional collapse and assuring her that he had her best interests at heart. He even offered to increase her allowance if she would just have a "civilized affair" while keeping up the framework of her marriage. Only after repeatedly "falling into his traps" did Helen recognize that he sought justification of his own marital pattern.

As Helen proceeded with her divorce plans, her parents became increasingly vindictive and cut off her financial support. They threatened to have her declared an unfit mother and urged Dan to have detectives follow her to report on her "promiscuous behavior." In view of this last, her lawyer advised her to stop all personal contact with her friend, and Helen was left to struggle alone against her husband and parents.

With a great deal of support from me, she was able to differentiate between her parents' overreaction to her situation and her own diminishing investment in her ties with Dan. Although initially he had agreed to the divorce, he contested every step in the procedure and Helen was often left emotionally and physically exhausted by the struggle. She finally decided to move out of the house and rented a small apartment for herself and the two children. She suffered acutely as their own house, into which she had poured so much effort, was sold and their household effects were divided up. She devoted most of her time to the children and was pleased to report that they appeared to make the transition to the new neighborhood smoothly. Since she no longer worked for the family business, she found herself a part-time job during the summer to help eke out the meager support she received from her husband.

By the middle of the summer, Helen reported jubilantly that the divorce was finally granted and she was free. Dan continued alternately to neglect the children when he was supposed to take them and to appear unexpectedly to demand them when she planned outings with them. She had broken off relations completely with her mother, although her father continued to call her to "nag" at her for her neglect. However, she felt more able to handle his pressure and found he no longer had the power to influence her as he once did.

In the final phase of treatment, the tenor of our discussions shifted considerably. Much less time was spent considering Helen's past, except for occasional annoying incidents which would crop up. Instead, she became much more introspective and concerned about her own feelings of lack of self-worth. Slowly she began to examine what sort of a person she had been and was becoming. She was able to assess her own strengths and weaknesses and consider what she wanted for herself and for her children in the future. Her friend was abroad for most of the summer, taking advanced training in his specialty, and Helen began to experiment with going out with other men. She was gratified to find that she was considered attractive as well as intellectually stimulating. For the first time she made a few good women friends, two of whom were also going through divorce processes, and found that her feelings were shared by others.

Also for the first time, Helen began to consider her own future, outside of her nebulous plans to marry "some day." She had received her B.A. by this time, placing in the top tenth of her class, and decided to go on for teacher training in order to give herself a career alternative.

END PHASE: CLOSING

After a two-month break, Helen came in at the start of the fall term to report that things were coming along much better. Timmy was starting first grade and Suzy kindergarten. She was still planning to enroll in graduate school, although there was a possibility that she would take a year off first. She had resumed seeing her friend and things were fine between them, although she was still wary of making any long-term commitment. She rarely saw her parents, although occasionally her father would call and seemed to want to resume ties. Dan still worked for the family business, and she heard from her father that he was going out with a woman and was thinking of getting married again. She still experienced occasional periods of depression when she thought of the past, but she felt cautiously optimistic that things were getting better for her.

Notes

1. These are expressed most clearly in Erik H. Erikson, *Identity and the Life Cycle,* Psychological Issues, vol. 1 (New York: International Universities Press, 1959), pp. 116–121. It is presumed that

both Erikson's epigenetic stages and the core conflicts are familiar enough not to require recapitulation at this point. See Table 2, pp. 152–154.

2. See Nancy Datan and Leon H. Ginsberg, eds., *Life-Span Developmental Psychology: Normative Life Crises* (New York: Academic Press, 1975), for a report of a recent conference on this subject.

3. A number of these papers can be found in Barbara S. Dohrenwend and Bruce P. Dohrenwend, *Stressful Life Events: Their Nature and Effects* (New York: Wiley-Interscience, 1974). See also Thomas A. Holmes and Richard H. Rahe, "The Social Readjustment Rating Scale," *Journal of Psychosomatic Research* 11 (1967): 213–218; R. Dean Coddington, "The Significance of Life Events as Etiological Factors in the Diseases of Children," *Journal of Psychosomatic Research* 16 (1972): 7–18, 205–213; Eric K. E. Gunderson and Richard H. Rahe, *Life Stress and Illness* (Springfield, Ill.: Charles C Thomas, 1974).

4. A fine example of applicable research is Hope J. Leichter and William E. Mitchell, *Kinship and Casework* (New York: Russell Sage Foundation, 1967).

5. For example, Frances H. Scherz, "The Crisis of Adolescence in Family Life," *Social Casework* 48 (April 1967): 209–215, and Barbara Fried, *The Middle-Age Crisis,* revised ed. (New York: Harper and Row, 1976).

6. Martin Strickler, "Crisis Intervention and the Climacteric Man," *Social Casework* 56 (February 1975): 85–89.

7. Harriett M. Bartlett, *The Common Base of Social Work Practice* (New York: NASW, 1970), pp. 93–97.

8. Carol H. Meyer, *Social Work Practice,* 2nd ed. (New York: Free Press, 1976), pp. 70–74. Reprinted by permission of the author and publisher.

9. A great deal of work has been done in this area by family sociologists. See, for example, Evelyn M. Duvall, *Family Development,* 2nd ed. (Philadelphia: Lippincott, 1962), chaps. 12–14; William F. Kenkel, *The Family in Perspective,* 2nd ed. (New York: Appleton-Century-Crofts, 1966), chaps. 17–20; Robert R. Bell, *Marriage and Family Interaction,* 3rd ed. (Homewood, Ill.: Dorsey Press, 1971), Parts 2 and 3.

10. The following discussion has been condensed and adapted from

Frances H. Scherz, "Maturational Crises and Child Interaction," *Social Casework* 52 (June 1971): 362–369. Reprinted with permission of *Social Casework*. Despite its occasional complexity, I have chosen this interpretation because Scherz, as a practitioner-teacher, tended to see the individual and family developmental tasks from the practice viewpoint.

11. See Blanca N. Rosenberg, "Planned Short-Term Treatment in Developmental Crises," *Social Casework* 56 (April 1975): 195–204, for focused treatment in this area.

12. Barbara Smith, "Adolescent and Parent: Interaction Between Developmental Stages," *Center Quarterly Focus* (Minneapolis: University of Minnesota Center for Youth Development and Research, Fall 1976), p. 3.

13. Erik. H. Erikson, *Identity, Youth and Crisis* (New York: W. W. Norton, 1968), p. 96.

14. Rhona Rapoport, "Normal Crises, Family Structure, and Mental Health," *Family Process* 2, 1 (1963). Reprinted in H. J. Parad, ed. *Crisis Intervention: Selected Readings* (New York: FSAA, 1965). p. 75.

15. Phyllis Silverman, "Caregiver During Critical Role Transition in the Normal Life Cycle," Paper presented at NIMH Continuing Education Seminar on Emerging Mental Health Service, Washington, D. C., June 22, 1973. Cited with permission of the author.

16. Rhona Rapoport and Robert Rapoport, "New Light on the Honeymoon," *Human Relations* 17 (1964): 33–56.

17. E. E. LeMasters, "Parenthood as Crisis," *Marriage and Family Living* 19, no. 4 (1957), reprinted in Parad, 1965, 111–117; Everett Dyer, "Parenthood as Crisis: a Restudy," *Marriage and Family Living,* 25, no. 2 (1963), reprinted in Parad, 1965, 312–323; Daniel F. Hobbs, "Parenthood as a Crisis: a Third Study," *Journal of Marriage and the Family,* 27 (1965): 367–372. Also Therese Benedek, "Parenthood as a Developmental Phase," *Journal of the American Psychoanalytic Association* 7 (1959): 389–417.

18. Donald C. Klein and Ann Ross, "Kindergarten Entry: A Study of Role Transition," *Orthopsychiatry and the School* (New York: American Orthopsychiatric Association, 1958), reprinted in Parad, 1965, pp. 140–148.

19. J. S. Tyhurst and Libuse, "Displacement and Migration; A Study in Social Psychiatry," *American Journal of Psychiatry* 107 (1951): quoted in James S. Tyhurst, "The Role of Transitional States," *Symposium on Preventive and Social Psychiatry* (Washington, D.C.: Walter Reed Army Institute of Research, 1957), pp. 154–155; Naomi Golan and Ruth Grushka, "Integrating the New Migrant: A Model for Social Work Practice in Transitional States," *Social Work* 16 (April 1971): 82–87.

20. Gordon F. Streib and Clement J. Schneider, *Retirement in American Society: Impact and Process* (Ithaca, N. Y.: Cornell University Press, 1971).

21. Introduction to Elisabeth Kübler-Ross, *On Death and Dying* (New York: Macmillan, 1969); Ira O. Glick, Robert S. Weiss, and C. Murray Parkes, *The First Year of Bereavement* (New York: John Wiley and Sons, 1974).

22. Marjorie F. Lowenthal, Majda Thurnher, David Chiriboga, and associates, *Four Stages of Life* (San Francisco: Jossey-Bass, 1975). For a lively, intriguing examination of transitional states, see Gail Sheehy, *Passages: Predictable Crises of Adult Life* (New York: E. P. Dutton, 1974).

23. Golan, 1975, pp. 369–374.

24. In a recent research study, it was found that, despite expectations, persons with social-transition problems did not respond to the use of short-term treatment to the same degree that other types of cases did. This was interpreted to indicate that the transitional process has its own tempo which, in some situations, resists time-limited intervention. See Golan, 1976, p. 43.

25. Bell, 1971, pp. 514–516.

26. Paul Bohannan, ed., *Divorce and After* (Garden CIty, N. Y.: Anchor Books, 1971), pp. 33–62.

27. Reva S. Wiseman, "Crisis Theory and the Process of Divorce," *Social Casework* 56 (April 1975): 206–211. Reprinted in condensed version with permission of the author and *Social Casework*.

28. For further discussion of these issues, see Bernard Steinzor, *When Parents Divorce* (New York: Pantheon, 1969), pp. 11–21; Vicki L. Rose and Sharon Price-Bonham, "Divorce Adjustment: a Woman's Problem?," *Family Coordinator* 22 (July 1973): 291–297.

29. See, for example, Robert S. Weiss, "The Contributions of an

Organization of Single Parents to the Well-Being of Its Members,"
Family Coordinator 22 (July 1973): 321–326.

30. Also see David D. Schmidt and Edward Messner, "The Role of the Family Physician in the Crisis of Impending Divorce," *Journal of Family Practice,* 2 (April 1975): 99–102.

31. Kathryn Hallett, *A Guide for Single Parents: Transactional Analysis for People in Crisis* (Millbrae, Cal.: Celestial Arts, 1974).

32. For a structured educational program in the transition of "becoming marrieds," see Sherod Miller, Elam Nunnally, and Daniel B. Wackman, "A Communication Training Program for Couples," *Social Casework* 57 (January 1976): 9–18.

33. E. D. Grollman, ed., *Explaining Divorce to Children* (Boston: Beacon Press, 1969).

Chapter 9

Situational Crises

Situational crises, of varying levels of acuteness, form the large bulk of cases in which crisis intervention occurs. They can be found in a wide range of settings: hospital emergency rooms, crisis clinics, family agencies, public welfare departments, and private psychotherapists' offices. They represent such a variety and complexity of conditions that it is virtually impossible to categorize them adequately. What they do have in common is that they are usually triggered by some unanticipated or accidental hazardous event which starts off a chain of reactions in an individual or system, in which the themes of loss or threat figure prominently, and which precipitates at least some of the persons involved into states of active crisis.

Some years ago, following the classifications developed by family sociologists,[1] I attempted to categorize unexpected hazardous events into those involving a loss or impending loss to the applicant or a significant other, and those involving the introduction of a new person into the social orbit.[2] In actual practice, however, it soon becomes evident that although the initial event can sometimes be clearly defined (often after the crisis has abated and the dust has settled), it is often intermingled with and

187

superimposed upon other events which have occurred previously but which the individual has, until this point, been able to handle by his customary coping patterns. The event may also, as discussed in Chapter 8, bring to the surface other conflicts and pressures which aggravate or distort the current situation.

Moreover, as noted in Chapter 4, the hazardous event may be unanticipated in the sense that it was totally unexpected or adventitious, such as a traffic accident or a mugging. On the other hand, it may merely have been unexpected in its timing, as in the case of the premature birth of a child or a middle-aged man's heart attack.

Some events affect a whole family or network simultaneously. When a home is destroyed by fire, although the family members' reactions may vary depending upon the subjective importance of the home to each of them at this time and place, nevertheless intervention can usually be carried out from the same baseline of loss of dwelling and can be dealt with largely in terms of the generic consequences of the current situation.

This is a very different type of situation from, say, the effect of the suicide of a seventeen-year-old college freshman on his parents, his twelve-year-old sister, his friends, his favorite instructor, and the school authorities. Not only will the range of reactions be far broader and more closely interwoven with personal interpretations in terms of past and present experiences, but intervention will probably have to be individual and comprehensive.

Undoubtedly the key to being able to work intelligently with situational crises is to become aware of the specific effects that particular stressful events tend to have upon persons and systems and to be able to forecast with some degree of certainty the problem-solving tasks that need to be carried out during the different phases of the total situation so that the crisis can be resolved adaptively.[3]

Such information can be obtained by reviewing the theoretical knowledge base that has been developed about the event. In the case of the death of a loved one, for example, we learn, on the basis of Bowlby's work, that the bereavement process usually consists of three stages: protest and denial, despair and disorganization, and, finally, reorganization on a new level.[4] More specifically in terms of the problem-solving tasks, on the basis of Lindemann's observations we can say that grief work involves the individual's ability to free himself from his attachment to the deceased, to readjust to the environment from which the deceased is now missing, and to form new relationships.[5] We find that, when death of a member occurs, the family must carry out four primary psychological tasks: they must allow mourning to occur, give up the memory of the deceased person as a force in family affairs, realign intrafamilial roles, and readjust extrafamilial roles.[6] Similar task explications have been and continue to be carried out for other types of crisis situations.

In addition, by now we have a considerable number of reports from the field on how practitioners have worked with individuals and families during periods of unanticipated crisis. While the variables of agency function, practice experience, and client commitment may differ, a respectable body of practice wisdom has accumulated over the past twenty years which can serve to guide us in working with these clients.

In this chapter, rather than enumerate different crises, we have chosen to present two typical situational crises in detail: physical illness and rape. Not only does each illustrate clearly the phases in the situation, but the intervention modes clearly illustrate some of the basic principles of crisis resolution.[7]

Physical Illness

Serious illness, by definition, usually represents a stressful experience both for the sick person and for his family. Warren Miller points out that the stresses to which sick individuals are subject may be placed in three categories:

> 1. The *loss* of functional ability and the debilitation, pain, and threat of death which result directly from the disease itself. Associated with these stresses are others which result from the various threatening procedures and experiences to which the patient may be subjected during the course of his evaluation and treatment.

2. The *dependency* and *passivity* and the resulting regression which the patient must accept, especially during the early phase of a severe illness. A corollary stress which may occur toward the end of an illness is the resumption of previous levels of self-determination and emotional investment in the outside world, with its associated need to "de-regress." In illnesses which leave a permanent residual, this recuperative psychological process may even assume the proportions of new identity formation.

3. The *separation* and *aloneness* which follow the removal of the sick individual, both psychologically and spatially, from his supportive social network.[8]

Some years ago, Davis, describing how polio victims and their families experienced the crisis of this illness, tried to fit his analysis into the disaster formula and listed five sequential stages through which they passed: prelude, warning, impact, inventory, and recovery.[9] As an overall process, however, we find it simpler to talk of the *onset phase,* when the illness is developing and being diagnosed; the *acute phase* of treatment, including hospitalization and surgical procedures; the *recuperation phase,* which encompasses the gradual recovery of normal functions; and the post-hospital *restoration phase,* including adjustment to new limitations and disabilities and re-establishment of systems relationships.

The tasks of coping with stress, according to Kaplan, occur in order and relate to the characteristic sequential phases of the illness. These phase-related tasks must be resolved in proper sequence within the time limits set by the duration of the successive phases of the illness. Failure to resolve them in this manner is likely to jeopardize the total coping process of the entire family and the outcome of the stressful situations.[10]

ONSET PHASE

If we consider the first phase of a serious, life-threatening illness to last from the onset of symptoms and the recognition that "something is not right" to the confirmation of the diagnosis and setting up of a treatment plan, it is obvious that there is a wide range of types of medically connected crisis situations. At the one extreme we have the flash explosion in a factory, causing extensive injuries, or the sudden massive myocardial infarction in an athlete, in which the first phase lasts only minutes and the person and his family are thrust almost immediately into the acute second phase. This lack of forewarning and sudden change in social forces frequently bring about what Korner calls the "shock crisis," as described in Chapter 4.

At the other extreme, when the onset of the illness is gradual, as in heart disease or cancer, we find patients living for weeks and months with the nagging awareness that their normal level of functioning has been reduced, yet reluctant to admit or confirm it despite increasingly urgent warning signs. In the case of parents' recognition of their children's illness, Davis found three main types of reaction during this period: rationalization, reinterpretation, and vacillation.[11]

Miller presents a profile of the two types of patient who react maladaptively to the onset of illness.

The *denier* is the individual who typically takes great pride in his self-reliance, health, and ability to control his own life, including his bodily functions. Such an individual will often delay attending to signs and symptoms and then will avoid interpreting them in terms of illness as long as possible. He will be reluctant to acknowledge to his family and friends that he is ill and even more reluctant to ask for help from a physician. If he cannot avoid becoming a patient, he will minimize his illness and avoid his appointments or treatments. If he is hospitalized, he will create problems with the staff by denying or minimizing his illness and attempting to resume his usual activities too quickly. In general, this sort of individual comes to treatment too late, often after the disease has progressed extensively, and when he does come to treatment, resists it in a variety of ways.

...At the other extreme, the *hypochondriac* is extremely dependent and anxious about even the mildest phsyical illness. He is hyperalert to the signs and symptoms of illness and too quick to interpret any bodily change as a signal of disease . . . . In the face of real and severe physical illness, [he] will tend to rely excessively on others for help and reassurance . . . . If he is hospitalized, he is inclined to regress to an anxious and dependent state, often characterized by a demanding and controlling quality. In general, this sort of individual comes to a physician too early and too often. As a result of his behavior he often creates antagonism and may be rejected by his family, friends, and physician for excessive complaints and demands; on the other hand he may be medically and surgically overtreated.[12]

Many medical situations fall somewhere in between these extremes, with both patient and family worried but able to cope with their customary problem-solving methods. It may take the shock of actually learning the diagnosis and/or prognosis to confirm their fears and push them into a state of crisis. Engelmann describes the typical reaction of a patient who has learned that he has developed diabetes:

The new diabetic may be shocked, frightened, and even have moments of panic. He may feel a sense of despair because he faces a lifelong incurable condition. The amount of technical information he must absorb about diet and insulin therapy can seem overwhelming and he may have doubts about his ability to care for himself. Along with this great increase in anxiety can come feelings of inadequacy and insecurity as he is faced with the awareness of physical limitation, dependency on insulin, and continuous medical supervision.[13]

Spink found that parents of a deaf infant may have suspected their child's deafness long before a definitive diagnosis is made. Four psychological processes can be identified in this stage: denial, rationalization, shock, and overidentification. At first the mother may insist that the child is hearing when actually he is responding to vibrations or a shifting of light patterns. She may rationalize instances when he does not respond to sound by saying that he is stubborn or "hearing only what he wants to hear." When faced with a professional diagnosis of deafness, the parents may react with a number of feelings associated with shock: grief, helplessness, guilt, anger, and a sense of isolation from society. And, finally, they may tend to overidentify with the child by assuming an inaccurate or exaggerated concept of the situation as they view his life circumstances more through their own frame of reference than through his.[14]

In the case of a terminal illness, Kübler-Ross describes the first stage as one of denial and isolation. She finds that in some ways this is a healthy way of dealing, temporarily, with the uncomfortable and painful situation which the patient and family may have to live with for a considerable time.[15]

According to Kaplan, the coping tasks in the initial phase are associated with confirmation of the patient's diagnosis. In their study of childhood leukemia, he and his associates found that it was important for both parents to understand the essential nature of the illness as early as possible and to cope adaptively with the fact that they have a seriously ill child. They must inform the rest of the family about the true nature of the illness and open the way for a period of mourning as a healthy, natural response to news of the impending loss.

They found, however, that eighty-seven percent of the families interviewed were unable to resolve these initial tasks successfully. The most common reactions were a denial of the reality of the diagnosis and an attempt to conceal it from the child. Other maladaptive coping responses included postponement of grief until the illness had reached an advanced stage, "flight into activity" such as moving or starting a new pregnancy, display of overt and massive hostility to members of the medical staff, shopping elsewhere for a cure, and early abdication of parental responsibility.[16]

ACUTE PHASE

Once the diagnosis is confirmed and a plan of treatment set up, the patient usually enters the second phase of the illness process.

This generally centers on the medical and surgical procedures for treating the illness, usually within the confines of a hospital or medical center.

Hospitals, with their complex, sophisticated machinery for treatment and their impersonal, busy, often-masked staff, tend to be confusing, frightening places for the patient in serious discomfort and pain. It has been suggested that the environment of the recovery room to which patients are brought following cardiac surgery, with its strange equipment, "science-fiction" atmosphere, hypnotically monotonous and repetitive sounds, and disruptions of usual sleep-waking patterns, may explain why many patients have episodes of acute delirium.[17]

During the first period of hospitalization, the patient is often in severe physical and emotional trauma. He may be given massive doses of sedatives or narcotics to numb the pain, which adds to his sense of disorientation and dissociation and increases the feelings of anxiety, depression, fear, and shock which, according to Ezra, are common reactions to the sudden and unexpected assault of an acute heart attack.[18]

Meanwhile, the family of the sick person is also going through a parallel phase of serious upset. Brodland and Andreasen found that the first reactions of relatives of severely burned patients are acute shock and grief. On arriving at the hospital, they often express relief that he has not died or been burned more severely. At times, interwoven with the fear that the injury may prove fatal can be found the well-repressed wish that he *should* die and thus avoid the pain and frustration that lie ahead. At this stage they show little concern about potential scarring and worry primarily about the patient's recovery, no matter what his appearance will be.[19]

Soon after admission, some burn patients may experience confusion and disorientation as the result of the acute brain syndrome that often accompanies this trauma. Others may regress psychologically so that individuals who previously were quite self-sufficient now become complaining, demanding, and dependent. The family, unused to such behavior, becomes alternately confused and angry, feeling that the patient does not give them credit for their supportive efforts.

During this phase, both relatives and patients develop strong feelings of either trust or mistrust toward the medical staff. Because they are concerned that everything possible should be done to ensure the sick person's comfort and recovery, the family may question the competence of the doctors and feel that they are experimenting on the patient. In burn cases, the extended waiting period before skin grafting begins is often seen as abandonment and may lead to feeling of mistrust and anger.[20]

The patient's coping tasks during this acute phase of the illness are, primarily, to cooperate with the medical staff in carrying out the complex procedures prescribed and to endure, as patiently as possible, the pain and discomfort that accompany them. Relatives, who tend to feel neglected and shunted aside in the staff's preoccupation with the sick person, must cope with their own and each other's misgivings, fears, and anxieties without disturbing either the patient or the medical and nursing staffs.

The process is at times attenuated by differences of opinion among physicians, the ordering of additional tests or operations, or the waiting for a suitable donor in, say, a kidney- or heart-transplant case. The family may have to deal with the very real prospect that the patient may not survive and that death is a serious threat. The extent to which the possibility of death in the event of cardiac transplant is recognized and anticipatory grief is begun is reflected in the responses of the families of patients who die before a donor heart becomes available:

> Grief is immediate and strong, accompanied by a sense of "having lost the battle," as well as the realization that "we knew this might happen." Close family members often express gratitude that they could communicate so freely with the patient during the last days of his life. A process seems to occur by which the physicians, nurses, and social worker become "family." The intensity of the shared efforts and mutual caring during the days preceding the patient's death facilitates open expression of grief by staff members as well as by members of the patient's family.[21]

RECUPERATION PHASE

Once the acute phase is over and the patient starts on the long road to recovery, both patients and their families become immersed in the treatment procedures. As the shock wears off, the pain the patient suffers is a primary problem. He begins to verbalize his suffering, at times desperately. In burn cases, additional surgical procedures, such as autografting, engender further pain and frustration, since he must lie quietly for fear of disturbing the graft. Later on the pain is supplanted by itching, which produces further discomfort and stress.

Relatives must often stand by helplessly while the healing proceeds at its own pace. Their own sense of powerlessness produces conflict in that they try to aid the patient by making him physically comfortable and providing emotional support, while often feeling that the staff is not doing enough to relieve the pain by administering analgesic medication. Again, they find themselves in the precarious position of trying to balance good relations with both the patient and the medical staff.

As recovery continues, fear of deformity and permanent scarring makes the patient hypersensitive to the reactions of others. Relatives must attempt to hide their own dismay and revulsion and to provide reassurance which they may not sincerely feel. Family members may also carry the additional burden of guilt that they may have contributed to or caused the accident in which the patient was injured. Even if they were not directly involved, they may feel that they should have foreseen the possibility of the accident and prevented it. Occasionally relatives become so overwhelmed by the emotional stress of sitting at the bedside of a suffering loved one and so depressed or anxious that they may be asked to leave the ward until they regain their emotional equilibrium.[22]

In a coronary care unit, the initial trauma of the heart attack is usually over quickly for most patients, and they begin to feel better soon. His sudden brush with death makes the sick person aware of his own feelings and at the same time awakens the realization that, from this point on, he will be different, now that his heart has been damaged. He must cope with his own changed self-image and his fears of dependency and of changed life style.[23]

During this period, families must also prepare themselves physically and psychologically for the patient's extended hospital stay. Practically, they must make arrangements to spend entire days or parts of days at the patient's bedside, find nearby sleeping accommodations if they live at a distance, and arrange for leave from jobs and for care of the rest of the family. They must cope with the hours of boredom and enforced inactivity during the recuperation phase. Even though they may provide valuable assistance in helping to feed the patient, providing companionship, and encouraging and assisting him in his exercises and physical therapy, their role is still a secondary supportive one to the medical staff. For active people, cessation of customary activities and learning to accommodate to the hospital's routine are a strain.

The family member's task in this emotionally draining situation is difficult unless he himself receives support from others. This is often supplied by relatives of other patients. As they sit together in waiting rooms and on sun porches, they may pool information about treatment methods, compare notes on the conditions of the patients, and console one another when setbacks occur.

Restoration Phase

Leaving the hospital or convalescent home, with the worst of the illness behind, by no means implies a return to a pre-illness state of health for the sick person. The operation or debilitating illness may have left permanent damage and limitations, as in the case of a heart occlusion or lung resection. If the hazardous event persists, as in the case of aging, the patient may become more vulnerable to new blows. Lipner and Sherman found, in their study of hip fractures among the elderly, that a number of patients sustained a second fracture, either before their discharge from the hospital or shortly thereafter.[24] Post-hospital follow-ups and repeated re-examinations may be an essential part of the medical treatment, and extensive aftercare may be required.

When the illness is long-term or chronic, with frequent relapses and regressions, the repeated recycling through the phases of the illness may leave the patient and family emotionally and physically depleted. In addition, the repeated efforts to grapple with the economic and social concomitants of the situation may become intolerable in time and put the entire family into a precarious position, where one final pressure may tip the balance and send them into the state of "exhaustion crisis" described by Korner (see Chapter 4).

Macnamara found that, in prolonged renal disease, the patient who requires dialysis and eventually a kidney transplant must face significant changes in his living patterns. He must adjust to a strict diet, limit his social life, and return periodically to the hospital for checkups, dialysis, and, in time, surgery. Economic and social problems arise as the family has to adjust to reduced income, loss of job or business, even bankruptcy. The patient's need to curtail his activity and remain under continuous medical supervision disturbs the rest of the family network, who feel depressed, shamed, anxious, guilty, and angry as they have to take over his former roles. Children become disturbed and confused by their parents' frequent absences from home and by shifts in caregivers.[25]

Coping tasks during this phase revolve to a large extent around readjustment to the major realignments in family roles and to the provision of material and emotional support. Kaplan notes that the family as a group must offer its members access to its collective coping experience:

> In the family system of reciprocal relationships, in which one function is to provide mutual assistance to members under stress, members expect others in the family to help them meet their needs—whether these needs are for emotional support or assistance with family functions and labors. When one family member

fails to respond to what another considers legitimate expectations under stress, the inevitable resentment and dissatisfactions that follow decrease the effectiveness of the joint effort essential for successful family coping.[26]

Intervention in Physical Illness

Some years ago, Perlman defined the purpose of social casework in a medical setting as twofold: "to deal with those social-psychological factors that impede the patient's good use of recuperative aids and to provide such material, social, and psychological services as will enhance the patient's motivation, capacity, and opportunity to regain or build up his sense of well-being."[27] Within this overall framework, treatment in cases of physical illness seems to consist of intervals of intense, focused crisis intervention alternating with periods of sustained, supportive casework during which the medical social worker serves as a "sounding board, balance wheel, and resident philosopher for both patients and families."[28]

Since it is difficult to predict exactly what elements or combinations of elements will precipitate a crisis response, the worker must keep a careful, concerned eye on the total situation to become quickly aware of shifts in reactions and coping patterns. Knowing the potential danger points in the process, the strengths and weaknesses in the network, and the material-arrangemental and psychosocial tasks that patient and family must face, he makes a series of professional judgments as to when to leave them to their own coping devices and when to intervene actively. As part of the medical team, he balances his own role against those of the rest of the helping network: the physician, surgeon, nurses, physiotherapist, aides, and, in some cases, psychiatrist.

Thus we can only offer some general guidelines for treatment in medical crises, following the basic crisis model outlined in Part 2, adapted to the nature of the setting and the illness. We know, for example, that, if the condition is new, learning the diagnosis is one of the critical points at which the patient and/or his family may become disequilibrated. The practitioner's role at this time is to focus on helping them clarify the meaning of the diagnosis and its implications and encouraging them to express their fears, anxieties, and other feelings of loss or threat.

Although the physician or surgeon usually reserves the right to inform the patient of the diagnosis, he may present it in a way that is too technical for the upset, physically weakened patient to understand. On the other hand, he may, for his own reasons, choose to be deliberately vague, uncommunicative, or even unavailable. He may prefer not to discuss the situation with the family or may concentrate on only one person in the network. The social worker may have to facilitate communications between the doctor, the patient, and the family. He may, in addition, have to take on the educative role of reinterpreting and elaborating this material in a way the patient and family can grasp and of helping them consider its short- and long-term practical implications.

For example, the worker may have to spell out the genetic aspects of a medical condition, as Spink reports:

> One important function of the social worker...is to educate the parents on matters such as the causes of deafness, the meaning and implications of audiological terms such as "decibel loss" and "residual hearing," and the opportunities available to their child through school programs for the deaf and through the deaf community. Here is seen the directive, educative function of crisis intervention. The worker in the medical setting has early access to the parent in their crisis—that is, immediately after diagnosis—and can begin giving concrete services and information at that time.[29]

During the acute phase of the illness, patients are often too absorbed in the medical procedures to deal with their own feelings. Brown notes, however, that in the case of proposed cardiac surgery, some patients ask for help in dealing with the mysteries and intricacies of the surgical experience itself. He feels that for persons who tend to use intellectual techniques to gain a sense of mastery, providing full and complete information gives them the tools to cope with the threatening situation. Other patients may merely seek general reassurance that the hospital staff is concerned; they prefer to be spared the details of what awaits them.[30]

Hickey states that before and after a patient undergoes kidney transplantation and during the recovery period, the social worker's major function is to help him and his family face their current situation, work through their feelings, and set up a realistic adjustment and post-discharge plan. She suggests focusing on the family interaction and dynamics—attitudes, ways of communication, and patterns of coping—with the emphasis on helping the family retain its integrity and functions.[31]

In dealing with the long-term, post-hospitalized patient faced with a deteriorating level of functioning, the social worker may expect to intervene periodically to help the network cope with the changed aspects of the situation during what become, in effect, a series of transitional phases. Lambert found that as patients with progressive neurological diseases became increasingly helpless and disabled, the practitioner was called on repeatedly to help them and their families express and clarify their reactions to each new stage of deterioration, to cope with the reality aspects of the situation, and to redefine their responsibilities in a constructive way.[32]

If the illness turns out to be terminal, the patient and family may need the opportunity to ventilate their feelings of sadness and grief, loss and fear of death. The importance of helping them pass through this period of anticipatory mourning runs as a theme through all the social work literature on work with fatally ill patients and has been explored extensively.[33] Meetings with groups of patients,[34] with families,[35] and with both of them together[36] are considered effective methods of providing support in dealing with the cognitive and affective aspects of approaching death.

As a final point, Goldstein reminds us that crisis resolution can be viewed not merely as curative or preventive but as ego-enhancing as well. Dying can be seen as a developmental phase involving active preparation by the individual and positive involvement by the family. Helping them focus on the positive aspects of the terminal process can be a constructive experience, for the dying patient, for his family who live on after him, and for the professional staff members who guide the intervention.[37]

The following intervention involving physical illness is a condensed version of part of a case presented by Bender.[38] Although the medical situation itself was not life-threatening, the crisis aspects of the situation were aggravated by the patient's acute hospital anxiety.

THE CASE OF MRS. R.

ONSET PHASE

Mrs. R. had been having problems for some time with exceptionally heavy menstrual bleeding. Her doctor decided to try to clear up the problem by means of a dilation and curettage. Mrs. R. was distraught at the news of the procedure, which required an overnight stay in the hospital. She was overwhelmed with anxiety, sure she would not survive the hospitalization. She was unable to sleep or to manage the house and the children. Her inability to cope with her feelings about the impending hospitalization was compounded by the fact that her illness had left her chronically weak and anemic.

Mrs. R. and the worker undertook the task of enabling her to deal with the hospitalization, the dilation and curettage, and the disruptive attendant anxiety so that she could return to her former level of functioning. Although her emotional crisis concerning her hospitalization seemed to be exaggerated, it was clear that the chief precipitant was indeed reactivation of an earlier trauma. It soon emerged that she had undergone a very traumatic hospitalization for ear surgery at the age of five, for which she had been completely unprepared. Apparently her parents had tended to handle all medical procedures with denial and evasion. At the time of her ear surgery, her parents took her to the hospital with the usual deception about "a nice drive" and left her there, feeling abandoned, with no explanations. She had vivid memories of the operating room, where she was surrounded by masked figures whom she thought were monsters rather than people. She was terrified by the ether mask and thought that the monsters were trying to kill her.

Together, Mrs. R. and the worker determined that their prime task was to make the hospitalization as different as possible from the former one. They isolated the chief anxiety-provoking factors of the earlier situation: (1) her lack of control over what was happening to her and (2) the fact that she did not understand what was wrong and had not been told why she was in the hospital or what would be done to her. The task of treatment was thus seen as engaging the healthy portions of her shaky ego in regaining a sense of mastery and control over her life situation.

Once a focused exploration revealed these prime anxiety-producing elements, it became clear that the next and most important step was for Mrs. R. to get a clearer understanding of what her doctor planned to do and more detailed information about the dilation and curettage procedure. Characteristically she had asked no questions of her doctor and had been given no facts at all.

The probable steps involved in going into the hospital were discussed and the worker outlined for Mrs. R. the general procedures of a dilation and curettage, including the possiblity of having it done on an outpatient basis. She stressed, however, the importance of her arranging another appointment with her doctor to get the detailed medical information she needed and wanted, underlining that it was her right as an adult patient to request and obtain the facts. Cognitive aspects of the situation were focused on, since she was an intelligent woman whose thought processes were relatively intact even in face of her irrational feelings. It was the worker's intention to bring her intellect to bear in better evaluating reality and in correcting her considerable misinformation about anatomical structures, physical illness, and medical procedures.

The worker encouraged Mrs. R. to get more information for herself rather than giving it to her, because it seemed important to engage her in an active coping process whereby she would have the sense that her own efforts had an impact on her situation, to change her subjective perception of the crisis from a threat to that of a challenge which could mobilize energy and problem-solving behavior. This approach was successful; the worker got a triumphant call from Mrs. R. detailing her visit with her busy doctor. He not only gave her a thorough explanation of what he planned to do and why but also agreed to arrange for the operation to be done on an outpatient basis.

ACUTE PHASE

The next stage involved Mrs. R. and the worker rehearsing together the anticipated sequence of events, going over and discussing the various routines and procedures she would undergo at the hospital, and predicting the aspects that might be particularly difficult for her. This further served to strengthen her cognitive grasp of the situation and thus her sense of control.

It became apparent that one of the things that most frightened Mrs. R. was the anesthesia: she felt she was more susceptible than other people to the effects of medication. With support, she was able to verbalize her fears of never waking up from the anesthesia, of succumbing to an overdose. With this aspect of her fears, reality factors and her own potential mastery of the situation were stressed: she was told that an anesthesiologist generally comes to talk to his patient just before surgery and that it would be up to her to share her concerns with him. The worker tried to convey the idea that Mrs. R. deserved the best for herself, that she was deserving of and should insist on respect and attention. The themes "It doesn't have to be the way it was when you were five" and "You're not a child now, you can make it different" were repeatedly underlined.

Another aspect of treatment was helping Mrs. R. manage her overwhelming affect, primarily fear and anger. She was encouraged to express her feelings, even the most irrational, and the worker tried to put them in a sensible framework by connecting them with past events, such as her childhood feelings of fright and abandonment when left by her parents. The last step in this process was helping Mrs. R. to be more available to her own children in their fear and upset surrounding her hospitalization. Her anxiety ultimately lessened to the point where she was able to give some attention to the children's needs and to move from the conviction that they were acting up on purpose to an understanding of their fright. Again, taking an active role in reassuring the children that she would return from the hospital all right seemed to help her master her own fears.

Mrs. R. also was helped to make better use of the neighbors, who were eager and willing to help with child care. This resulted in enhancing her continuing relationships with some of her neighbors, from whom she had previously been isolated.

RECUPERATION AND RECOVERY PHASES

The worker arranged to see Mrs. R. the day after she had had her dilation and curettage. When Mrs. R. came in she gave an interesting account of how she had handled the hospitalization, which was "not as bad as I expected." Apparently she had been able to make use of support from a sympathetic nurse while waiting to go to the operating room and had also asked to speak to the anesthesiologist, who had considerably allayed her fears about medication. In the operating room she looked around and said to herself, "It really *is* different from when I was five!"

Mrs. R.'s most vivid memory, which clearly reveals the extent to which this hospitalization was an ego-strengthener rather than a destructive experience for her, was of waking up in the recovery room. A little boy was crying for his mother, and her immediate reaction was not the empathy that one might have expected but rather, "I'm coming!" Thus she was able to maintain her role as an adult in reworking and mastering the traumatic experience of a five-year-old. She went on to describe her anger at the doctor because of the way he handled another woman who had had a dilation and curettage at the same time; he told her abruptly that she would have to have a hysterectomy and walked away. Enraged on this woman's behalf, Mrs. R. had attempted to comfort her.

Since her hospitalization experience, Mrs. R. seems to find it easier to express anger and anxiety and to channel them appropriately. About two weeks after the dilation and curettage, Mrs. R. found herself unexpectedly panicky about a follow-up pelvic examination but was able to handle this well on her own. She asked the physician to explain everything he was going to do, and this was enough to calm this brief resurgence of anxiety. Thus Mrs. R. well demonstrates that a crisis has growth-enhancing potential and can serve as a catalyst for the development of new adaptive mechanisms.

Rape

In contrast to physical illness, rape represents an acute situational hazard of a completely different kind. It is frequently a sudden, violent assault characterized by physical force and psychological coercion, and sometimes repeated a number of times in rapid succession by one or several assailants. The stressful combination of sexual violation plus brutal aggression almost invariably thrusts the woman into a state of crisis; indeed, these two elements have become part of the definition of the traumatic experience used by workers in emergency rooms of general hospitals and rape-counseling centers. The predominant subjective reaction is that of threat, rather than loss, with the accompanying affect of high anxiety.

Within the last several years, rape has become the subject of much discussion and controversy, with increasing attention being paid to its effect on the victim rather than on the rapist. Abarbanel estimates that at least 259,000 women were probably raped in this country during 1977 and that only one in 3.5 victims reported the crime.[39]

We cannot enter here into the sociological background of rape[40] or into its politics from the viewpoint of the victim,[41] although an understanding of both is vital to intervention in the consequences. Moreover, we shall limit this discussion to instances of violent rape among adolescent and adult women, though its implications can be broadened to cover other types of situations. As a simple working definition, rape is taken to refer to the "forced sexual penetration of a woman by a man accomplished under actual or implied threat of severe bodily harm."[42]

Hardgrove is emphatic about the frame of reference in which the act should be placed:

> Rape is a hostile, forcible act by one person against another, with the object of dominating, degrading, humiliating, and subjugating the victim. It is not an act that is primarily for sexual gratification. It is a violent crime against the person, a violation of another's self. In fact, rape is the ultimate violation of self short of homicide.[43]

TIME SEQUENCE

In keeping with our view of crisis situations as differentiated into time phases, reactions to rape can be separated into two and sometimes three stages. On the basis of personal interviews with victims, Sutherland (Fox) and Scherl divide the process into phases of acute reaction, outward adjustment, and integration and resolution.[44] Burgess and Holmstrom speak of the acute phase of disorganization and the long-term process of reorganization.[45]

PHASE ONE: ACUTE REACTION

In the hours and days immediately following the attack, the victim's acute reactions include shock and disbelief, followed by fear, anxiety, and outrage. When seen in the hospital emergency room or police station, she appears agitated, incoherent, and highly volatile. Sometimes she is unable to talk about her experience or describe her assailant. Burgess and Holmstrom identify two types of reactions: the *expressed style,* in which feelings of fear, anger, and anxiety are demonstrated by crying, sobbing, restlessness, tenseness, or even smiling; and the *controlled style,* in which feelings are masked or hidden and a calm, composed, or subdued affect is displayed.

It has been observed that women who feel there has been no invitation, seduction, or willing compliance on their part generally call the police immediately or go to the nearest medical emergency station. If they feel some degree of guilty involvement, they tend to delay reporting and then do so by indirect means, such as by telling a roommate or employer.

In addition to the first shock reactions, victims also display in the several weeks following the rape acute symptoms of physical trauma (soreness and bruising of throat, neck, breasts, thighs, legs, arms, and throat); skeletal-muscle tension (tension headaches, fatigue, and sleep-pattern disturbances); gastrointestinal irritability (stomach pains, decreased appetite, nausea);

genitourinary disturbance (vaginal discharge and itching, chronic vaginal infections, generalized genital pains, and burning sensation on urination); and rectal bleeding and pain.

Emotional reactions, as the initial shock wears off, range from embarrassment, humiliation, and fear to anger, vengefulness, and fury. Fear of physical violence and death is primary. Self-blame also is evident, with women wondering whether, if they had acted differently, the outcome might have been avoided.

PHASE TWO: OUTWARD ADJUSTMENT

Once the acute phase, which may last from a few hours to weeks, has passed, the victim generally returns to her usual pursuits at work, school, and home. She often says she is over the shock and needs no further help. Sutherland and Scherl feel this period of pseudo-adjustment does not represent a final resolution of the traumatic event and contains a considerable amount of denial and suppression.

During this phase, the woman makes the effort to deal with her feelings about the attacker and tries to rationalize her reactions, to put the entire rape incident "in its place." As precautionary measures, she often changes her living arrangements; perhaps even moving to a new apartment or neighborhood. She puts extra safety locks on her door and asks for an unlisted telephone number. She takes a course in judo or other means of self-defense and sometimes even buys a weapon as a safeguard.

Haunted by the fear or the threat that her assailant may return, she may go away—take a trip back home to visit her family, go on a vacation to a different part of the country or even abroad. If she has close friends, she often turns to them for support. Outwardly, she appears to have made an adjustment.

PHASE THREE: INTEGRATION AND RESOLUTION

This period begins when the woman develops an inner sense of depression and the urge to talk. Sutherland and Scherl see two major themes emerging in this phase: the need to integrate a new view of herself and the need to resolve her own feelings about the assailant and her relations to him.

This phase may be precipitated by a specific incident: a request to identify her attacker in a police line-up, a diagnosis of pregnancy, a marriage proposal, an attempt to engage in sexual activity with her boyfriend, a glimpse of someone who looks like the rapist. Sometimes, however, no specific precipitant can be identified and the phase is merely marked by a more general deterioration and breakdown of previous defenses.

Burgess and Holmstrom report a number of specific symptoms which occur at this time: frightening fantasies and nightmares in which violence and fear are the outstanding motifs, phobias such as fear of indoors or outdoors (depending on where the attack occurred), fear of being alone, fear of crowds, fear of people coming up from behind, and fear of sexual activity.

A significant syndrome these authors have noted is what they call the "silent reaction to rape," which can be found in the woman who had been raped or molested in the past and never told anyone about the attack. She carries a tremendous psychological burden. The current rape often reactivates her previous experience, and she now feels pressure to talk, not only about the current event, but about the earlier one as well.

At times the rape incident becomes the precipitating factor for consideration of broader issues in the woman's life and the need to re-examine her attitudes, her relations to significant others in her various networks, and her own overall style of life.

The following case study is an abridged version of an anonymous self-report by a social work student who was raped.[46] It illustrates graphically both the phases in the sequence and the emotional reactions of the victim.

RAPE—A PERSONAL ACCOUNT

THE EVENT

Early on Easter morning, 1974, as my boyfriend and I were waiting in the elevator in my building, two young men forced their way into the elevator and began what was for me the most frightening experience of my life.

The men immediately grabbed us and clamped their hands over our faces, saying, "This is a stick-up." They forced us to go to my apartment and let them in. They demanded all of our money. We gave them what we had but it wasn't enough. They tore out my phone and tied up my friend with the cord. One of the men took me into my bedroom and insisted that I had more money in there. When I told him that we had really given them everything we had, he repeated that we were lying and forced me to lie face down on my bed.

At this point I felt sure I was about to be raped and I couldn't see any way out of it. I was becoming more frightened and anxious by the second. I also wanted to know what was happening to my friend in the living room. The man rolled me over with one hand, keeping the other over my eyes. He insisted that I not look at him, although I kept attempting to see what he looked like. He told me that if I didn't make a sound he wouldn't hurt me. He threw himself on top of me and began to rape me. He also managed to force his shoulder into my mouth so that any sounds I tried to make couldn't be heard.

As the man became more involved in the rape, I felt more and more helpless. He was a good deal bigger than I and overpowered me physically. I was shaking with fright and was trying to think of ways to stay calm. It was probably for that reason that I asked him his name. I really didn't expect him to answer but he told me his nickname—Peewee. He left me on my bed and motioned to his partner to trade places with him. The other man came in and asked me if his friend had hurt me. By that I assumed he meant had his friend beat me up, and I said no.

He asked me if I had ever been "fucked in the ass." I told him I hadn't. At this point I was thinking to myself how I'd always thought I would die if I were raped, but now I was really frightened of anal rape. It seemed as if that would be truly intolerable. The man asked me if I wanted to be fucked anally. I didn't know what to say. If I said yes, I wasn't sure that it would discourage him, and if I said no, I felt sure it would encourage him. I took a deep breath and told him, "No."

For a split second I thought he would leave the room, but no, he raped me too. He also told me not to look at him and kept checking to see if my eyes were closed. He didn't seem especially involved in it, but he was still keeping me firmly in his grip. I was becoming more and more numb from the shock of what was being done to me. I felt completely helpless and out of control.

The next thing I knew, I heard someone rummaging through my kitchen drawers. Both men then took me through the living room, one holding the butcher knife that he found. I could see my boyfriend lying face down, tied up, with a chair placed over his head. He wasn't moving or making a sound. Somehow I didn't think he was dead, but I couldn't be sure.

The men forced me to wake up a neighbor. They were holding the knife against my neck. They pushed their way into her apartment and made both of us lie face down on her bed. They asked her for her money and she gave them what she had, but again it didn't satisfy them. They tied her up with her phone cord.

Since they had netted very little money from the three of us, they started threatening to kill us if we didn't come up with more money. We offered them every possession we had in the hope that they would be satisfied. I even told them to take my car, but they refused on the ground that it would be auto theft. Finally they decided to make a "deal." If we didn't call the police, they would leave us. Of course we agreed and they left.

We lay still for a few minutes; then I looked around the apartment. No one was there so I ran back to my apartment to check on my boyfriend. I was frantic about him. My door was locked, so we woke up the occupants of another apartment and called the police. They were there almost instantly. As we stood around the door trying to get in, my boyfriend opened the door—he was all right.

PHASE ONE

The rest of the night brought a welcome release of tension. We answered the immediate request of the police to describe the attackers, and I then went to a hospital to be examined and treated. I was asked if I was using any form of birth control, and a "morning-after pill" was offered if I was not. Tests for venereal disease were done and I was counseled to see my gynecologist or return to the hospital in six weeks for a follow-up examination.

On returning to my apartment I was asked many more questions about the intimate details of the rape by one policeman. His manner was professional and he explained that such questions were necessary because rapists usually have their own "method of operation." I understood this and felt numb and very tired, so I was able to answer his questions directly. He did not subject me to the notorious humiliating questions that many rape victims have described, such as what my sexual history was or if I had enjoyed being raped.

PHASE TWO

Approximately three days after I was raped, I visited a psychiatrist. My parents had suggested this, but I had already decided on my own that it would be a good idea to talk with a professional at least once. I knew there were thoughts on my mind that I hadn't shared with anyone—not even my boyfriend, with whom I had talked a great deal. There was no mental health worker at the hospital the night I was raped, and I think I might have liked to have spoken with someone then or at least have had someone wait with me in the examining room rather than wait alone.

I told the psychiatrist what had happened to me and he asked me a few questions that I'd expected to be asked. After we talked for an hour, he said that I seemed perhaps a little too rational just then but that this might be better than the other extreme. We didn't set up another appointment, but he told me to feel free to return at any time.

I found this interview valuable, even though I had also talked a great deal with my family and my peers. There were certain aspects of the rape that I felt embarrassed about, certain aspects I felt were too "brutal" for others to hear about, and other issues concerning the rape that I couldn't talk about with anyone who knew me. Also, certain feelings of messiness and dirtiness I have been able to share only with another victim.

PHASE THREE

I found that almost eight months afterward, I was still thinking a great deal about my experience. I felt that I was able to do this thinking because I had adequate defenses against possible repercussions. During the time immediately after I was raped, I could think very little and only superficially about what had happened. Even when I wanted to think a great deal about it, I found that I protected myself and couldn't. I didn't dream about rape until after it occurred and feel certain that this was again due to defenses. I feel that I dealt with only as much as I was able to cope with at any given time. Eight months later, I began thinking about my rape again. I felt distant enough by then to think more deeply about my experience.

In some ways I felt that members of my family were suffering more than I had over the rape. Their fantasies and their guilt over "letting" the rape happen to me were consuming their energy. I found that I was shielding some of my thoughts from my family and friends because I felt they wouldn't be able to cope with them and at times I felt that I was making a better recovery than they were.

My boyfriend and I were never able to really talk about his feelings about that evening. After the rape, I received more attention than he, but although I had been through living hell, surely he must have, too. He also visited a psychiatrist once. I wondered what feelings of guilt and impotence he must be dealing with and I think he felt guilty about raising his feelings in view of what I'd been through.

The main factor that helped me pull through this experience was that, after I was raped, my life was threatened. This was by far more traumatic and threatening than being raped. I re-experienced the fear of losing my life many times after the real danger had passed.

There are many moments of despair after being raped. At times I felt that I would never be able to integrate the experience. I wondered, too, if I could ever be acceptable to any man or if I had been "ruined for life." I was not a fearful person before the rape, but afterward I found that I became frightened when alone and less likely to stay out as late as I had been before.

Treatment in Rape Situations

Women who have been raped have very special needs. Abarbanel has identified six specific areas:

1. Information about what to do and where to go after the rape in order to obtain medical, mental health, social, and legal services.

2. Immediate and follow-up medical care for physical trauma, collection of medicolegal evidence, prevention of venereal disease, and protection against unwanted pregnancy.
3. Immediate and follow-up professional counseling for emotional trauma and consequent social disruption.
4. Skilled, sensitive treatment by police officers, social workers, nurses, physicians, lawyers, and others who treat or question the victim.
5. Support from significant others, because talking about the experience with friends and relatives who are understanding is helpful in resolving the crisis.
6. Legal assistance, including information about rights, advocacy, and representation in the criminal-justice system.[47]

In addition, Hardgrove stresses that a victim needs to feel that she is safe and will not be brutalized further. She needs to be listened to and helped to talk about her experience as well as to be given basic information and assistance in making decisions about further steps to be taken.

The discussion here will be limited to direct treatment of victims by helping professionals, even though the preventive, educational, and organizational aspects are equally important and must be dealt with concurrently. Unfortunately, because of the prevalent unwillingness of victims to report rape attacks, the professional may not be brought into the picture until considerable time has elapsed.

PHASE ONE

Intervention immediately after the rape attack often takes place in the emergency room of the hospital to which the police, relatives, or friends have brought the victim. It is being offered increasingly in special rape-counseling centers set up to deal with this crisis. It may require the worker, in the beginning, to see the client daily for a period of time to carry out all the pressing activities that need to be done.

Fox and Scherl see treatment in the acute phase as focusing upon a range of issues.[48] If the victim has not received medical attention, arrangements should be made for an immediate physical examination to attend to her health needs and to furnish medical evidence for possible legal action. The examination should include tests for and prophylactic steps against venereal disease and possible pregnancy. The worker should know which hospitals and clinics treat rape cases and under what circumstances; he should explain carefully ahead of time what will be done and why and should wait with the victim for the doctor.

Although initially the victim may be too upset and confused to consider pressing charges, the worker should encourage her to discuss her situation as soon as possible with an attorney or other competent legal counseling service. If she has not already reported the attack to the police, she should be helped to decide whether she wants to do so and what lies in store for her if she does. It may be appropriate, in this instance, for the worker to accompany the victim to the police station to relieve her anxiety. If she decides not to report the rape, she should be made aware of possible future consequences of her decision.

The victim's anxiety often abates markedly once she has talked with a close relative or friend. The worker can help her decide who should be informed of the attack and how it should be done: whether by the woman alone, together with the worker, or by the worker in her presence. Generally, the victim should be encouraged to do as much as possible herself, along the crisis-intervention principle of helping her regain the sense of being in control of her situation. However, if she is unable to take the necessary first steps, at least she should be present when this is done for her, to reduce the possibility of misunderstanding, distortion, and fantasies about what has been said or done.

Practically, the worker should provide the victim with basic information about what has happened to her sexually and physically and what its implications can be. She should be prepared for possible publicity arising out of the assault and what steps to take to maintain her privacy. Arrangements should be made to repair windows, doors and locks in instances of break-ins; money should be provided to attend to her immediate needs in cases where robbery has been involved; and protective measures should be taken to keep her from becoming frightened of further attacks or threats of revenge by the attacker.

Along with these material arrangements, the worker must help the victim cope with her inner feelings about herself in the light of this new experience. Fox and Scherl advise an attitude of warmth, calmness, empathy, and firm consistency as being most useful. The worker must become personally involved, yet at the same time remain professionally objective. Throughout this phase, he (or she) should be coming to a tentative diagnostic formulation about the rape attack (why here, why now?) and an assessment of the strengths and weaknesses of both the woman herself and the social situation around her.

Finally, through techniques of support and anticipatory guidance, the worker should help her understand that her current feelings are similar to those experienced by others in the same position and that in time they will pass. Together, they should project what lies ahead in the next weeks and months and what resources are available to help her cope with the situation and her reactions to it over time. If psychiatric evaluation or intervention is indicated at this point, the worker should arrange to have this made available.

PHASE TWO

Once the acute phase has passed, the worker's direct activity decreases considerably. His role becomes one of providing support and back-up in order to help the client absorb and integrate what has happened to her. Although the worker may be tempted to challenge defenses, Fox and Scherl feel that such interference is unwarranted and nonproductive in this stage. Instead, the worker should, for the most part, assume a stand-by position. He should encourage the woman to keep her follow-up medical appointments, though she may often fail to do so during this interval of denying and forgetting.[49]

Although there may be relatively little for him to do with the victim, the worker may become active during this phase with relatives and friends who want to deal with their own reactions to the rape incident. They may feel extremely angry with the woman for having been careless, seductive, or unmindful of their prior warnings and may engage in punitive accusations against her. On the other hand, they may feel guilty over having "allowed" the rape to occur and become oversolicitous in keeping her from discussing the event openly. Supportive, educative work can be done to help them examine their preconceived attitudes about rape and seduction and reconcile these with their picture of their own daughter or girlfriend.

PHASE THREE

At some point, the woman client often begins to feel depressed and expresses the desire to talk out and rework the rape experience at a different level. The practitioner who sees her in this final stage—whether at the same rape-counseling center or as a referral from emergency service—often finds two intermingled issues on which to focus: her feelings about herself and her feelings about the assailant. She may want to discuss her feelings of having been soiled and spoiled, her sense of guilt over possibly having provoked the rape, and her need to punish herself for her part in what has happened.[50]

Hardgrove feels that ventilation of these emotions is very important; if they are cut off by reassurances, she will only repress them further. She should be encouraged to direct her anger appropriately at the rapist rather than turn it inward on herself. In this connection, Abarbanel points out that, in contrast to general clinical practice, wherein the worker encourages the client to assume personal responsibility for his part in events, in the case of unanticipated rape, this approach is contraindicated. Instead, the worker should communicate that the woman was *not* responsible, that blame lies with the rapist.[51]

Fox and Scherl, however, caution against challenging such guilt feelings prematurely.[52] Often, in such instances, the woman feels the worker does not understand and therefore cannot help her. Even though realistically the worker may believe that there was nothing she could have done to prevent the attack, it is preferable for the victim to arrive at this conclusion herself, guided by appropriate questions and observations. In the event that she does bear some partial responsibility (for example, in having gone out alone late at night in an area where rapists might lurk), she should be helped to examine her own behavior as part of integrating the total experience.

Feelings of having been dirtied or defiled, if they persist at this stage, may be harder to deal with and require going into the entire issue of her self-image. In such cases, as indicated earlier, the rape may become the springboard for an overall consideration of herself as a person and her relations with significant others. If her feelings of depression, unworthiness, and anxiety continue and even increase, if her sleeping and eating patterns have not returned to normal by this time, and/or if she suffers from generalized fears, phobias, or compulsive rituals, a psychiatric examination or referral is certainly appropriate.

The extent of treatment during this phase depends to a large degree on the client's overall personality, her current level of functioning, and the extent to which she has successfully mastered the earlier phases in the crisis situation. It may be necessary for her to be seen at close intervals at the start of this stage, to help her overcome her subjective reactions of loss of self-esteem and cope adaptively with the consequences of the rape event which continue to arise (e.g., her inability to act normally toward any young man who may want to date her).

Treatment in this phase is usually brief. After several weeks of extensive work, most women tend to integrate the experience and place it appropriately in their past. Should the client be unable to master the trauma within a reasonable time, the worker may evaluate the need for continued therapeutic treatment in the light of the ego's inability to handle stress of this magnitude. In any event, the worker should emphasize the continued availability of help if related issues arise in the future.

As a final point, if the worker dealing with the extremely value- and prejudice-loaded situation of rape should find himself "stuck" and unable to help the victim overcome the crisis, he may find it advisable to examine his own inner reactions and to ask for consultation.

Practitioners who have worked with rape victims stress that the way in which the rape crisis is resolved will have enormous implications for the ongoing functioning of the individual involved. Immediate, positive intervention can take advantage of the increased ability and willingness available during the time of crisis to learn and to use more functional ways of coping. On the other hand, lack of intervention or help that comes too late or is inappropriate can result in a lifetime of emotional problems for the victim.

Notes

1. See, for example, Reuben Hill, "Generic Features of Families Under Stress," *Social Casework* 39 (February–March, 1958). Reprinted in Parad, 1965, pp. 38–39.
2. Naomi Golan, "When is a Client in Crisis?" *Social Casework* 50 (July 1969): 390.
3. Lydia Rapoport, "Crisis Intervention as a Mode of Brief Treatment," in Robert W. Roberts and Robert H. Nee, eds., *Theories of Social Casework* (Chicago: University of Chicago Press, 1970), pp. 282–285.
4. John Bowlby, "Grief and Mourning in Infancy and Early Childhood," *Psychoanalytic Study of the Child* 15 (New York: International Universities Press, 1960), pp. 9–52.
5. Erich Lindemann, "Symptomatology and Management of Acute Grief," *American Journal of Psychiatry 101* (September 1944). Reprinted in Parad, 1965, pp. 10–11.

6. Stanley B. Goldberg, "Family Tasks and Reactions in the Crisis of Death," *Social Casework* 54 (July 1973): 400–401.

7. Since so much has already been written on death and dying and suicide, I decided not to address myself specifically to these topics, although they represent significant acute situational crises.

8. Warren B. Miller, "Psychiatry and Physical Illness; The Psychosomatic Interface," in C. Peter Rosenbaum and John E. Beebe, *Psychiatric Treatment: Crisis/Clinic/Consultation* (New York: McGraw-Hill, 1975), pp. 475–495.

9. Fred Davis, *Passage Through Crisis: Polio Victims and Their Families* (New York: Bobbs-Merrill, 1963), pp. 18–44. A very recent book on this subject is Rudolf H. Moos, *Coping with Physical Illness* (New York: Plenum, 1977).

10. David M. Kaplan, Aaron Smith, Rose Grobstein, and Stanley E. Fischman, "Family Mediation of Stress," *Social Work* 18 (July 1973): 62–69.

11. Davis, 1963, p. 26.

12. W. Miller, 1975, p. 280. In the last instance the "cry wolf" phenomenon may occur.

13. Mary W. Engelmann, "The Diabetic Client," *The Social Worker* 35 (February 1967). Reprinted in Francis J. Turner, ed., *Differential Diagnosis and Treatment in Social Work,* 2nd ed. (New York: Free Press, 1976), p. 431.

14. Diane Spink, "Crisis Intervention for Parents of the Deaf Child," *Health and Social Work* 1 (November 1976): 147–154.

15. Kübler-Ross, 1969, pp. 35–38.

16. Kaplan, et al., 1973, pp. 62–67.

17. Elliot C. Brown, Jr., "Casework with Patients Undergoing Cardiac Surgery," *Social Casework* 52, (December 1971): 612.

18. Julia Ezra, "Casework in a Coronary Care Unit," *Social Casework* 50 (May 1969): 276.

19. Gene A. Brodland and N. J. C. Andreasen, "Adjustment Problems of the Family of the Burn Patient," *Social Casework* 55 (January 1974); 14–15.

20. Ibid., p. 15.

21. Lois K. Christopherson, "Cardiac Transplant: Preparation for Dying or for Living," *Health and Social Work* 1 (February 1976): 65–66.

22. Brodland and Andreasen, 1974, pp. 15–16.

23. Kathleen Obier and L. Julian Haywood, "Role of the Medical Social Worker in a Coronary Care Unit," *Social Casework* 53 (January 1972): 15–16.

24. Joan Lipner and Etta Sherman, "Hip Fractures in the Elderly—A Psychodynamic Approach," *Social Casework* 56 (February 1975): 100.

25. Margaret Macnamara, "The Family in Stress: Social Work Before and After Renal Homotransplantation," *Social Work* 14 (October 1969): 89–97.

26. Kaplan et al., 1973, p. 68.

27. Helen H. Perlman, "Family Diagnosis in Cases of Illness and Disability," in *Family-Centered Social Work in Illness and Disability: A Preventive Approach* (New York: NASW, 1961), p. 8.

28. Christopherson, 1976, p. 66.

29. Spink, 1976, p. 145.

30. Brown, 1971, p. 407.

31. Kathleen M. Hickey, "Impact of Kidney Disease on Patient, Family, and Society," *Social Casework* (July 1972): 391–392.

32. Gladys Lambert, "Patients with Progressive Neurological Diseases," *Social Casework* 55 (March 1974): 154–159.

33. Among others, see Lillian P. Cain, "Casework with Kidney Transplant Patients," *Social Work* 18 (July 1973): 76–83; Audrey T. McCollum and A. Herbert Schwartz, "Social Work with the Mourning Parent," *Social Work* 17 (January 1972): 25–36; Jeannette R. Oppenheimer, "Use of Crisis Intervention in Casework with the Cancer Patient and his Family," *Social Work* 12 (April 1967): 44–52; Carleton Pilsecker, "Help for the Dying," *Social Work* 20 (May 1975): 190–194; Lillian M. Weisberg, "Casework with the Terminally Ill," *Social Casework* 55 (June 1974): 337–342.

34. Judith R. Singler, "Group Work with Hospitalized Stroke Patients," *Social Casework* 56 (June 1975): 348–354.

35. Vrinda S. Knapp and Howard Hansen, "Helping the Parents of Children with Leukemia," *Social Work* 18 (July 1973): 70–73; Chancellor B. Driscoll and A. Harold Lubin, "Conferences with Parents of Children with Cystic Fibrosis," *Social Casework* 53 (March 1972): 140–146.

36. Grace H. Lebow, "Facilitating Adaptation in Anticipatory Mourning," *Social Casework* 57 (July 1976): 456–465.

37. Eda G. Goldstein, "Social Casework and the Dying Person," *Social Casework* 54 (December 1973): 605–608.

38. Barbara Bender, "Management of Acute Hospitalization Anxiety," *Social Casework* 57 (January 1976): 19–26. Reprinted with permission of the author and *Social Casework*. Since this case was condensed, for futher explanation of the theory behind the practice in this specific situation, we suggest that the full case be read.

39. Gail Abarbanel, "Helping Victims of Rape," *Social Work* 21 (November 1976): 478.

40. Menachem Amir, in *Patterns of Forcible Rape* (Urbana, Ill.: University of Illinois Press, 1971), offers a comprehensive bibliography.

41. Diana E. H. Russell, *The Politics of Rape: The Victim's Perspective* (New York: Stein and Day, 1975); Carole V. Horos, *Rape* (New Canaan, Conn.: Tobey, 1974), which also contains a directory of rape crisis centers; and Andrea Medea and Kathleen Thompson, *Against Rape* (New York: Farrar, Straus and Giroux, 1974), are among recent publications offered from the point of view of the women's movement.

42. Sandra Sutherland and Donald J. Scherl, "Patterns of Response Among Victims of Rape," *American Journal of Orthopsychiatry* 40 (April 1970): 504. It should be noted that the legal definitions of rape are more explicit and vary among different states.

43. Grace Hardgrove, "An Interagency Service Network to Meet Needs of Rape Victims," *Social Casework* 57 (April 1976): 246.

44. Sutherland and Scherl, 1970, pp. 503–511. Also, Sandra Sutherland Fox and Donald J. Scherl, "Crisis Intervention with Victims of Rape, *Social Work* 17 (January 1972): 37–42.

45. Ann W. Burgess and Lynda L. Holmstrom, "Rape Trauma Syndrome," *American Journal of Psychiatry,* 131 (1974): 981–986.

Reprinted in S. F. J. Turner, ed., *Differential Diagnosis and Treatment in Social Work,* 2nd ed. (New York: Free Press, 1976), pp. 692–702.

46. "Rape—A Personal Account," *Health and Social Work* 1 (August 1976): 84–95. Reprinted with permission of the National Association of Social Workers.

47. Abarbanel, 1976, p. 478.

48. Fox and Scherl, 1972, pp. 38–39.

49. Ibid., pp. 39–40.

50. Ibid., pp. 40–41.

51. Hardgrove, 1976, pp. 248–249.

52. Fox and Scherl, p. 41.

Chapter 10

Overview and Outlook

Summary

In this volume, we have made an effort to outline the theoretical foundations on which the crisis approach is built and to present the academic, philosophic, and professional matrices out of which it emerged. A basic treatment model was presented as the bridge between theory and practice. This offers a format for helping troubled persons in various crisis situations by stressing (1) the need for clarifying the key issues with which the client is struggling and, (2) the importance of identifying the tasks that have to be carried out in order to cope effectively with the difficulties.

Mindful of the fact that this model may be criticized as being a blanket formula, we have emphasized that it must be applied selectively and appropriately and that intervention must be based on a rapid but thorough evaluation of the person-in-his-social-context. It is seen as a guide to providing some semblance of order and planning to the professional's helping role during periods of disruption.

Three common types of stressful situations were analyzed: community disasters, developmental and transitional events, and
224

situational crises. The original crisis theory has been broadened and modified so that, instead of viewing each situation as a simple, unilateral process of increasing disruption, disequilibrium, and reintegration, it is seen as composed of a series of unique phases, each of which carries the potential for invoking a state of crisis.

Some crises are simple in that they have one common hazardous event with a high probability of disorganization; they can usually be resolved by dealing generically with the common threat or loss aspects in the immediate situation. Other situations are far more complex and consist of a series of danger points to which different persons react in different ways; these must be dealt with individually and differentially by using focused crisis-intervention techniques during acute phases, interspersed with other forms of treatment during less critical intervals.

This last point offers a tie-in between crisis intervention and other treatment strategies. The tendency in recent years has been to search for certain types of problems, certain kinds of clients, and certain settings in which to practice this form of treatment.[1] This has resulted in streamlining admission requirements and offering treatment quickly and appropriately in separate crisis-intervention centers or in special emergency units within larger services. It has brought about the development of a number of imaginative and effective interdisciplinary programs, as described in Chapter 1.

On the other hand, this separation of crisis treatment from other forms of services has, in some cases, brought about an artificial distinction between treatment offered during periods of high anxiety and pressure and treatment given at other periods. If crisis intervention is to become a viable practice modality, it must be considered part of the practice repertoire of *all* social workers and other helping professionals and must be offered differentially and as the treatment of choice under specific conditions where it promises the maximal return. It should be usable in long-term cases of chronic and recurrent crises as well as in short-term, limited-problem situations. The key would seem to lie in the professional's ability to engage the client immediately, to carry out a quick differential diagnosis, and to focus on rapid resolution of the crisis aspects of the disturbed predicament in order to effect substantial progress in the total case situation.

Uncovered Issues

Several topics originally envisaged as part of this book have been omitted for lack of space. Current research efforts have been referred to only fleetingly. Actually, recent research programs in the crisis area appear to be lagging somewhat, partly because of methodological problems of measuring outcome and attributing causality and partly because support funds have decreased. Some research is being carried out within the overall framework of evaluation of treatment services in psychiatric settings to measure the relative efficacy of crisis intervention as opposed to other forms of treatment[2] and to measure the effectiveness of services offered.[3]

One promising area for study which is just beginning to be tapped is the follow-up on cases seen previously for crisis intervention, to check on the durability of treatment advances and of referrals to other sources. McGee notes that clinic clients appreciated the follow-up procedure in the area he studied, provided that the calls were made within two months after the case was closed.[4]

Another important issue not discussed here is the relationship between professional and nonprofessional workers in crisis services. This area was omitted because our discussion was specifically addressed to professionals and, especially, to graduate social workers; nonetheless, problems of intrastaff communication and role relationships must be dealt with if crisis services are to be run successfully. In addition, the use of volunteers, whether as an integral part of crisis programs or as adjuncts out in the community, and the relationship between hotline and referral sources and crisis-intervention services are recurrent issues in considering the establishment and operation of such programs.

The question of ethical standards has rarely been raised in discussing crisis treatment. Motto and his associates found that a fundamental consideration, often not discussed sufficiently, is that of confidentiality.[5] Although this is a basic question in all helping services, it becomes crucial when a client calls at a point of high vulnerability such as a suicide attempt. To what extent, for example, does the worker guard the client's right to privacy when his life is at stake? To what degree does he respect the client's right to autonomy and self-determination when it conflicts with the need to make a referral to an appropriate agency—or when a child's well-being is involved? In the heat of the crisis, when it seems important for several agencies to work together to achieve maximal impact, what efforts are made to guard privileged information and to obtain the necessary releases to impart it?

When value systems clash—as in the question whether to inform a terminally ill patient or his family of his diagnosis, or whether to give the police information on drug abuse by a client—to what extent do we yield to outside pressure and to what extent do our own professional ethics take precedence? These points are currently being raised and debated among crisis workers, not as abstract issues but as matters of daily practice. Their resolution is often based on the weighing of viable alternatives and probable consequences for both the worker and the client.

Training for Crisis Work

Special training for crisis intervention is a pivotal question which often determines the extent to which it becomes part of a worker's practice armamentarium. If crisis intervention is to be regarded as an integral tool in practice, at what level and in what context should it be taught? An examination of current programs of study at a number of graduate schools of social work, reveals that it is rarely taught as a separate treatment methodology. Its inclusion as a teaching unit within basic treatment courses is more prevalent but still relatively infrequent.

When this was discussed with methods instructors, many replied that crisis intervention was usually left to be covered in field instruction by supervisors, more or less on an ad hoc basis, when a crisis would crop up in an ongoing case.

For practitioners in the field, crisis intervention has often been the subject of in-service training and staff-development programs within agencies[6] or of special short-term workshops given by an outside "expert" under the auspices of a university or professional association.

Each of these approaches presents some drawbacks. In attempting to teach crisis treatment as part of a practice curriculum, many instructors find that students are unable to function at a pace rapid and advanced enough to make the autonomous decisions necessary to help clients in severe distress. In fieldwork settings, many agencies and supervisors seem reluctant to trust clients in acute crises to the care of students who lack practice skills and whose hours of availability to the client are limited.[7] And staff-development programs frequently follow the latest "fashion"; in recent years, crisis intervention as a topic of interest seems to have been superseded by more novel treatment approaches.

Nevertheless, social workers and other professionals are operating in settings in which crisis situations arise. Much of current practice appears to have been learned informally through practice wisdom gleaned over the years, the interchange of ideas, observations, and experiences among staff members, and independent examination of the professional literature. Only recently have practice manuals devoted to this area begun to appear.[8]

With treatment in crisis situations a significant part of practice in the helping professions, its inclusion as an integral part of social work practice curricula would seem to be strongly indicated.

Notes

1. See Naomi Golan, "Crisis Theory," in F. J. Turner, ed., *Social Work Treatment* (New York: Free Press, 1974), pp. 441–443, for a discussion of clients considered suitable for crisis intervention.

2. Ronald Maris and Huell E. Connor, "Do Crisis Services Work? A Follow-up of a Psychiatric Outpatient Sample," *Journal of Health and Social Behavior* 14 (December 1973): 311–322.

3. Constance A. Katzenelson, "The Effectiveness of Crisis Therapy," Ph.D. Dissertation, Dept. of Psychiatry, University of Chicago, 1971.

4. Richard K. McGee, *Crisis Intervention in the Community* (Baltimore: University Park Press, 1974), p. 206

5. Jerome A. Motto, Richard M. Brooks, Charlotte P. Ross, and Nancy H. Allen, *Standards for Suicide Prevention and Crisis Centers,* American Association of Suicidology (New York: Behavioral Publications, 1974), Chap. 7, "Ethical Standards," pp. 66–75.

6. See Gertrude Einstein, ed., *Learning to Apply New Concepts to Casework Practice* (New York: FSAA, 1968), pp. 9–33, for a typical staff development seminar.

7. In my own experience in offering a year-long seminar on treatment in crisis situations to senior students, I was pleasantly surprised at their maturity and responsibility in working with clients in seriously disturbed crisis states. They generally reported that their field instructors tended to have more misgivings than they did over their active involvement.

8. See notes 1–5 following the Introduction to Part 2 of this book.

Bibliography

ABARBANEL, GAIL. "Helping Victims of Rape." *Social Work,* 21 (November 1976): 478–482.

ADAMS, JOHN E., and ERICH LINDEMANN. "Coping with Long-Term Disability." In G. V. Coehlo, D. A. Hamburg, and J. E. Adams, eds., *Coping and Adaptation,* pp. 127–138. New York: Basic Books, 1974.

AGUILERA, DONNA C., JANICE M. MESSICK, and MARLENE S. FARRELL. *Crisis Intervention: Theory and Methodology.* St. Louis: C. V. Mosby, 1970.

ALEXANDER, FRANZ. *Psychoanalysis and Psychotherapy.* New York: W. W. Norton, 1956.

_____. "Psychoanalytic Contributions to Short-Term Psychotherapy." In Lewis R. Woldberg, ed., *Short-Term Psychotherapy,* pp. 53–55. New York: Grune and Stratton, 1965.

_____. "Sandor Rado: the Adaptational Theory." In F. Alexander, S. Eisenstein, and M. Grotjahn, eds., *Psychoanalytic Pioneers,* pp. 240–248. New York: Basic Books, 1966.

AMIR, MENACHEM. *Patterns of Forcible Rape.* Urbana, Ill.: University of Illinois Press, 1971.

AUSTIN, LUCILLE N. "Trends in Differential Treatment in Social Casework." *Journal of Social Casework,* June 1948. Reprinted in

C. Casius, ed., *Principles and Techniques in Social Casework,* pp. 324–338. New York: FSAA, 1950.

BABCOCK, CHARLOTTE G. "Inner Stress in Illness and Disability." In H. J. Parad and R. R. Miller, eds., *Ego-Oriented Casework,* pp. 45–64. New York: FSAA, 1963.

BAKER, G. W., and D. W. CHAPMAN, eds. *Man and Society in Disaster.* New York: Basic Books, 1962.

BALDWIN, KATHARINE A. "Crisis-Focused Casework in a Child Guidance Clinic." *Social Casework* 49 (January 1968): 28–34.

BARTEN, HARVY H., and SYBIL S. BARTEN. "New Perspectives on Child Mental Health." In Barten and Barten, eds., *Children and Their Parents in Brief Therapy.* New York: Behavioral Publications, 1973.

BARTLETT, HARRIETT M. *The Common Base of Social Work Practice.* New York: NASW, 1970.

BARTON, ALLEN. *Communities in Disaster.* New York: Doubleday, 1969.

BECK, DOROTHY F. *Patterns in Use of Family Agency Service.* New York: FSAA, 1962.

BELL, ROBERT R. *Marriage and Family Interaction.* Homewood, Ill.: Dorsey Press, 1971.

BENDER, BARBARA. "Management of Acute Hospitalization Anxiety." *Social Casework* 57 (January 1976): 19–26.

BENEDEK, THERESE. "Parenthood as a Developmental Phase." *Journal of the American Psychoanalytic Association* 7 (1959): 389–417.

BERGMAN, ANNE. "Emergency Room: A Role for Social Workers." *Health and Social Work* 1 (February 1976): 32–44.

BERNE, ERIC. *Games People Play.* New York: Grove Press, 1964.

BIRNBAUM, FREDA, JENNIFER COPLON, and IRA SCHARFF. "Crisis Intervention after a Natural Disaster." *Social Casework* 54 (November 1973): 545–551.

BITTERMANN, CATHERINE M. "Serving Applicants When There Is a Waiting List." *Social Casework* 39 (June 1958): 356–360.

BLAUFARB, HERBERT and JULES LEVINE. "Crisis Intervention in an Earthquake." *Social Work* 17 (July 1972): 16–19.

BLOOM, BERNARD L. "Definitional Aspects of the Crisis Concept." *Journal of Consulting Psychology* 27, no. 6 (1963). Reprinted in

H. J. Parad, ed., *Crisis Intervention: Selected Readings,* pp. 303–311. New York: FSAA, 1965.

BOHANNAN, PAUL, ed. *Divorce and After.* Garden City, N.Y.: Anchor Books, 1971.

BOWLBY, JOHN. "Grief and Mourning in Infancy and Early Childhood." *Psychoanalytic Study of the Child* vol. 15, pp. 9–52. New York: International Universities Press, 1960.

BRECHENSER, DONN M. "Brief Psychotherapy Using Transactional Analysis." *Social Casework* 53 (March 1972): 173–176.

BRODLAND, GENE A., and N. J. C. ANDREASEN. "Adjustment Problems of the Family of the Burn Patient." *Social Casework* 55 (January 1974): 13–18.

BROWN, ELLIOT C. JR. "Casework with Patients Undergoing Cardiac Surgery." *Social Casework* 52 (December 1971): 611–617.

BRUNER, JEROME. *Studies in Cognitive Growth.* New York: John Wiley and Sons, 1966.

BURGESS, ANN W., and LYNDA L. HOLMSTROM. "Rape Trauma Syndrome." *American Journal of Psychiatry* 131 (1974): 981–986. Reprinted in F. J. Turner, ed., *Differential Diagnosis and Treatment in Social Work,* 2nd ed., pp. 692–702. New York: Free Press, 1976.

BURGESS, ERNEST W. "Family Living in the Later Decades." In Marvin B. Sussman, ed., *Sourcebook on Marriage and the Family,* 2nd ed., pp. 425–431. Boston: Houghton Mifflin, 1963.

BURNETT, BRUCE B., JOHN J. CARR, JOHN SINAPI, and ROY TAYLOR. "Police and Social Workers in a Community Outreach Program." *Social Casework* 57 (January 1976): 41–49.

CAIN, LILLIAN P. "Casework with Kidney Transplant Patients." *Social Work* 18 (July 1973): 76–83.

CALDWELL, J. M. "Military Psychiatry," in A. M. Freedman, H. I. Kaplan, and H. S. Kaplan, eds., *Comprehensive Textbook of Psychiatry.* Baltimore: William and Wilkins, 1967.

CAPLAN, GERALD. "A Public Health Approach to Child Psychiatry." *Mental Health* 35 (1951): 235–249.

——. "The Role of the Social Worker in Preventive Psychiatry for Mothers and Children." In *Concepts of Mental Health Consultation.* Washington, D.C.: U.S. Dept. of Health, Education, and Welfare, 1958.

————, ed. *Prevention of Mental Disorders in Children*. New York: Basic Books, 1961.

————. *Principles of Preventive Psychiatry*. New York: Basic Books, 1964.

————. *Support Systems and Community Mental Health*. New York: Behavioral Publications, 1974.

————, EDWARD A. MASON, and DAVID M. KAPLAN. "Four Studies of Crisis in Parents of Prematures." *Community Mental Health Journal* 2, no. 2 (Summer 1965).

CARTER, ROBERT D., and RICHARD B. STUART. "Behavior Modification Theory and Practice: A Reply." *Social Work* 15 (January 1970): 37–50.

CHILMAN, CATHERINE S. *Growing Up Poor*. Washington, D.C.: U.S. Dept. of Health, Education, and Welfare, 1966.

CHRISTOPHERSON, LOIS K. "Cardiac Transplant: Preparation for Dying or for Living." *Health and Social Work* 1 (February 1976): 58–72.

CLARK, ELEANOR. "Round the Clock Emergency Psychiatric Services." *Social Work Practice, 1963*. New York: Columbia University Press, 1963. Reprinted in Parad, 1965, pp.261–273.

CODDINGTON, R. DEAN. "The Significance of Life Events as Etiological Factors in the Diseases of Children." I: "A Survey of Professional Workers," 7–18. II: "A Study of a Normal Population," 205–213. *Journal of Psychosomatic Research* 16 (1972).

COELHO, GEORGE V., DAVID A. HAMBURG, and JOHN E. ADAMS, eds. *Coping and Adaptation*. New York: Basic Books, 1974.

COHEN, NATHAN E. *Social Work in the American Tradition*. New York: Holt, Rinehart, and Winston, 1958.

COLLINS, ALICE H., and DIANE L. PANCOAST. *Natural Helping Networks*. Washington, D.C.: NASW, 1976.

CUMMING, JOHN and ELAINE. *Ego and Milieu*. New York: Atherton Press, 1966.

DARBONNE, ALLEN. "Crisis: A Review of Theory, Practice, and Research." *International Journal of Psychiatry* 6 (November 1968): 371–379.

DATAN, NANCY, and LEON H. GINSBERG, eds. *Life-Span Developmental Psychology: Normative Life Crises*. New York: Academic Press, 1975.

DAVIS, FRED. *Passage Through Crisis: Polio Victims and Their Families.* New York: Bobbs-Merrill, 1963.

DAVIS, INGER P. "Advice Giving in Parent Counseling." *Social Casework* 56 (June 1975): 343–347.

DAWLEY, ALMENA. "Professional Skills Requisite to a Good Intake Service." *Proceedings of the National Council of Social Welfare, 1937,* pp. 256–265. Chicago: University of Chicago Press, 1937.

DOHRENWEND, BARBARA S., and BRUCE P. DOHRENWEND. *Stressful Life Events: Their Nature and Effects.* New York: Wiley-Interscience, 1974.

DRABEK, THOMAS E., and KEITH E. BIGGS. "Families in Disaster: Reactions and Relations." *Journal of Marriage and the Family* 30 (August 1968): 403–451.

DRISCOLL, CHANCELLOR B., and A. HAROLD LUBIN. "Conferences with Parents of Children with Cystic Fibrosis." *Social Casework* 53 (March 1972): 140–146.

DUBLIN, LOUIS I. *Suicide: A Sociological and Statistical Study.* New York: Ronald Press, 1963.

DUCKWORTH, GRACE L. "A Project in Crisis Intervention." *Social Casework* 48 (April 1967): 227–231.

DUVALL, EVELYN M. *Family Development,* 2nd ed. Philadelphia: Lippincott, 1962.

DYER, EVERETT. "Parenthood as a Crisis: A Restudy." *Marriage and Family Living* 25, no. 2 (1963). Reprinted in Parad, 1965, pp. 312–323.

EINSTEIN, GERTRUDE, ed. *Learning to Apply New Concepts to Casework Practice.* New York: FSAA, 1968.

ENGELMANN, MARY W. "The Diabetic Client." *The Social Worker* 35 (February 1967). Reprinted in Turner, 1976, 430–433.

ERIKSON, ERIK H. *Identity and the Life Cycle.* Psychological Issues vol. 1, 1, pp. 116–121. New York: International Universities Press, 1959.

——. *Identity, Youth and Crisis.* New York: W. W. Norton, 1968.

ESCALONA, SIBYLLE K. *The Roots of Individuality.* Chicago: Aldine, 1968.

EWALT, PATRICIA L. "The Crisis Treatment Approach in a Child Guidance Clinic." *Social Casework* 54 (July 1973): 406–411.

————. "An Examination of Advice Giving as a Therapeutic Intervention." Paper presented at the Annual Meeting of the American Association of Psychiatric Services for Children, November 1975. Mimeo.

————. "The Case for Immediate Brief Intervention." *Social Work* 21 (January 1976): 63–65.

EZRA, JULIA. "Casework in a Coronary Care Unit." *Social Casework* 50 (May 1969): 276–281.

FAMILY SERVICE ASSOCIATION. *Scope and Method of Family Service.* New York: FSAA, 1953.

FANTL, BERTA. "Preventive Intervention." *Social Work* 7 (July 1962): 41–48.

FARBER, BERNARD. "Some Effects of a Retarded Child on the Mother." In Sussman, 1963, pp. 324–333.

FARBEROW, NORMAN L., and EDWIN L. SHNEIDMAN. *The Cry for Help.* New York: McGraw-Hill, 1961.

FELD, ALLEN. "Reflections on the Agnes Flood." *Social Work* 18 (September 1973): 46–51.

FELL, ELISE. "An Experiment in Short-Term Treatment in a Child Guidance Clinic." *Journal of the Jewish Communal Service* 36 (Winter 1959): 144–149.

FISCHER, JOEL, and HARVEY L. GOCHROS. *Planned Behavioral Change: Behavior Modification in Social Work.* New York: Free Press, 1975.

FISHER, SHEILA A. *Suicide and Crisis Intervention: Survey and Guide to Services.* New York: Springer, 1973.

FOECKLER, MERLE M. "Dynamics of Coping with a Medical Crisis." *Public Welfare* 23 (January 1965): 41–46.

FOX, SANDRA SUTHERLAND, and DONALD J. SCHERL. "Crisis Intervention with Victims of Rape." *Social Work* 17 (January 1972): 37–42.

FRIED, BARBARA. *The Middle-Age Crisis,* rev. ed. New York: Harper and Row, 1976.

FRITZ, CHARLES E., and J. H. MATHEWSON. *Convergence Behavior in Disasters: A Problem in Social Control.* Disaster Study No. 9, Commission on Disaster Studies. Washington, D.C.: National Academy of Sciences–National Research Council, 1957.

_____. "Disasters." In Robert K. Merton and Robert A. Nisbet, eds. *Contemporary Social Problems,* pp. 651–669. New York: Harcourt, Brace, and World, 1961.

GARRISON, JOHN. "Network Techniques: Case Studies in the Screening-Linking-Planning Conference Method." *Family Process* 13 (September 1974): 337–353.

GARVIN, CHARLES D., WILLIAM REID, and LAURA EPSTEIN. "A Task-Centered Approach." In Robert W. Roberts and Helen Northen, eds., *Theories of Social Work with Groups,* pp. 239–267. New York: Columbia University Press, 1976.

GELB, L. A., and M. ULLMAN. "Instant Psychotherapy Offered at an Outpatient Psychiatric Clinic." *Frontiers of Hospital Psychiatry* 4 (August 1967).

GELFAND, BERNARD. "Emerging Trends in Social Treatment." *Social Casework* 53 (March 1972): 156–162.

GEORGE, ALEXANDER L. "Adaptation to Stress in Political Decision Making: the Individual, Small Group, and Organizational Contexts," in Coelho, Hamburg, and Adams, 1974, pp. 176–245.

GETZ, WILLIAM, ALLEN E. WEISEN, STAN SUE, and AMY AYERS. *Fundamentals of Crisis Counseling.* Lexington, Mass.: D. C. Heath, 1974.

GILL, MERTON M. *The Collected Papers of David Rapaport.* New York: Basic Books, 1967.

GLICK, IRA O., ROBERT S. WEISS, and C. MURRAY PARKES. *The First Year of Bereavement.* New York: John Wiley and Sons, 1974.

GOBLE, FRANK G. *The Third Force: The Psychology of Abraham Maslow.* New York: Grossman, 1970.

GOLAN, NAOMI. "Federal Participation in Mental Health Programs: From Mann to Mental Health Centers." School of Social Service Administration, University of Chicago, 1965. Unpublished paper.

_____. "When Is a Client in Crisis?" *Social Casework* 50 (July 1969): 389–394.

_____. "Short-Term Crisis Intervention: An Approach to Serving Children and Their Families." *Child Welfare* 50 (February 1971): 101–107.

_____. "Social Work Intervention in Medical Crises." *Hospital and Community Psychiatry* 23 (February 1972): 41–45.

————. "Crisis Theory." In F. J. Turner, ed., *Social Work Treatment: Interlocking Theoretical Approaches,* pp. 420–456. New York: Free Press, 1974.

————. "Wife to Widow to Woman." *Social Work* 20 (September 1975): 369–374.

————. "A Field Study of the Task-Centered Model of Short-Term Treatment: Final Research Report." School of Social Work, University of Haifa, April 1976. Mimeo.

————. "Work with Young Adults in Israel," in William J. Reid and Laura Epstein, eds., *Task-Centered Practice,* pp. 270–284. New York: Columbia University Press, 1977.

————, and RUTH GRUSCHKA. "Integrating the New Immigrant: A Model for Social Work Practice in Transitional States." *Social Work* 16 (April 1971): 82–87.

————, and SHLOMO SHARLIN. "Using Natural Helping Systems to Intervene." Paper presented at the American Orthopsychiatric Association Annual Meeting, Atlanta, Ga., March 1976. Mimeo.

————, and BATYA VASHITZ. "Social Services in a War Emergency. *Social Service Review* 48 (September 1974): 422–427.

GOLDBERG, STANLEY B. "Family Tasks and Reactions in the Crisis of Death." *Social Casework* 54 (July 1973): 398–405.

GOLDSTEIN, EDA G. "Social Casework and the Dying Person." *Social Casework* 54 (December 1973): 601–608. Reprinted in Turner, 1976, pp. 156–166.

GOODE, WILLIAM J. *After Divorce.* Glencoe, Ill.: Free Press, 1956.

GRINKER, ROY R., and JOHN P. SPIEGEL. *Men Under Stress.* New York: Blackeston, 1945.

GROLLMAN, E. D., ed. *Explaining Divorce to Children.* Boston: Beacon Press, 1969.

GROSSER, GEORGE H., HENRY WECHSLER, and MILTON GREENBLATT, eds. *The Threat of Impending Disasters.* Cambridge, Mass.: M.I.T. Press, 1964.

GROSSMAN, LEONA. "Train Crash: Social Work and Disaster Services." *Social Work* 18 (September 1973): 38–44.

GRUMET, GERALD W., and DAVID L. TRACHTMAN. "Psychiatric Social Worker in the Emergency Department." *Health and Social Work* 1 (August 1976): 114–131.

GUNDERSON, E. K., and RICHARD H. RAHE. *Life Stress and Illness.* Springfield, Ill.: Charles C. Thomas, 1974.

GURIN, GERALD, JOSEPH VEROFF, and SHEILA FELD. *Americans View Their Mental Health.* New York: Basic Books, 1960.

HALLETT, KATHRYN. *A Guide for Single Parents: Transactional Analysis for People in Crisis.* Millbrae, Cal.: Celestial Arts, 1974.

HAMILTON, GORDON. *Theory and Practice of Social Work,* 2nd ed. New York: Columbia University Press, 1951.

HARDGROVE, GRACE. "An Interagency Service Network to Meet Needs of Rape Victims." *Social Casework* 57 (April 1976): 245–253.

HARRIS, F. G., and R. W. LITTLE. "Military Organizations and Social Psychiatry," in *Symposium on Preventive and Social Psychiatry,* pp. 173–184. Washington, D.C.: Walter Reed Army Institute of Research, 1957.

HARTMANN, HEINZ. *Ego Psychology and the Problem of Adaptation.* New York: International Universities Press, 1958.

HAUXWELL, JULIA. "A Social Worker's View of an Emergency Clinic—Its Workers and Users." *British Journal of Social Work* 1 (Autumn 1971): 305–314.

HENDERSON, HOWARD E. "Helping Families in Crisis: Police and Social Work Intervention." *Social Work* 21 (July 1976): 314–315.

HENDRICK, IVES. "Discussion of the Instinct to Master." *Psychoanalytic Quarterly* 12 (1943): 561–565.

HICKEY, KATHLEEN M. "Impact of Kidney Disease on Patient, Family, and Society." *Social Casework* 53 (July 1972): 391–398.

HILGARD, E., and G. BOWER, *Theories of Learning,* 4th ed. New York: Appleton-Century-Crofts, 1974.

HILL, REUBEN. "Generic Features of Families Under Stress." *Social Casework* 39 (February–March 1958): 139–150. Reprinted in Parad, 1965, pp. 32–52.

————— and DONALD A. HANSEN. "Families in Disaster." In Baker and Chapman, 1962, pp. 185–221.

HIRSCH, JOSEPHINE S., JACQUELYNNE GAILEY, and ELEANOR SCHMERL. "A Child Welfare Agency's Program of Service to Children in Their Own Homes." *Child Welfare* 55 (March 1976): 193–204.

HOBBS, DANIEL F. "Parenthood as a Crisis: A Third Study." *Journal of Marriage and the Family* 27 (August 1965): 367-372.

HOFFMAN, DAVID L., and MARY L. REMMEL. "Uncovering the Precipitant in Crisis Intervention." *Social Casework* 56 (May 1975): 259-267.

HOLLIS, FLORENCE. *Casework: A Psychosocial Therapy,* 1st ed. New York: Random House, 1964. 2nd ed., 1972.

HOLMES, THOMAS H., and MINORU MASUDA. "Life Changes and Illness Susceptibility." In Dohrenwend and Dohrenwend, 1974, pp. 45-72.

———, and RICHARD H. RAHE. "The Social Readjustment Rating Scale." *Journal of Psychosomatic Research* 11 (1967): 213-218.

HOOKER, CAROL E. "Learned Helplessness." *Social Work* 21 (May 1976): 194-198.

HOROS, CAROL V. *Rape.* New Canaan, Conn.: Tobey Publications, 1974.

ICHIKAWA, ALICE. "Observations of College Students in Acute Distress." *Student Medicine* 10, no. 2 (1961). Reprinted in Parad, 1965, pp. 167-173.

IRELAN, LOLA M., ed. *Low-Income Life Styles.* Washington, D.C.: U.S. Dept. of Health, Education, and Welfare, 1966.

JACOBSON, GERALD F. "Crisis Theory and Treatment Strategy: Some Sociocultural and Psychodynamic Considerations." *Journal of Nervous and Mental Diseases* 141 (August 1965): 209-218.

———. "Programs and Techniques of Crisis Intervention." In Silvano Arieti, ed., *American Handbook of Psychiatry,* 2nd ed. New York: Basic Books, 1974, pp. 810-825.

———, MARTIN STRICKLER, and WILBUR E. MORLEY. "Generic and Individual Approaches to Crisis Intervention." *American Journal of Public Health* 58 (February 1968): 338-343.

———, D. M. WILNER, W. E. MORLEY, S. SCHNEIDER, M. STRICKLER, and G. J. SOMMER. "The Scope and Practice of an Early Access Brief Treatment Psychiatric Center." *American Journal of Psychiatry* 121 (June 1965): 1176-1182.

JACOBSON, SYLVIA R. "Individual and Group Responses to Confinement in a Skyjacked Plane." *American Journal of Orthopsychiatry* 43 (April 1973): 459-469.

JANIS, IRVING L. *Psychological Stress*. New York: John Wiley and Sons, 1958.

————. "Psychological Effects of Warnings." In Baker and Chapman, 1962, pp. 55–92.

————. *Stress and Frustration*. New York: Harcourt Brace Jovanovich, 1969.

————. "Vigilance and Decision Making in Personal Crises." In Coelho, Hamburg, and Adams, 1974, pp. 139–175.

JOINT COMMISSION ON MENTAL ILLNESS and HEALTH. *Action for Mental Health: Final Report*. New York: John Wiley and Sons, 1961.

JOLESCH, MIRIAM. "Strengthening Intake Practice Through Group Discussion." *Social Casework* 40 (November 1959): 504–510.

KAFRISSEN, STEVEN, EDWARD S. HEFFRON, and JACK ZUSMAN. "Mental Health Problems in Environmental Disaster." In H. L. P. Resnik and Harvey L. Ruben, eds., *Emergency Psychiatric Care*, pp. 159–170. Bowie, Md.: Charles Press, 1975.

KALIS, BETTY L., M. R. HARRIS, A. R. PRESTWOOD, and E. H. FREEMAN. "Precipitating Stress as a Focus in Psychotherapy." *Archives of General Psychiatry* 5 (September 1961): 219–226.

KAMEN, CHARLES. "Crisis, Stress and Social Integration: The Case of Israel and the Six-Day War." Ph.D. Dissertation, Dept. of Sociology, University of Chicago, 1971.

KAPLAN, DAVID M. "A Concept of Acute Situational Disorders." *Social Work* 7 (April 1962): 15–23.

————, AARON SMITH, ROSE GROBSTEIN, and STANLEY E. FISCHMAN. "Family Mediation of Stress." *Social Work* 18 (July 1973): 60–69.

KARDINER, ABRAHAM. *The Individual and His Society*. New York: Columbia University Press, 1939.

KATZ, SANFORD N., ed. *Creativity in Social Work: Selected Writings of Lydia Rapoport*. Philadelphia: Temple University Press, 1975.

KATZENELSON, CONSTANCE A. "The Effectiveness of Crisis Therapy." Ph.D. Dissertation, Dept. of Psychiatry, University of Chicago, 1971.

KENKEL, WILLIAM F. *The Family in Perspective,* 2nd ed. New York: Appleton-Century-Crofts, 1966.

KLEIN, DONALD C., and ERICH LINDEMANN. "Preventive Intervention in Individual and Family Crisis Situations." In Caplan, 1961, pp. 283-306.

KLEIN, DONALD C., and ANN ROSS. "Kindergarten Entry: A Study in Role Transition." In M. Krugman, ed., *Orthopsychiatry and the School.* New York: American Orthopsychiatric Association, 1958. Reprinted in Parad, 1965, pp. 140-148.

KLIMAN, ANN S. "The Corning Flood Project: Psychological First Aid Following a Natural Disaster." In Howard J. Parad, H. L. P. Resnik, and Libbie G. Parad, eds., *Emergency and Disaster Management: A Mental Health Sourcebook,* pp. 309-323. Bowie, Md.: Charles Press, 1976.

KNAPP, VRINDA S., and HOWARD HANSEN. "Helping the Parents of Children with Leukemia." *Social Work* 18 (July 1973): 70-75.

KORNER, I. N. "Crisis Reduction and the Psychological Consultant." In Gerald A. Specter and William L. Claiborn, eds., *Crisis Intervention,* pp. 30-45. New York: Behavioral Publications, 1973.

KRIDER, JAMES. "A New Program and Its Impact on a Small Agency." *Social Casework* 50 (November 1969): 508-512.

KÜBLER-ROSS, ELISABETH. *On Death and Dying.* New York: Macmillan, 1969.

LAMAR, HELEN. "The Intake Process in a Growing Community." *Social Casework* 34, no. 4 (April 1953). Reprinted in *The Intake Process,* pp. 8-15. New York: FSAA.

LAMBERT, GLADYS. "Patients with Progressive Neurological Diseases." *Social Casework* 55 (March 1974): 154-159.

LAMPE, HELEN. "Diagnostic Considerations in Casework with Aged Clients." *Social Casework* 42 (May-June): 1971; 241-244.

LANG, JUDITH. "Planned Short-Term Treatment in a Family Agency." *Social Casework* 55 (June 1974): 369-374.

LANGSLEY, DONALD, and DAVID KAPLAN. *Treatment of Families in Crisis.* New York: Grune and Stratton, 1968.

LAZARUS, RICHARD S. *Psychological Stress and the Coping Process.* New York: McGraw-Hill, 1966.

————, JAMES R. AVERILL, and EDWARD M. OPTON, JR. "The Psychology of Coping: Issues of Research and Assessment." In Coelho, Hamburg, and Adams, 1974, pp. 249–315.

LEBOW, GRACE H. "Facilitating Adaptation in Anticipatory Mourning." *Social Casework* 57 (July 1976): 456–465.

LEICHTER, HOPE J., and WILLIAM E. MITCHELL. *Kinship and Casework*. New York: Russell Sage Foundation, 1967.

LEMASTERS, E. E. "Parenthood as Crisis." *Marriage and Family Living* 19, no. 4 (1957). Reprinted in Parad, 1965, pp. 111–117.

LEOPOLD, ROBERT L. "Crisis Intervention: Some Notes on Practice and Theory." In Gertrude Einstein, ed., *Learning to Apply New Concepts to Casework Practice,* pp. 9–49. New York: FSAA, 1968.

LEVINE, RACHEL A. "A Short Story on the Long Waiting List." *Social Work* 8 (January 1963): 20–22.

LEWIN, KURT. *Field Theory in Social Sciences*. New York: Harper, 1951.

LIEB, JULIAN, IAN L. LIPSITCH, and ANDREW E. SLABY. *The Crisis Team*. Hagerstown, Md.: Harper and Row, 1973.

LIEBERMAN, MORTON A. "Adaptive Processes in Late Life." In Datan and Ginsberg, 1975, pp. 139–159.

LINDEMANN, ERICH. "Symptomatology and Management of Acute Grief." *American Journal of Psychiatry* 101, no. 2, (September 1944). Reprinted in Parad, 1965, pp. 7–21.

LION, AVIVA, and NAOMI GOLAN. "Crisis-Oriented Brief Treatment: A Side Effect of the War in Israel." *Journal of Jewish Communal Service* 40 (Fall 1968): 97–101.

LIPNER, JOAN, and ETTA SHERMAN. "Hip Fractures in the Elderly—a Psychodynamic Approach." *Social Casework* 56 (February 1975): 97–103.

LOWENTHAL, MARJORIE FISKE, MAJDA THURNHER, DAVID CHIRIBOGA, and Associates. *Four Stages of Life*. San Francisco: Jossey-Bass, 1975.

LOWRY, FERN. "The Caseworker in Short-Contact Services." *Social Work* 2 (January 1957).

LUCAS, REX A. *Men in Crisis: A Study of a Mine Disaster*. New York: Basic Books, 1969.

LUKTON, ROSEMARY C. "Crisis Theory: Review and Critique." *Social Service Review* 48 (September 1974): 384–402.

McCOLLUM, AUDREY T., and A. HERBERT SCHWARTZ. "Social Work and the Mourning Parent." *Social Work* 17 (January 1972): 25–36.

McCUBBIN, HAMILTON I., BARBARA B. DAHL, PHILIP J. METRES, JR., EDNA J. HUNTER, and JOHN A. PLAG. *Family Separation and Reunion: Families of Prisoners of War and Servicemen Missing in Action.* San Diego, Cal.: Center for Prisoners of War Studies, Naval Health Research Center, 1974.

McGEE, RICHARD K. *Crisis Intervention in the Community.* Baltimore: University Park Press, 1974.

————, and EDWARD HEFFRON. "The Role of Crisis Intervention Services in Disaster Recovery." In Parad, Resnik, and Parad, 1976, pp. 309–323.

MACNAMARA, MARGARET. "The Family in Stress: Social Work Before and After Renal Homotransplantation." *Social Work* 14 (October 1969): 89–97.

MALAN, DAVID H. *The Frontier of Brief Psychotherapy.* New York: Plenum, 1977.

MALUCCIO, ANTHONY N. "Action as a Tool in Casework Practice." *Social Casework* 55 (January 1974): 30–35.

MANTELL, JOANNE E., ESTHER S. ALEXANDER, and MARK ALLEN KLEIMAN. "Social Work and Self-Help Groups." *Health and Social Work* 1 (February 1976): 86–100.

MARCUS, GRACE F. "Helping the Client to Use His Capacities and Resources." *Proceedings of the National Conference of Social Welfare, 1948,* pp. 251–259. New York: Columbia University Press, 1948.

MARIS, RONALD , and HUELL E. CONNOR. "Do Crisis Services Work? A Follow-up of a Psychiatric Outpatient Sample." *Journal of Health and Social Behavior* 14 (December 1973): 311–322.

MECHANIC, DAVID. *Mental Health and Social Policy.* Englewood Cliffs, N. J.: Prentice-Hall, 1969.

————. "Social Structure and Personal Adaptation: Some Neglected Dimensions," In Coelho, Hamburg, and Adams, 1974, pp. 32–44.

MEDEA, ANDREA, and KATHLEEN THOMPSON. *Against Rape.* New York: Farrar, Straus, and Giroux, 1974.

MERBAUM, MICHAEL, and ALBERT HEFEZ. "Some Personality Characteristics of Soldiers Exposed to Extreme War Stress." *Journal of Consulting and Clinical Psychology* 44 (1): 1–6.

MEYER, CAROL H. *Social Work Practice*, 2nd ed. New York: Free Press, 1976.

MEYER, CAROL H., ed. *Preventive Intervention in Social Work.* Washington, D.C.: NASW, 1974.

MILLER, JAMES G. "A Theoretical Review of Individual and Group Psychological Reactions to Stress." In Grosser, Wechsler, and Greenblatt, 1964, pp. 11–33.

MILLER, SHEROD, ELAM NUNALLY, and DANIEL B. WACKMAN. "A Communication Training Program for Couples." Social Casework 57 (January 1976): 9–18.

MILLER, WARREN B. "Psychiatry and Physical Illness: The Psychosomatic Interface." In C. P. Rosenbaum and John E. Beebe III, eds., *Psychiatric Treatment: Crisis/Clinic/Consultation,* pp. 475–495. New York: McGraw-Hill, 1975.

MITTELMANN, BELA. "Motility in Infants, Children, and Adults." *Psychoanalytic Study of the Child,* 9. New York: International University Press, 1954.

MOOS, RUDOLF H., ed. *Coping with Physical Illness.* New York: Plenum Medical Book Co., 1977.

MORLEY, WILBUR E. "Treatment of the Patient in Crisis." *Western Medicine* 3 (March 1965): 1–10.

———. "Theory of Crisis Intervention." *Pastoral Psychology,* April 1970, pp. 1–6.

———, and VIVIAN B. BROWN. "The Crisis Intervention Group: A Natural Mating or a Marriage of Convenience?" *Psychotherapy: Theory, Research, and Practice* 6 (Winter 1969): 30–36.

MORRIS, BETTY. "Crisis Intervention in a Public Welfare Agency." *Social Casework* 49 (December 1968): 612–617.

MOTTO, JEROME A., RICHARD M. BROOKS, CHARLOTTE P. ROSS, and NANCY H. ALLEN. *Standards for Suicide Prevention and Crisis Centers.* New York: Behavioral Publications, 1974.

MURPHY, LOIS B. "Preventive Implications in the Preschool Years." In Caplan, 1961, pp. 218–248.

————, and ALICE E. MORIARTY. *Vulnerability, Coping, and Growth.* New Haven: Yale University Press, 1976.

National Mental Health Programs and the States. Public Health Service Pub. 629, rev. 1962. Washington, D.C.: U.S. Government Printing Office, 1962.

NEISSER, U. *Cognitive Psychology.* New York: Appleton-Century-Crofts, 1967.

NELSON, ZANE P., and DWIGHT D. MOWRY. "Contracting in Crisis Intervention." *Community Mental Health Journal.* 12 (September 1976): 37–44.

NICHOLS, BEVERLY B. "The Abused Wife Problem." *Social Casework* 57 (January 1976): 27–32.

OBIER, KATHLEEN, and L. JULIAN HAYWOOD. "Role of the Medical Social Worker in a Coronary Care Unit." *Social Casework* 53 (January 1972): 14–18.

OPPENHEIMER, JEANNETTE R. "Use of Crisis Intervention in Casework with the Cancer Patient and His Family." *Social Work* 12 (April 1967): 44–52.

OZARIN, LUCY D., and BERTRAM S. BROWN. "New Directions in Community Mental Health Programs." *American Journal of Orthopsychiatry* 35 (January 1965): 11–17.

PARAD, HOWARD J. "Brief Ego-Oriented Casework with Families in Crisis." In H. J. Parad and R. R. Miller, eds., *Ego-Oriented Casework: Problems and Perspectives,* pp. 145–164. New York: FSAA, 1963.

————, ed. *Crisis Intervention: Selected Readings.* New York: FSAA, 1965.

————. "Crisis Intervention." In *Encyclopedia of Social Work,* 16th issue, vol. 1, pp. 197–202. New York: NASW, 1971.

————, and GERALD CAPLAN. "A Framework for Studying Families in Crisis." *Social Work* 5 (July 1960). Reprinted in Parad, 1965, pp. 53–72.

————, and LIBBIE G. PARAD. "A Study of Crisis-Oriented Planned Short-Term Treatment." Part I: *Social Casework* 49 (June 1968): 346–355. Part II: *Social Casework* 49 (July 1968): 418–426.

————, and H. L. P. RESNIK. "The Practice of Crisis Intervention in

Emergency Care." In H. L. P. Resnik and L. L. Ruben, eds., *Emergency Psychiatric Care*, pp. 23–34. Bowie, Md.: Charles Press, 1975.

———, H. L. P. RESNIK, and LIBBIE G. PARAD. *Emergency and Disaster Management: A Mental Health Sourcebook*, Bowie, Md.: Charles Press, 1976.

———, LOLA SELBY, and JAMES QUINLAN. "Crisis Intervention with Families and Groups." In Robert W. Roberts and Helen Northen, eds., *Theories of Social Work with Groups*, pp. 304–330. New York: Columbia University Press, 1976.

PARAD, LIBBIE G. "Short-Term Treatment: An Overview of Historical Trends, Issues, and Potentials." *Smith College Studies* 41 (February 1971): 119–146.

PASEWARK, RICHARD, and DALE A. ALBERS. "Crisis Intervention: Theory in Search of a Program." *Social Work* 17 (March 1972): 70–77.

PAVENSTADT, ELEANOR, and VIOLA W. BERNARD, eds. *Crises of Family Disorganization*. New York: Behavioral Publications, 1971.

PERGAMENTER, RUTH. "Group Work with Child Nurses in a Border Kibbutz." Paper presented at Conference on Child Psychiatry, Jerusalem, 1970. Mimeo.

PERLMAN, HELEN H. *Social Casework: A Problem-Solving Process*. Chicago: University of Chicago Press, 1957.

———. "Family Diagnosis in Cases of Illness and Disability." In *Family-Centered Social Work in Illness and Disability: A Preventive Approach*. New York: NASW, 1961.

———. "Some Notes on the Waiting List." *Social Casework* 44 (April 1963): 200–205. Reprinted in Parad, 1965, pp. 193–201.

———. "The Problem-Solving Model in Social Casework." In Robert W. Roberts and Robert H. Nee, eds., *Theories of Social Casework*, pp. 129–179. Chicago: University of Chicago Press, 1970.

PIAGET, JEAN. *The Origins of Intelligence in Children*. New York: W. W. Norton, 1963.

PILSECKER, CARLETON. "Help for the Dying." *Social Work* 20 (May 1975): 190–194.

PITTMAN, FRANK, CAROL DEYOUNG, KALMAN FLOMENHAFT, DAVID KAPLAN, and DONALD LANGSLEY. "Crisis Family Therapy." In

J. H. Masserman, ed., *Current Psychiatric Therapies,* 6, pp. 187–196. New York: Grune and Stratton, 1966.

POWELL, J. W., J. E. FINESINGER, and M. H. GREENHILL. "An Introduction to the Natural History of Disaster." In *Final Contract Report, II,* Disaster Research Project, Psychiatric Institute, University of Maryland, 1954.

POWELL, J. W., and J. RAYNER. *Progress Notes: Disaster Investigation.* Edgewood, Md.: Chemical Corps Medical Laboratories, Army Chemical Center, 1952.

QUARANTELLI, E. L., and RUSSELL DYNES. "Looting in Civil Disorders: An Index of Social Change." In L. H. Masotti and D. R. Bowen, eds., *Riots and Rebellion.* Beverly Hills, Cal.: Sage Publications, 1968.

RABINER, EDWIN L., CARL F. WELLS, and JOEL YAGER. "A Model for the Brief Hospitalization Treatment of the Disadvantaged Psychiatrically Ill." *American Journal of Orthopsychiatry* 43 (October 1973): 774–782.

"Rape—A Personal Account." *Health and Social Work* 1 (August 1976): 84–95.

RAPOPORT, LYDIA. "The State of Crisis: Some Theóretical Considerations." *Social Service Review* 6 (June 1962): 211–217. Reprinted in Parad, 1965, pp. 22–31.

———. "Working with Families in Crisis: An Exploration in Preventive Intervention." *Social Work* 7 (3): 48–56. Reprinted in Parad, 1965, pp. 129–139.

———. "Crisis-Oriented Short-Term Casework." *Social Service Review* 41 (March 1967): 31–42.

———. "Crisis Intervention as a Mode of Brief Treatment." In Roberts and Nee, 1970, pp. 267–311.

RAPOPORT, RHONA. "Normal Crises, Family Structure, and Mental Health." *Family Process* 2, no. 1 (1963). Reprinted in Parad, 1965, pp. 75–87.

——— and RAPOPORT, ROBERT. "New Light on the Honeymoon." *Human Relations* 17 (1964): 33–56.

RAYMOND, MARGARET, ANDREW E. SLABY, and JULIAN LIEB. "Familial Responses to Mental Illness." *Social Casework* 56 (October 1975): 492–498.

REID, WILLIAM J., and LAURA EPSTEIN. *Task-Centered Casework.*
New York: Columbia University Press, 1972.

———, eds. *Task-Centered Practice.* New York: Columbia University
Press, 1976.

RESNIK, L. P., and H. L. RUBEN, eds. *Emergency Psychiatric Care:
The Management of Mental Health Crises.* Bowie, Md.: Charles
Press, 1975.

REYNOLDS, BERTHA C. *An Uncharted Journey.* New York: Citadel
Press, 1963.

RICH, MARGARET E. *A Belief in People.* New York: FSAA, 1956.

RIPPLE, LILIAN, with ERNESTINA ALEXANDER and BERNICE W.
POLEMIS. *Motivation, Capacity, and Opportunity.* Social Service
Monographs, 2nd series. School of Social Service Administration,
University of Chicago, 1964.

ROSE, VICKI L., and SHARON BRICE-BONHAM. "Divorce Adjustment:
A Woman's Problem?" *Family Coordinator* 22 (July 1973): 291–
297.

ROSENBAUM, C. PETER, and JOHN E. BEEBE III. *Psychiatric Treatment:
Crisis/Clinic/Consultation.* New York: McGraw-Hill, 1975.

ROSENBERG, BLANCA N. "Planned Short-Term Treatment in Developmental Crises." *Social Casework* 56 (April 1975): 195–204.

RUMMEL, KATHRYN. "Helping the Older Client Involve His Family in
Future Plans." *Social Casework* 39 (November 1958): 508–512.

RUSSELL, BETTY, and SYLVIA SCHILD. "Pregnancy Counseling with
College Women." *Social Casework* 57 (May 1976): 324–329.

RUSSELL, DIANA E. H. *The Politics of Rape: The Victim's Perspective.*
New York: Stein and Day, 1975.

SATIR, VIRGINIA. *Peoplemaking.* Palo Alto, Cal.: Science and Behavior
Books, 1972.

SCHERZ, FRANCES H. "The Crisis of Adolescence in Family Life."
Social Casework 48 (April 1967): 209–215.

———. "Maturational Crises and Parent-Child Interaction." *Social
Casework* 52 (June 1971): 362–369.

SCHMIDT, DAVID D., and EDWARD MESSNER. "The Role of the Family
Physician in the Crisis of Impending Divorce." *Journal of Family
Practice* 2 (April 1975): 99–102.

SCHULBERG, HERBERT C. "Disaster, Crisis Theory, and Intervention Strategies." *Omega* 5 no. 1 (1974): 77–87.

SELYE, HANS. *The Stress of Life*. New York: McGraw-Hill, 1956.

SHADER, RICHARD I., and ALICE J. SCHWARTZ. "Management of Reaction to Disaster." *Social Work* 11 (April 1966): 99–105.

SHEEHY, GAIL. *Passages: Predictable Crises of Adult Life*. New York: E. P. Dutton, 1974.

SHERIDAN, MARY S., and DORIS R. JOHNSON. "Social Work Services in a High-Risk Nursery." *Health and Social Work* 1 (May 1976): 86–103.

SHNEIDMAN, EDWIN S., NORMAN L. FARBEROW, and ROBERT E. LITMAN. *The Psychology of Suicide*. New York: Science House, 1970.

SIFNEOS, PETER E. "A Concept of Emotional Crisis." *Mental Hygiene* 44 (April 1960): 169–170.

———. "Two Different Kinds of Psychotherapy of Short Duration." *American Journal of Psychiatry* 123 (March 1967): 1069–1073.

———. *Short-Term Psychotherapy and Emotional Crisis*. Cambridge, Mass.: Harvard University Press, 1972.

SILVERMAN, PHYLLIS. "Caregiver During Critical Role Transactions in the Normal Life Cycle." Paper presented at NIMH Continuing Education Seminar on Emergency Mental Health Service, Washington, D.C., 1973. Mimeo.

———, Dorothy MacKenzie, Mary Pettipas, and Elizabeth Wilson, eds. *Helping Each Other in Widowhood*. New York: Health Services, 1974.

SIMONDS, JOHN F. "A Foster Home for Crisis Placements." *Child Welfare* 52 (February 1973): 82–90.

SINGLER, JUDITH R. "Group Work with Hospitalized Stroke Patients." *Social Casework* 56 (June 1975): 348–354.

SIPORIN, MAX. "Social Treatment: A New-Old Helping Method." *Social Work* 15 (July 1970): 13–25.

———. "Disaster Aid." In *Encyclopedia of Social Work* 16th issue, vol. 1. pp. 245–254. New York: NASW, 1971.

———. *Introduction to Social Work Practice*. New York: Macmillan, 1975.

————. "Altruism, Disaster, and Crisis Intervention." In Parad, Resnik, and Parad, 1976, pp. 213–229.

SLABY, ANDREW E., JULIAN LIEB, and LAURENCE TANCREDI. *Handbook of Psychiatric Emergencies*. New York: Medical Examination Publishing Co., 1975.

SMALL, LEONARD. *The Briefer Psychotherapies*. New York: Brunner/Mazel, 1971.

SMALLEY, RUTH E. "The Functional Approach to Casework Practice." In Roberts and Nee, 1970, pp. 79–128.

SMITH, BARBARA. "Adolescent and Parent: Interaction Between Developmental Stages." *Center Quarterly Focus*. University of Minnesota Center for Youth Development and Research, Fall 1976, pp. 1–7.

SPECK, ROSS V., and CAROLYN L. ATTNEAVE. *Family Networks*. New York: Pantheon, 1973.

SPECTER, GERALD A., and WILLIAM L. CLAIBORN, eds. *Crisis Intervention*. New York: Behavioral Publications, 1973.

SPIEGEL, JOHN. "The Resolution of Role Conflict Within the Family." In Norman W. Bell and Ezra F. Vogel, eds., *The Family*, pp. 361–381. New York: Free Press, 1960.

SPINK, DIANE. "Crisis Intervention for Parents of the Deaf Child." *Health and Social Work* 1 (November 1976): 141–160.

STEIN, EDWARD H., JESSICA MURDAUGH, and JOHN A. MACLEOD. "Brief Psychotherapy of Psychiatric Reactions to Physical Illness." *American Journal of Psychiatry*. 125 (1969): 1040–1047.

STEINZOR, BERNARD. *When Parents Divorce*. New York: Pantheon, 1969.

STREIB, GORDON F., and CLEMENT J. SCHNEIDER. *Retirement in American Society: Impact and Process*. Ithaca, N.Y.: Cornell University Press, 1971.

STRICKLER, MARTIN. "Applying Crisis Theory in a Community Clinic." *Social Casework* 46 (March 1965): 150–154.

————. "Crisis Intervention and the Climacteric Man." *Social Casework* 56 (February 1975): 85–89.

————, and JEAN ALLGEYER. "The Crisis Group: A New Application of Crisis Theory." *Social Work* 12 (July 1967): 28–32.

————, ELLEN G. BASSIN, VIRGINIA MALBIN, and GERALD F. JACOBSON. "The Community-Based Walk-in Center: A New Resource for

Groups Underrepresented in Outpatient Treatment Facilities." *American Journal of Public Health* 55 (March 1965): 377–384.

————, and MARGARET BONNEFIL. "Crisis Intervention and Social Casework: Similarities and Differences in Problem Solving." *Clinical Social Work Journal* 2 (Spring 1974): 36–44.

————, and BETSY LASOR. "The Concept of Loss in Crisis Intervention." *Mental Hygiene* 54 (April 1970): 301–305.

STUDT, ELLIOT. "Social Work Theory and Implications for the Practice of Methods." *Social Work Education Reporter* 16 (June 1968): 22–24, 42–46.

SUSSMAN, MARVIN B., ed. *Sourcebook in Marriage and the Family,* 2nd ed. Boston: Houghton Mifflin, 1963.

SUTHERLAND, SANDRA, and DONALD J. SCHERL. "Patterns of Response Among Victims of Rape." *American Journal of Orthopsychiatry* 40 (April 1970): 503-511.

TAFT, JESSIE. *Dynamics of Therapy in a Controlled Relationship.* New York: MacMillan, 1933. Reissued by Dover, 1962.

TAPLIN, JULIAN R. "Crisis Theory: Critique and Reformulation." *Community Mental Health Journal* 7 (March 1971): 13–23.

TAYLOR, JAMES B., LOUIS A. ZUICHER, and WILLIAM H. KEY. *Tornado: A Community Responds to Disaster.* Seattle: University of Washington Press, 1970.

THOMAS, DOROTHY V. "The Relationship Between Diagnostic Services and Short-Contact Cases." *Social Casework* 32 (February 1951). Reprinted in *The Intake Process,* pp. 26–33. New York: FSAA.

TIDMARSH, SHEILA. *Disaster.* Harmondsworth, Middlesex: Penguin Books, 1969.

TOMARO, MICHAEL P., and DAVID L. HOFFMAN. "Crisis Psychotherapy." Milwaukee: Family Service of Milwaukee, March 1971. Mimeo.

TOWLE, CHARLOTTE. *Common Human Needs.* Washington, D.C.: Federal Security Agency, 1945. Reissued by NASW, 1957.

TROSSMAN, BERNARD. "Adolescent Children of Concentration Camp Survivors." *Canadian Psychiatric Association Journal* 13 (April 1968): 121–123.

TYHURST, JAMES S. "The Role of Transition States—Including Disasters—in Mental Illness." *Symposium on Preventive and Social*

Psychiatry, pp. 149–169. Walter Reed Army Institute of Research, Walter Reed Army Medical Center, Washington, D.C., 1958.

————, and LIBUSE. "Displacement and Migration. A Study in Social Psychiatry." *American Journal of Psychiatry* 107 (1951).

VOGEL, EZRA F., and NORMAN W. BELL. "The Emotionally Disturbed Child as the Family Scapegoat." In Bell and Vogel, eds., *The Family*. pp. 382–397. New York: Free Press, 1960.

VOLLMAN, RITA R., AMY GANZERT, LEWIS PICKER, and W. VAIL WILLIAMS. "The Reactions of Family Systems to Sudden and Unexpected Death." *Omega* 2 (May 1971): 101–106.

WALLACE, ANTHONY F. C. *Tornado in Worchester: An Exploratory Study of Individual and Community Behavior in an Extreme Situation*. Committee on Disaster Studies, 3. Washington, D.C.: National Academy of Science–National Research Council, 1956.

WASSER, EDNA. *Creative Approaches in Casework with the Aged*. New York: FSAA, 1966.

WEAKLAND, JOHN H., RICHARD FISCH, PAUL WATZLAWICK, and ARTHUR M. BODIN. "Brief Therapy: Focused Problem Resolution." *Family Process* 13 (June 1974): 141–167.

WEISBERG, LILLIAN M. "Casework with the Terminally Ill." *Social Casework* 55 (June 1974): 337–342.

WEISS, ROBERT S. "The Contributions of an Organization of Single Parents to the Well-Being of Its Members." *Family Coordinator* 22 (July 1973): 321–326.

WHITE, ROBERT W. "Strategies of Adaptation: An Attempt at Systematic Description," in Coelho, Hamburg, and Adams, 1974, pp. 47–60.

WHITTAKER, JAMES K. *Social Treatment*. Chicago: Aldine, 1974.

WILSON, ROBERT S. *The Short Contact in Social Case Work*, vol. 1. New York: National Association for Travelers Aid and Transient Service, 1937.

WINNIK, HEINRICH, RAPHAEL MOSES, and MORTIMER OSTROW. *Psychological Bases of War*. Jerusalem: Jerusalem Academic Press, Quadrangle, 1973.

WISEMAN, REVA S. "Crisis Theory and the Process of Divorce." *Social Casework* 56 (April 1975): 205–212.

WITHEY, STEPHEN B. "Reaction to Uncertain Threat." In Baker and Chapman, 1962, pp. 93–123.

WOLFENSTEIN, MARTHA. *Disaster*. New York: Free Press, 1957.

YANOOV, BINYAMIN. "Short-Term Intervention: A Model of Emergency Services for Times of Crisis." *Mental Health and Society* 3 (1976) 33–52.

Index